German Women's Writing in the Twenty-First Century

Studies in German Literature, Linguistics, and Culture

German Women's Writing in the Twenty-First Century

Edited by
Hester Baer and Alexandra Merley Hill

CAMDEN HOUSE
Rochester, New York

Copyright © 2015 by the Editors and Contributors

All Rights Reserved. Except as permitted under current legislation, no part of this work may be photocopied, stored in a retrieval system, published, performed in public, adapted, broadcast, transmitted, recorded, or reproduced in any form or by any means, without the prior permission of the copyright owner.

First published 2015 by Camden House
Reprinted in paperback 2018

Camden House is an imprint of Boydell & Brewer Inc.
668 Mt. Hope Avenue, Rochester, NY 14620, USA
and of Boydell & Brewer Limited
PO Box 9, Woodbridge, Suffolk IP12 3DF, UK
www.boydellandbrewer.com

Paperback ISBN-13: 978-1-64014-025-7
Hardcover ISBN-13: 978-1-57113-584-1

Library of Congress Cataloging-in-Publication Data

German Women's Writing in the Twenty-First Century / Edited by Hester Baer and Alexandra Merley Hill.
   pages cm. — (Studies in German literature, linguistics, and culture)
"This book has its roots in a conversation that began at the Women in German conference in 2006."—Preface.
   Summary: "What is the status of women's writing in German today, in an era when feminism has thoroughly problematized binary conceptions of sex and gender? Drawing on gender and queer theory, including the work of Lauren Berlant, Judith Butler, and Michel Foucault, the essays in this volume rethink conventional ways of conceptualizing female authorship and re-examine the formal, aesthetic, and thematic terms in which "women's literature" has been conceived. With an eye to the literary and feminist legacy of authors such as Christa Wolf and Ingeborg Bachmann, contributors treat the works of many of contemporary Germany's most significant literary voices, including Hatice Akyün, Sibylle Berg, Thea Dorn, Tanja Dückers, Karen Duve, Jenny Erpenbeck, Julia Franck, Katharina Hacker, Charlotte Roche, Julia Schoch, and Antje Rávic Strubel—authors who, through their writing or their role in the media, engage with questions of what it means to be a woman writer in twenty-first-century Germany."—Provided by publisher.
   Includes bibliographical references and index.
   ISBN-13 978-1-57113-584-1 (hardcover: alk. paper)—
   ISBN-10 1-57113-584-7 (hardcover: alk. paper)
   1. German literature—Women authors—History and criticism—Congresses. 2. German literature—21st century—History and criticism—Congresses. I. Baer, Hester, editor. II. Hill, Alexandra Merley, editor.

PT167.G466 2015
830.9′928709051—dc23

2014048698

To our mothers,

Elizabeth Baer and Maria Cisyk

Contents

Acknowledgments   ix

Introduction: German Women's Writing Beyond the
Gender Binary   1
Hester Baer and Alexandra Merley Hill

1: Language-Bodies: Interpellation and Gender Transition
in Antje Rávic Strubel's *Kältere Schichten der Luft* and
Judith Hermann's "Sonja"   18
Necia Chronister

2: Matrilineal Narrative and the Feminist Family Romance   37
Valerie Heffernan

3: The Pitfalls of Constructing a Female Genealogy: Cultural
Memory of National Socialism in Recent Family Narratives   54
Katherine Stone

4: Reckoning with God: Attitudes toward Religion
in German-Language Women's Writing in the
Twenty-First Century   74
Sheridan Marshall

5: Muslim Writing, Women's Writing   95
Lindsay Lawton

6: Popfeminism, Ethnicity, and Race in Contemporary
Germany: Hatice Akyün's Popfeminist Autobiographic
Works *Einmal Hans mit scharfer Soße* (2005) and
Ali zum Dessert (2008)   113
Mihaela Petrescu

7: The Awkward Politics of Popfeminist Literary Events:
Helene Hegemann, Charlotte Roche, and Lady Bitch Ray   132
Carrie Smith-Prei and Maria Stehle

8: The Indictment of Neoliberalism and Communism
in the Novels of Katharina Hacker, Nikola Richter,
Judith Schalansky, and Julia Schoch   154
Helga Druxes

9: Sounds of Silence: Rape and Representation in
Juli Zeh's Bosnian Travelogue   175
Jill Suzanne Smith

Bibliography   197

Notes on the Contributors   203

Index   205

Acknowledgments

THIS BOOK HAS ITS ROOTS in a conversation that began at the Women in German conference in 2006. We thank our colleagues and friends at WiG conferences and panels over the years for many intriguing discussions of intersectionality and women's cultural production "beyond the gender binary." Special thanks to Maria Stehle and the faculty research seminar on Modern German and Central European Studies at the University of Tennessee-Knoxville for feedback on an early draft of the introduction. We also thank all the contributors to this volume for taking our thinking about contemporary women's writing in new directions. We owe a debt of gratitude to our institutions, the University of Portland and the University of Maryland, for assistance with publication costs. Jim Walker has been a fantastic editor and a pleasure to work with; we thank him for his support of this project from its earliest stages through the publication process. Thanks also to Ryan Peterson, Rosemary Shojaie, Julia Cook, and the rest of the marketing and production team at Camden House. Finally, we are especially grateful to our families, Della Baer, Ryan Long, and Jamie Hill, for their support of our work on this project.

H. B. and A. M. H.
November 2014

Introduction: German Women's Writing Beyond the Gender Binary

Hester Baer and Alexandra Merley Hill

THIS BOOK INVESTIGATES the way women's writing and feminist literary criticism constitute key sites for imagining, critiquing, and troubling gender in the twenty-first century. We aim to instigate an invigorating discussion of German women's writing by emphasizing the intersectional qualities of both women's literature and feminist analysis today. Making the case for renewed attention to women's writing appears particularly crucial at the present moment, defined by neoliberal capitalism and proclamations of postfeminism, when the study of literature in general, and women's literature in particular, is waning. Yet as the contributions to this volume show, contemporary women's writing engages in important and nuanced ways with the seismic social, political, and economic transformations of the present, many of which affect women in particular. Moreover, women's literature provides imaginative possibilities—both for understanding the present and for envisioning change—that carry renewed significance in the twenty-first century.

In arguing for new attention to women's writing, we do not seek to revive an outdated concept, engage in a nostalgic excavation, or reassert essentialized, normative categories. In contrast to the twentieth century, when the literary canon largely excluded works by female authors, and feminist criticism emphasized projects of recovery and reevaluation, today women's literature is commonplace, mainstream, and widely accepted. At the same time, contemporary feminists have thoroughly problematized any unified conception of "woman" (as a category of political agency, or indeed of authorship) by emphasizing the constitutive role of difference in understanding both the construction of identity and the complexity of oppression. Trenchant critiques by poststructuralist and queer theorists emphasizing the fluidity, contingency, and performativity of gender and sexuality have underscored the normativity and instability of identity categories. Together, these developments have sometimes made gender seem either redundant or empty as a category of analysis, and at times they have appeared to stymie feminist theory and criticism.

As Toril Moi has argued, these developments also help to explain "why feminist theory stopped being concerned with women and writing" after the 1980s:[1] how can one speak of women's literature if "woman" has been theoretically deconstructed? Indeed, in the past two decades, excellent scholarship on contemporary women authors has been published, but much of it was not explicitly organized by gender or feminism: a chapter in a monograph here, an article in a journal there, a section of a study somewhere else. Not unique to German Studies, the tendency to avoid questions of women's writing and aesthetics is "symptomatic of a theoretical malaise."[2] While feminist scholars can justify attention to women's writing on political grounds, the category "women's literature" has become theoretically fraught. In response to this predicament, we argue for the continued relevance of the category of women's writing. Picking up where past decades of feminist literary criticism left off,[3] we bring together multiple voices in order to develop some theoretical tools for analyzing women's literature and to carry the conversation forward in light of new ways of conceptualizing gender and feminism.

In her 2004 book *Undoing Gender*, Judith Butler points out that the norms governing gender "both constrain and enable life, . . . they designate in advance what will and will not be a liveable existence."[4] Butler identifies the inherent paradox here—whereby norms may simultaneously allow the recognizability that makes life liveable and impose terms of recognition that constrain livability—as the juncture from which (feminist) critique emerges (4). For the double nature of gender norms means that "we cannot do without them [but] we do not have to assume that their form is given or fixed. Indeed, even if we cannot do without them, it will be seen that we can also not accept them as they are" (207). Butler's description of feminism as a project "about the social transformation of gender relations" emphasizes the sense in which gender is a normative fiction that entails specific consequences on human lives and bodies (204). Motivated by contemporary feminist thought, the essays collected here consider women's writing by examining how the politics of gender continue to inform practices of reading, writing, and representation; at the same time they examine how women's writing participates in the feminist project of transforming gender relations.

Although this volume uses the broad term "German women's writing," it supports no single definition of what that is. As Moi reminds us, "After all, the whole point is *to avoid laying down requirements for what a woman's writing must be like*."[5] Instead, the essays collected here examine diverse representations of gendered social, sexual, and political experience in contemporary German-language literature. The literary works under discussion grapple with urgent issues in Germany, Europe, and the world: sexuality, politics, labor, race, class, migration, history, globalization, power, violence, identity, and agency, all of which intersect with and are shaped by gender. The contributors to this volume argue that examining literature by, for, and about women can illuminate these intersections and lead to a more nuanced understanding of the role of the gendered subject in society.

Many of contemporary Germany's significant literary voices, both emergent and well established, are treated here, including Hatice Akyün, Jenny Erpenbeck, Katharina Hacker, Katharina Hagena, Helene Hegemann, Judith Hermann, Anja Jonuleit, Ursula Krechel, Nikola Richter, Charlotte Roche, Judith Schalansky, Julia Schoch, Antje Rávic Strubel, and Juli Zeh—authors who, through their writing, their role in the media, or both, engage with questions of what it means to be a woman writer in twenty-first-century Germany. They also consistently attend to questions of gender and sexuality in their works. Many reject the notion of categorizing their work as "women's literature" and even repudiate a connection between their gender politics and their writing. For example, Julia Franck, Judith Hermann, and Juli Zeh have all denied that their works are feminist.[6] By contrast, Charlotte Roche identifies herself and her books with her own definition of feminism, based on improving the relationship between women and their bodies.[7] Regardless of their formal relationship to feminism—and it should be noted that these relationships evolve as feminism does—the writers discussed in this collection are all living and creating within the context of a revival of interest in feminism and gender in German culture.

Contemporary Feminisms

Interest in feminism has experienced a resurgence in Germany since the turn of the twenty-first century, spurred on by natalist debates about Germany's declining birthrate; increasing economic precarity that has disproportionately affected women and minorities; controversies about migration and multiculturalism; and the rise of widespread Islamophobic discourse, all topics addressed in a literary context by writers discussed in the following chapters. A number of specific political and media events have shaped the conversation about feminism in Germany in the last decade. The adoption of the Hartz IV welfare-reform package in 2005 has led to declining employment opportunities for women in Germany, who were already underrepresented in the labor force and significantly underpaid in comparison to women in other Western countries.[8] At the same time, public discourse has blamed women for the effects of neoliberal policies such as Hartz IV, especially in the long-standing debate about demographic shifts in twenty-first-century German society. Notable contributions to this debate have included bestsellers such as Eva Herman's *Das Eva-Prinzip* (The Eve Principle, 2007), a critique of the supposed selfishness of women who choose to prioritize a career over raising children, and Thilo Sarrazin's *Deutschland schafft sich ab* (Germany Is Abolishing Itself, 2010), a racist screed expressing anxieties about the declining birth rate and the growing immigrant population.[9] Women have responded strongly to these interpretations of and assumptions about gender roles, from the former conservative Federal Minister for Family Affairs, Senior Citizens, Women and Youth Ursula von der Leyen to feminists of the women's movement, such as Alice Schwarzer.[10] In 2012, the government took action by implementing a new family leave policy (*Bundeselterngeld- und Elternzeitgesetz*).[11]

Young feminists have played a significant role in these debates through both writing and activism. Contributions encompass a range of approaches to feminism, including transnationally inflected forms of postfeminism,[12] generationally informed attempts to build on 1970s feminism, and the specifically German movement known as popfeminism. These overlapping and mutually influential contemporary feminisms articulate various attitudes toward the media, sexuality, and consumerism, and also toward the historical German women's movement itself, ranging from critique to reclamation. The evolution of recent feminisms has not been a linear progression, and tensions exist between generations (for example, Alice Schwarzer [b. 1942] and Charlotte Roche [b. 1978] have famously and publicly sparred) and between different contemporary feminist groups—popfeminists, for example, are criticized for their supposedly unreflective participation in patriarchal consumer culture.[13] Nonetheless, even those manifestations of contemporary feminism that outwardly reject a connection to the historical women's movement are in fact informed by it and continue discussions (for example, of the body, sexuality, gender norms, behavior, appearance) that it started.[14]

Manifestos such as *Wir Alphamädchen* (We Alpha Females, 2008) and *Neue deutsche Mädchen* (New German Girls, 2008) pick up the banner of feminism and move it forward, declaring that feminism is "jung und cool und kann dabei helfen, jede Menge Fragen zu beantworten" (young and cool and can help to answer any number of questions).[15] Cheerful and upbeat, these works attempt to strike a balance between pointing out what women have gained from feminism and what young women can do to continue empowering themselves. Another group of young feminists traces its evolution more directly from 1970s feminism. Thea Dorn's *Die neue F-Klasse* (The New F-Class, 2007) and Mirja Stöcker's *Das F-Wort* (The F-Word, 2007), while both playfully referencing the unpopularity of second-wave feminism in Germany, resist giving it the kind of face-lift that the *Mädchen* movement does, insisting more aggressively on a political and activist dimension.[16]

Despite key differences, these feminist writings have all been subsumed loosely under the banner of popfeminism, a movement that is given voice in Sonja Eismann's 2007 volume *Hot Topic: Popfeminismus heute* (Popfeminism Today). Eismann explains "dass es im deutschen Sprachraum keine medial präsente Kultur eines radikalen, popbezogenen Feminismus gibt" (that there is no media presence of a radical, pop-oriented feminist culture in the German-speaking world) equivalent to the widespread feminist media culture in the Anglo-American context.[17] Rather, until recently, feminism was represented almost exclusively through the persona of Alice Schwarzer, whose particular viewpoints remain anathema to many (including many feminists). For Eismann, popfeminism suggests a dialectical collision and synthesis of pop culture and feminism, a making-present of feminism in the public sphere as well as a renewed understanding of feminism's relevance. She writes that "Popkultur [sollte] durch feministische Strategien perforiert und erschüttert werden" (pop culture should be perforated and shaken up by feminist strategies); conversely, feminism should not be understood as an abstract concept but rather as something that "als gelebte Alltagskultur alle Lebensbereiche durchdringt" (permeates all spheres of everyday life).[18]

Since the emergence of this widespread discussion of feminism in the first decade of the twenty-first century, feminist activists have also taken up the mantle of popfeminism, initiating a protest culture that has proliferated through digital media. In connection with transnational feminist protest movements, German activists organized "Slutwalks," which called attention to sexual violence, marched in solidarity with the Russian feminist punk collective Pussy Riot, and staged protests both in affiliation with and in opposition to the Ukrainian group Femen, whose polarizing tactics of demonstrating topless garnered much media attention. In 2013, sexist comments made by several prominent politicians (most notably Rainer Brüderle, a candidate for the FDP in a major federal election) led to a renewed discussion of sexism in the German media, after feminists organized a Twitter campaign in which thousands of women broadcast personal stories of sexism under the title "#Aufschrei" (#Outcry).[19] All these actions engaged pop tactics while making feminism increasingly visible in the public sphere.

Feminism is also a touchstone for contemporary literature by women, including highly popular novels such as Roche's *Feuchtgebiete* (2008; published in English as *Wetlands*, 2009) and *Schoßgebete* (Lap Prayers, 2011; published in English as *Wrecked*, 2013), and *Axolotl Roadkill* (2010) by Helene Hegemann.[20] At first glance, such texts appear to eschew any continuity with a feminist tradition, in part by focusing on individual pleasure and desire and embracing consumerism and consumption (of sex, drugs, makeup, fashion, media, and so on) However, their resignification of feminist politics and literature dovetails with the strategies of popfeminism, suggesting new frameworks for contemplating questions of generational affiliation, influence, and aesthetics. Ultimately these works call into question the category of women's writing, while simultaneously underscoring its ongoing relevance, a paradoxical standpoint that Carrie Smith-Prei and Maria Stehle discuss in this volume as an "awkward provocation."

Women's Writing in Historical Perspective

The writers discussed here are indebted to the literary and feminist legacy of authors such as Ingeborg Bachmann, Elfriede Jelinek, Irmtraud Morgner, Verena Stefan, and Christa Wolf, women who forged pathways into the publishing world, created new generic models for expressing authenticity and gendered subjectivity, and broke with patriarchal stylistic conventions. *Frauenliteratur* (women's literature) of the 1970s and 1980s was a conscious, author-driven attempt to give voice to women's subjective experiences. Although the term has since been connected with the idea of *Trivialliteratur* (trivial literature), scholars have proposed a reclaiming and reinvigorating of the term as one that speaks to "the attempt to write through the lens of female experience, in search of a new language that could convey female subjectivity."[21] The *Fräuleinwunder* (girl wonder) trend of the late 1990s and early 2000s can be understood as the antithesis of *Frauenliteratur*, in that it was a label snatched up by publishers to group and market authors based on gender rather than commonality of subject matter, theme, or style.[22] Distinct from the *Fräuleinwunder* wave, but in some cases contemporaneous with it, came a series of publications understood to be the German answer to chick lit, a genre most commonly associated with British author Helen Fielding's *Bridget Jones's Diary* (1996). While some feminist literary critics voice skepticism of chick lit's literary merit, others argue for the value of German chick lit as a postfeminist subcategory of *Frauenliteratur*, one that gives voice to women's subjective experience.[23]

Whether in the context of *Frauenliteratur*, the *Fräuleinwunder*, chick lit, Berlin literature, or the trend of "neue Lesbarkeit" (new readability), in the postunification years women have increasingly gained the attention of the publishing industry. Despite their participation in these trends, however, their writing defies the limitations of such categories. The *Fräuleinwunder* authors have made significant contributions to the strongly male categories of the *Wenderoman* (novel of unification), the millennial novel, the historical novel, and the familial novel. Moreover, many German-language female authors have won nationally and internationally significant prizes for literature, even in just the last decade: the Nobel Prize for Literature (Elfriede Jelinek in 2004, Herta Müller in 2009), the Deutscher Buchpreis (Katharina Hacker in 2006, Julia Franck in 2007, Kathrin Schmidt in 2009, Melinda Nadj Abonji in 2010, and Ursula Krechel in 2012), the Fontane Preis (Emine Sevgi Özdamar in 2009), the Georg Büchner Preis (Brigitte Kronauer in 2005, Felicitas Hoppe in 2012, and Sibylle Lewitscharoff in 2013), and the most lucrative German literary prize, the Wilhelm-Raabe-Preis (Katja Lange-Müller in 2008, Sibylle Lewitscharoff in 2011, and Marion Poschmann in 2013). These prizes are of course a mark of respect and tend to both reflect and cause popularity and book sales. At the very least, marketing strategies and sales numbers indicate that the German-language publishing industry recognizes both that women writers are of significant interest to the book-buying public and that the white, educated, middle-class female is, statistically speaking, Germany's primary book buyer.[24]

The publishing phenomenon of the *Fräuleinwunder*, though driven by superficial marketing and generally rejected as a sloppy designation, inadvertently triggered a new wave of scholarly discussion of the feminine aesthetic—or perhaps a femin*ist* aesthetic—common to female authors. In 1976 Silvia Bovenschen asked whether writing style is affected by gender.[25] More than three decades later, Julia Franck put forth the term "weibliche Nüchternheit," or "female sobriety," to describe the restrained, matter-of-fact style adopted by many female authors as a means of evading accusations of employing sentimental or girlish prose.[26] Chick lit's first-person, confessional style of narration is another example of gender-specific writing conventions, though certainly not one that all female authors employ in the same way or to the same end.[27]

One cannot speak of an intentional, coherent aesthetic movement driven by or common to the authors included in this volume. Certainly there is no one style, just as there is no one story, for female authors today. Yet the very discussion "demonstrates [that] women's literature continues to be overdetermined in ways that 'men's literature' is not. . . ."[28] Our goal with this volume is not to continue to "overdetermine" the characteristics of women's literature or to insist on a direct lineage of German women's writing that precludes the influence of other (for example, male, international, or minority) authors. Instead we seek to illuminate the variety of structural and stylistic devices, traditions and breaks with tradition, and stories and subjectivities that make up the mosaic of contemporary women's writing.

In her recent history of German feminism, Myra Marx Ferree emphasizes the crucial role that writing played for feminists in the GDR: "East German women had a narrower window of opportunity for conventional political tools [than Western women], but they created a self-expressive space in fiction that they could not exercise in fact. GDR women's writing developed a counter-narrative to the socialist claim to have emancipated them, offering a critique of the double day that was heard around the world."[29] Feminists in postunification Germany do not face the same kind of challenges in overcoming state censorship or expressing political concerns publicly as women did in the GDR. Nevertheless, we suggest that women's writing plays a similarly crucial role in the neoliberal present, an era characterized by the absence of alternatives to capitalism and the waning of political structures fostering solidarity, collectivity, or resistance—all of which are quickly co-opted by neoliberalism's rhetorical commitment to "equality politics."[30] In this context, women's writing may provide a space for making visible the paradoxes of neoliberalism's promises, for imagining change, and for helping us understand how status—including gender, sexuality, race, ethnicity, and citizenship—still impacts individual lives.

Moreover, if neoliberal and consumerist ideologies co-opt the value of collective struggles and identity formations, then we can understand the continued trivialization of women's literature over the last two decades via marketable categories such as the *Fräuleinwunder* and chick lit as symptomatic. Again, we do not wish to recoup some essentialized notion of women's literature. But one key emphasis of this volume is to interrogate the ways in which women's writing—in aesthetic and representational terms—might contribute specifically to understanding the neoliberal present. As Rosalind Gill and Christina Scharff have pointed out, in neoliberalism "to a much greater extent than men, women are required to work on and transform the self, to regulate every aspect of their conduct, and to present all their actions as freely chosen."[31] To the extent that neoliberalism is *"always already gendered,"* women's writing may constitute a privileged place for the exploration of neoliberal subjectivities in general.[32]

Toward an Intersectional Feminist Literary Criticism

A key characteristic of contemporary feminist thought is its emphasis on differences between women, including ethnic, racial, sexual, class-based, and religious differences.[33] At the same time, anti-essentialist, post-structuralist, and queer critiques have problematized identity categories as normative and regulatory and therefore unsuitable as a basis for feminist politics. Together, these trajectories in contemporary feminism have led away from a unified conception of woman as the subject of feminist analysis or as a collective political agent.

These salient critiques, first articulated by women of color and lesbians (in the Anglo-American context) and by migrant and bicultural women (in the German context), have led to two key understandings of contemporary transnational feminist thought. First, feminist thinkers in the twenty-first century recognize the limitations of gender as a singular analytic category, cultural symbol, or personal status. Drawing on insights first articulated by the Combahee River Collective and other black feminists, contemporary feminists seek to account for the complexity of oppression by attending carefully to the intersections among identity categories.[34] Second, feminists have widely adopted Judith Butler's conception of gender as performative, as an effect of repetition with no underlying substance, something that one "does" rather than "has." As a result, feminists now view gender not only as a normative category but also as a highly unstable one.

As intersectionality and gender performativity have opened up new avenues for more complex thinking about gender and sexuality, they have also emphasized new possibilities for change, either via new forms of alliance or through personal transformation. However, as we pointed out at the start of this introduction, these developments within feminist thought, taken together, have sometimes created the paradoxical effect of making gender seem either redundant or empty as a category of analysis. What is more, intersectionality and Butlerian gender theory have often appeared theoretically incompatible for a number of reasons. For one thing, intersectionality appears to draw its analytic strength from emphasizing precisely those categories of identity (including gender and sexuality) that Butler's theory deconstructs, thereby making the two modes of thought appear contradictory. Moreover, intersectional feminism has often been yoked to empirical methodologies in the social sciences, leading feminist literary criticism in particular to reject it as simplistic and generally irreconcilable with postmodern, deconstructive theoretical approaches that are commonplace in literary studies. Finally, intersectionality remains methodologically tricky because it requires a complex approach, potentially involving attention to and expertise in multiple disciplines.

How can feminist literary criticism move beyond this aporia to develop new models for analysis? Feminist methodology offers a number of specific suggestions about where to begin. Sociologist Leslie McCall has argued for a multipronged approach to feminist intersectional research, one that does not seek to resolve these feminist debates but rather identifies the contradictions in contemporary feminist thought as a methodological advantage. McCall points out that intersectionality is perhaps the most significant theoretical contribution of women's studies as a discipline, and yet it poses ongoing challenges because of the methodological complexity it demands. By embracing a range of approaches and refusing unitary answers, feminist research is able to provide more robust accounts of power, discourse, narrative, and social life. Addressing feminist, queer, and antiracist concerns that categories are "simplifying social fictions that produce inequalities in the process of producing differences,"[35] McCall identifies the *anticategorical* trajectory within feminist thought as crucial because of its "radical potential to alter social practices—to free individuals and social groups from the normative fix of a hegemonic order and to enable a politics that is at once more complex and inclusive."[36] At the same time, McCall recognizes the complementary approach offered by feminists of color, who may not reject the social reality of categories altogether, even as they seek to confound and critique such categorization. This *intracategorical* trajectory in feminist thought is often best able to develop an account of the links among multiple positions of subordination, employing categories strategically to focus on neglected points of intersection. (McCall also identifies a third approach, *intercategorical* complexity, that typically emphasizes quantitative methods and is exclusive to the social sciences.)

As McCall argues, a major strength of feminist research is its ability to adapt methodologies from a range of disciplines that can produce different kinds of knowledge and can give us a more complex understanding of gender from a range of standpoints. McCall ultimately suggests that effective feminist intersectional research combines insights of feminist theory with knowledge from a home discipline; thus feminist literary criticism is singularly poised to provide accounts of the discursive construction and imbrication of categories, as well as to describe their instability and normativity, and these accounts can complement other accounts of race, class, gender, and sexuality that continue to insist on and help us understand lived reality, situated knowledge, and real-existing structures of oppression and domination. McCall's multipronged approach to feminist intersectional research helps describe the multiple ways in which women's writing is deployed as an analytic tool in this volume, invoking both anticategorical and intracategorical approaches to address the relationships among gender, sexuality, ethnicity, religion, and class, as well as those among authorship, narration, representation, and reception.

Ultimately, as the feminist philosopher Mary Hawkesworth suggests, feminist research should be designed to "confound gender."[37] That is, the aim of feminist literary criticism should be to draw attention to the "natural attitude" that conflates gender with biological sex (an attitude that continues to be all too persistent in social life today) along with "the oppressive social relations that the natural attitude legitimates" (149). For Hawkesworth, feminist research can best confound gender in two specific ways: first, it should analyze how gender operates in specific cultural and historical contexts while avoiding a deterministic view of gender (gender should never serve as an explanation or a "why"); and second, it must engage gender in a highly nuanced sense, employing many distinctions ("sexed embodiedness, sexuality, sexual identity, gender identity, gendered divisions of labor, gendered social relations, gendered institutions, and gender symbolism") rather than the singular category "gender" (175). The contributions to this volume seek to confound gender by examining its cultural and historical construction and by engaging gender in specific and nuanced ways; they also highlight the way contemporary women's writing itself continues to pursue the goal of confounding gender.

The Essays

In her reading of texts by Antje Rávic Strubel and Judith Hermann, Necia Chronister presents a paradigmatic analysis of literature's unique ability to confound gender by engaging the reader's imagination in constructing bodies that defy norms and expectations. Chronister emphasizes the function of language, interpellation, and performative speech in narratives of gender transition that destabilize both gender binaries and heteronormative sexuality. While she situates Strubel's and Hermann's works within a tradition of women's writing about the mutability of gender, Chronister argues that they depart from this tradition by emphasizing the relational quality of gender rather than its social construction. Taking a cue from gender and queer theory, these works participate in a new trend in German literature of thematizing the performativity and play of gender and sexuality.

Family narratives have played a significant role in contemporary German literature's engagement with questions of gender, generation, and nation. Valerie Heffernan examines the tendency within women's writing to restage the family novel in matrilineal terms. Focusing on mother-daughter relationships in three recent novels by Katharina Hagena, Anja Jonuleit, and Annette Pehnt, Heffernan situates these works both within the long-standing tradition of women's literature about maternity and alongside the motherhood debates in contemporary Germany. In her examination of the formal techniques used in these novels to give voice to multiple (including maternal) subjectivities, Heffernan argues that the authors offer a response to Marianne Hirsch's observation that mother-daughter narratives have been written largely from the viewpoint of the daughters. Moving beyond essentializing discourses of motherhood and generation, these novels "call attention to the role of the marginal and the powerless in the broader narrative of history."

Family narratives are also at the center of Katherine Stone's analysis of gender and the cultural memory of National Socialism, which examines three memoirists' responses to the muting of women's voices in family and cultural histories. By considering how women remember the Second World War, the memoirs by Gisela Heidenreich, Christina von Braun, and Alexandra Senfft undermine the dominant, masculine narrative of history and contest the assumption of female innocence, passivity, and victimhood in that narrative, still an urgent project in the twenty-first century amid recurrent discussions of German victimhood. Stone argues that generations play a crucial role in the politics of memory and the possibility for contesting or renegotiating hegemonic narratives of gender, although she does not hesitate to point out the authors' blind spots with regard to their own gender and/or generational biases.

A crucial site for the contestation of dominant gender narratives in twenty-first-century Germany is religion, which has taken on a new relevance in recent decades because of ongoing debates about the Nazi past, multiculturalism, and migration. Sheridan Marshall examines the intersections of gender and religion in works by Bettina Bàlaka, Sibylle Berg, Jenny Erpenbeck, and Ursula Krechel. In these novels, faith—both Christian and Jewish—is intimately connected with memories of National Socialism, and attitudes toward faith change significantly from one generation to the next. Marshall examines the gender dynamics of disappointment in religion expressed in the works of female writers, contextualizing their work within philosophical discourses about post-secular societies. These texts counter the trend of underrepresenting women's experiences of religious faith in German literature.

With an eye to dominant cultural assumptions about Islam, Lindsay Lawton investigates an emergent publishing phenomenon in twenty-first-century Germany: popular narratives about the abuse, oppression, and eventual liberation of Muslim women. Despite the tendency on the part of the publishing industry to shape and market these tales according to expected patterns, Lawton argues, "Muslim women's memoirs can offer complex portrayals of faith and gender, as well as of discrimination, sexuality, motherhood, the body, and labor." Lawton focuses particularly on the marketing and reception of these narratives to analyze how they confound readers' assumptions about Muslim women's victimhood and agency in German society.

Reading the humorous autobiographical works of Hatice Akyün within the framework of popfeminism, Mihaela Petrescu's intersectional analysis foregrounds their "exemplary interventions into the discursive representation of the Turkish-German woman in the twenty-first century." By deploying pop strategies such as sampling, resignification, and remixing, Akyün develops a critical account of racism and sexism in contemporary Germany. Her humorous texts, which convey a positive attitude toward sex, counteract dominant assumptions about Turkish-German and Muslim women, thereby also providing a crucial corrective to popfeminism, which has largely failed to attend to the intersections of gender with race, ethnicity, religion, and citizenship. Petrescu argues that as a result Akyün creates a new paradigm for transcultural women's writing.

The final three essays in this volume explicitly consider the political dimensions of contemporary women's writing, including its ability to imagine the present, figure change, or connect to a feminist tradition in women's literature. In their chapter on popfeminist literary events, Carrie Smith-Prei and Maria Stehle examine the performative dimensions of authorship as well as the public reception of "scandalous" works by Charlotte Roche, Helene Hegemann, and Lady Bitch Ray. Drawing on popfeminism as a methodology, Smith-Prei and Stehle develop a theory of awkwardness as a tool for political interpretation in an era when traditional modes of collective politics (especially feminism) have been co-opted such that they are no longer politically legible. Awkwardness offers a more productive way of reading authors whose reception has often been mired in debates about the feminist-political valence of their works, because it "draws attention to normative representations of sexuality, gender, and race and to the power of prescriptive regimes of representation while also representing the collapse of standard discursive frameworks that might easily describe these representations." Smith-Prei and Stehle's contribution is especially significant for this volume because of the way they rethink the category of women's writing for the twenty-first century. As they argue, awkwardness "problematizes the existence of the category of women's writing altogether, even while it confirms that in feminist literature, beginning a discussion with a notion of women's writing is potentially necessary."

Helga Druxes finds a strong critique of neoliberalism articulated in texts by Katharina Hacker, Nikola Richter, Judith Schlansky, and Julia Schoch, even as she diagnoses the waning influence of feminism in contemporary literature by women. Druxes argues that all four writers map the neoliberal present in works that address the evisceration of politics as a shared enterprise, the shifting of economic responsibility away from society and onto individuals, the eclipse of leisure by work, and the precarity that ensues from all of these. While they have a sharp eye for the "increasing saturation of everyday life by economic imperatives," for the most part these writers do not imagine alternatives, a fact that Druxes views as symptomatic.

Finally, Jill Smith examines the political and aesthetic dimensions of acclaimed author Juli Zeh's travelogue addressing sexual violence in the Balkan wars. Smith finds in Zeh's work an "aesthetics of restraint" in regard to the Balkan crisis and in particular to the systematic rape of women, an aesthetics that eschews the narrative conventions of melodrama (so often gendered as a feminine mode of narration) in order to engage more effectively with questions of justice, nationhood, and the European project. Smith argues that Zeh's intervention into narrative form makes visible gendered aspects of war, including sexual violence, that have remained obscured in dominant discourse about the Balkan war. As a result, her analysis resonates with the overarching argument of this volume: that contemporary women's writing continues to play a crucial role in confounding gender norms and expectations, and that it can lead to a more nuanced understanding of the role of the gendered subject in society today.

"Literature is the archive of a culture," Toril Moi states. "To turn women into second-class citizens in the realm of literature is to say that women's experiences of existence and of the world are less important than men's."[38] The contributors to this volume examine how German women's writing in the twenty-first century archives women's experiences of the neoliberal present; they ask how women experience precarity in the workplace, religious faith, romantic and familial relationships, political power structures, and their own bodies. By examining directly the literary representation of these experiences, we resist the postfeminist trend for women to "'eliminate' their gendered . . . subjectivity" and express hope that they will continue to confound gender by articulating their "highly specific and idiosyncratic" perspectives.[39] Together, the women writers and their works considered here give voice to a plurality of experience—of gender, race, ethnicity, class, religion, and citizenship—that demands to be heard.

Notes

[1] Toril Moi, "'I Am Not a Woman Writer': About Women, Literature, and Feminist Theory Today," *Feminist Theory* 9, no. 3 (2008): 261.

[2] Ibid., 264.

[3] See, for example, Sigrid Weigel, *Die Stimme der Medusa: Schreibweisen in der Gegenwartsliteratur von Frauen* (Dülmen-Hiddingsel, Germany: Tende, 1987); Inge Stephan, Regula Venske, and Sigrid Weigel, *Frauenliteratur ohne Tradition?* (Frankfurt am Main: Fischer, 1987); Chris Weedon, ed., *Post-War Women's Writing in German: Feminist Critical Approaches* (Providence, RI: Berghahn Books, 1997); Jo Catling, ed., *A History of Women's Writing in Germany, Austria, and Switzerland* (Cambridge: Cambridge University Press, 2000); Elke Frederiksen and Martha Wallach, eds., *Facing Fascism and Confronting the Past: German Women Writers from Weimar to the Present* (Albany, NY: SUNY Press, 2000); Brigid Haines and Margaret Littler, *Contemporary Women's Writing in German: Changing the Subject* (Oxford: Oxford University Press, 2004); Heike Bartel and Elizabeth Boa, eds., *Pushing at Boundaries: Approaches to Contemporary Women Writers from Karen Duve to Jenny Erpenbeck* (Amsterdam: Rodopi, 2006); Lyn Marven, "German Literature in the Berlin Republic—Writing by Women," in *Contemporary German Fiction: Writing the Berlin Republic*, ed. Stuart Taberner (Cambridge: Cambridge University Press, 2007), 159–77; and Valerie Heffernan and Gillian Pye, eds., *Transitions: Emerging Women Writers in German-Language Literature* (Amsterdam: Rodopi, 2013).

[4] Judith Butler, *Undoing Gender* (New York: Routledge, 2004), 206.

[5] Moi, "'I Am Not a Woman Writer,'" 268. Italics in original.

[6] On Julia Franck, see especially the introduction in Alexandra Merley Hill, *Playing House: Motherhood, Intimacy, and Domestic Spaces in Julia Franck's Fiction* (Oxford: Peter Lang, 2012). On Judith Hermann, see for example Anke S. Biendarra, "Gen(d)eration Next: Prose by Julia Franck and Judith Hermann," *Studies in Twentieth and Twenty-First Century Literature* 28, no. 1 (2004): 211–39. On Juli Zeh, see Patricia Herminghouse, "The Young Author as Public Intellectual: The Case of Juli Zeh," in *German Literature in a New Century: Trends,*

Traditions, Transitions, Transformations, ed. Katharina Gerstenberger and Patricia Herminghouse (New York: Berghahn Books, 2008), 268–84.

[7] Nicholas Kulish, "Germany Abuzz at Racy Novel of Sex and Hygiene," *New York Times,* 6 June 2008.

[8] See Myra Marx Ferree, "Gender Politics in the Berlin Republic: Four Issues of Identity and Institutional Change," *German Politics & Society* 28, no. 1 (2010): 189–214.

[9] Eva Herman, *Das Eva Prinzip: Für eine neue Weiblichkeit* (Munich: Goldmann Verlag, 2007); Thilo Sarrazin, *Deutschland schafft sich ab: Wie wir unser Land aufs Spiel setzen* (Munich: DVA, 2010).

[10] For an excellent overview of recent political changes affecting women in Germany, see especially chapters 7 and 8 of Myra Marx Ferree, *Varieties of Feminism: German Gender Politics in Global Perspective* (Stanford, CA: Stanford University Press, 2012).

[11] The new policy guarantees a maximum of fourteen months of *Elterngeld* (parental subsidy) during leave from a job to care for a child, as long as both parents take leave of at least two months each. This stipulation is intended to promote fathers' participation in parenting and to encourage middle-class, educated women to combine starting a family with continuing their careers. Bundesministerium für Familie, Senioren, Frauen, und Jugend, *Elterngeld und Elternzeit: Das Bundeselterngeld- und Elternzeitgesetz,* 11th ed., March 2012, 17.

[12] We recognize that the term "postfeminism" is contentious and evokes strong—and at times strongly opposed—responses, among them a critique of the suggestion that feminism is "over." As Anne Braithwaite articulates: "And if the 'post' in postfeminism in fact signifies some continuing relationship to feminism (as the 'post' in other theoretical languages such as postmodernism, postcolonialism and poststructuralism does), then postfeminism instead becomes a way to talk about the changes in feminist thinking over the last forty years rather than a rupture with it." Ann Braithwaite, "The Personal, the Political, Third-Wave and Postfeminisms," *Feminist Theory* 3, no. 3 (2002): 341. This is how we would argue for its use, but we remain aware of the negative associations with the term and have chosen to simply use "feminism" in this introduction instead, to make clear that feminism continues to evolve. For more on postfeminism, see Stéphanie Genz and Benjamin A. Brabon, eds., *Postfeminism: Cultural Texts and Theories* (Edinburgh: Edinburgh University Press, 2009), and Yvonne Tasker and Diane Negra, eds., *Interrogating Postfeminism: Gender and the Politics of Popular Culture* (Durham, NC: Duke University Press, 2007).

[13] See Emily Spiers, "The Long March through the Institutions: From Alice Schwarzer to Pop Feminism and the New German Girls," *Oxford German Studies* 43, no. 1 (March 2014): 69–88.

[14] Hester Baer, "Introduction: Resignifications of Feminism in Contemporary Germany," in "Contemporary Women's Writing and the Return of Feminism in Germany," special issue, *Studies in Twentieth and Twenty-First Century Literature* 35, no. 1 (Winter 2011): 8–17.

[15] Meredith Haaf, Susanne Klingner, and Barbara Streidl, *Wir Alphamädchen: Warum Feminismus das Leben schöner macht* (Hamburg: Hoffmann & Campe,

2008), 8. Jana Hensel and Elisabeth Raether, *Neue deutsche Mädchen* (Reinbek bei Hamburg: Rowohlt, 2008).

[16] Mirja Stöcker, ed., *Das F-Wort: Feminismus ist sexy* (Königstein: Helmer, 2007). Thea Dorn, *Die neue F-Klasse: Wie die Zukunft von Frauen gemacht wird* (Munich: Piper, 2007).

[17] Sonja Eismann, "Einleitung," in *Hot Topic: Popfeminismus heute* (Mainz: Ventil Verlag, 2007), 10–11.

[18] Eismann, "Einleitung," 10, 12. See also the contribution by Carrie Smith-Prei and Maria Stehle in this volume.

[19] See https://twitter.com/aufschreien.

[20] Charlotte Roche, *Feuchtgebiete* (Cologne: DuMont, 2008); Charlotte Roche, *Schoßgebete* (Munich: Piper, 2011); Helene Hegemann, *Axolotl Roadkill* (Berlin: Ullstein, 2010).

[21] Hester Baer, "Frauenliteratur 'after Feminism': Rereading Contemporary Women's Writing," in *Über Gegenwartsliteratur/About Contemporary Literature: Festschrift für/for Paul Michael Lützeler*, ed. Mark W. Rectanus (Bielefeld: Aisthesis, 2008), 70.

[22] For more on the "Fräuleinwunder," see for example Alexandra Merley Hill, "'Female Sobriety': Feminism, Motherhood, and the Works of Julia Franck," *Women in German Yearbook* 24 (2008): 209–28.

[23] Brenda Bethman, "Generation Chick: Reading *Bridget Jones's Diary*, *Jessica, 30.*, and *Dies ist kein Liebeslied* as Postfeminist Novels," in "Contemporary Women's Writing and the Return of Feminism in Germany," special issue, *Studies in Twentieth and Twenty-First Century Literature* 35, no. 1 (Winter 2011): 136–54. For an exploration of a new subcategory of "chick-lit alla turca," see Karin E. Yeşilada, "'Nette Türkinnen von nebenan'—Die neue deutsch-türkische Harmlosigkeit als literarischer Trend," in *Von der nationalen zur internationalen Literatur: Transkulturelle deutschsprachige Literatur und Kultur im Zeitalter globaler Migration*, ed. Helmut Schmitz (Amsterdam: Rodopi, 2009), 117–42.

[24] For more information on book marketing aimed at women, see Julia Karolle-Berg and Katya Skow, "From *Frauenliteratur* to *Frauenliteraturbetrieb*: Marketing Literature to German Women in the Twenty-First Century," in *German Literature in a New Century: Trends, Traditions, Transitions, Transformations*, ed. Katharina Gerstenberger and Patricia Herminghouse (New York: Berghahn, 2008), 220–36.

[25] Silvia Bovenschen, "Über die Frage: Gibt es eine 'weibliche' Ästhetik?," *Ästhetik und Kommunikation* 25 (1976): 60–75.

[26] Julia Franck, "The Wonder (of) Woman," *Women in German Yearbook* 24 (2008): 229–40. For a longer analysis of this essay, see Hill, "'Female Sobriety.'"

[27] See Bethman's analysis of the use of first-person narration in Marlene Streeruwitz's *Jessica, 30*. Bethman, "Generation Chick," 140–42.

[28] Baer, "Frauenliteratur," 78.

[29] Ferree, *Varieties of Feminism*, 55.

[30] See Lisa Duggan, *The Twilight of Equality? Neoliberalism, Cultural Politics, and the Attack on Democracy* (Boston: Beacon, 2003).

[31] Rosalind Gill and Christina Scharff, "Introduction," in *New Femininities: Postfeminism, Neoliberalism, and Subjectivity* (London: Palgrave Macmillan, 2011), 7.

[32] Gill and Scharff, "Introduction," 7, emphasis in the original.

[33] Though this emphasis is certainly not new—it dates back at least to the early 1980s—it has gained influence in Germany in the new millennium, changing the conversation about feminism significantly. As Myra Marx Ferree shows, German feminism in the twentieth century was strongly characterized by a discourse of solidarity among all women, including lesbians, based in part on an analysis of gender informed by class politics; this discourse began to change in the postunification period because of three primary influences: EU policy on gender mainstreaming, the voices of migrant women, and Judith Butler's gender theory. See Ferree, *Varieties of Feminism*.

[34] Combahee River Collective, "A Black Feminist Statement," in *All the Women Are White, All the Blacks Are Men, but Some of Us Are Brave: Black Women's Studies*, ed. Gloria T. Hull, Patricia Bell Scott, and Barbara Smith (New York: Feminist, 1982), 13–22.

[35] Leslie McCall, "The Complexity of Intersectionality," *Signs: Journal of Women in Culture and Society* 30, no. 3 (2005): 1773.

[36] McCall, "Complexity of Intersectionality," 1777.

[37] Mary Hawkesworth, *Feminist Inquiry: From Political Conviction to Methodological Innovation* (New Brunswick, NJ: Rutgers University Press, 2006).

[38] Moi, "'I Am Not a Woman Writer,'" 268.

[39] Ibid., 268.

1: Language-Bodies: Interpellation and Gender Transition in Antje Rávic Strubel's *Kältere Schichten der Luft* and Judith Hermann's "Sonja"

Necia Chronister

UNLIKE ANY OTHER MEDIUM, literature has the ability to employ the reader's imagination in the construction of bodies. When a narrator communicates information about a text's characters, the reader completes the act of constructing bodies by imagining their contours, postures, and gestures. A character's gender is thus dependent upon both the narrator's speech—his/her use of nouns, pronouns, and adjectives—and the reader's expectations regarding gender. If the narrator omits information about the character's gender, the reader finds clues in the text—social cues, behaviors, and actions—to fill in that information and assign one. Such moments activate literature's potential for "undoing" gender and bring to light the ways in which reading literature is an act of collaboration. Through this collaborative process between the reader and the narrator, the reader can become an active participant in the denaturalization of such basic categories as gender.

Two contemporary German authors exemplify literature's ability to employ the reader's imagination in this way. In Antje Rávic Strubel's *Kältere Schichten der Luft* (Colder Layers of Air, 2007), female protagonist and narrator Anja slowly transforms into a young man named Schmoll after a mysterious young woman (mis)recognizes her as him. Although Anja at first objects, the woman's insistence that Anja is Schmoll leads to Anja's physical and emotional transformation. Anja accepts Schmoll as a second identity within herself, experiencing a plurality of gender whenever Schmoll manifests himself in her body. Judith Hermann's short story "Sonja" (1998) similarly relies on a third party interlocutor to reveal information about the gender of the narrator. The reader may assume a female narrator until, halfway through the story, the protagonist's lover utters the pronoun "er" (he) and thereby forces the reader to reimagine the narrator as a man and her lesbian relationships as his heterosexual ones.[1] Just as in *Kältere Schichten der Luft*, the gender transition in

"Sonja" requires a third party interlocutor within the diegetic world to be initiated in the mind of the reader. In both texts, it is the moment in which heteronormativity is introduced into the lesbian relationship when queering happens—that is, the binary gender system breaks down. Anja/Schmoll experiences a doubling of gender and the unnamed narrator of "Sonja" undergoes a gender transformation.

In these two texts the determination of gender requires not only the character's expression of a gender identity but also an interlocutor to activate that character's gender potential. Moreover, the reader serves as a third agent in the construction of gender, the one who imagines (and thus, in a sense, performs) the respective character's gender transformation. In this chapter I take a cue from Judith Butler's writings on language and the body to examine the ways in which Strubel and Hermann experiment with interlocution, interpellation, and performative speech within their diegetic worlds. I then extend Butler's line of reasoning to examine the role of the reader in the interpellation process.

Interpellation and Performative Speech Acts

In her key works *Gender Trouble* and *Bodies That Matter*, Judith Butler challenges the sex/gender distinction that has been central to feminist theory since Gail Rubin's 1975 essay *The Traffic in Women: Notes on the "Political Economy" of Sex*. In this classic essay Rubin maintains that biological sex is the basis of male/female difference and that gender is its social overlay. Butler, in turn, questions the privileged position of the material body as existing prior to social meaning. Instead, she argues, the material body cannot be interpreted without preexisting social categories, and she illustrates her point with a well-known example. When a baby is born, the first pronouncement made about it is "it's a girl" or "it's a boy." Gender categories must first exist before the material body can be interpreted, and thus biological sex cannot be understood as essential or primary. Rather, biological sex is an interpretation of materiality made intelligible through discourse. In disrupting the assumption that the material body is primary, Butler gives privilege to language.[2]

In the introduction to *Excitable Speech*, Butler advances this analysis by positing language as the force behind the social orientation of the body. Building on both Louis Althusser's concept of interpellation and J. L. Austin's concept of performative speech acts, Butler demonstrates how the body comes into social existence through language. According to Althusser in his essay "Ideology and Ideological State Apparatuses," the subject does not precede the social ideologies in which s/he lives, but rather is formed through these ideologies. To demonstrate how the subject is formed through social structures that preserve and reproduce ideologies, he gives the example of a child being named at birth. He writes:

"It is certain in advance that [the child] will bear its Father's Name, and will therefore have an identity and be irreplaceable. Before its birth, the child is therefore always-already a subject, appointed as a subject in and by the specific familial ideological configuration in which it is 'expected' once it has been conceived."[3] Even before its birth, the child is appointed a subjectivity that is embedded in institutional structures that preserve social ideologies. The act of naming is essential to the process of calling the individual into subjectivity in the social world, a process that Althusser calls "interpellation."[4] The subject is always called into social existence through language, that is, by being addressed.

In *Excitable Speech* Butler applies the concept of interpellation to the body:

> Language sustains the body not by bringing it into being or feeding it in a literal way; rather, it is by being interpellated within the terms of language that a certain social existence of the body first becomes possible. To understand this, one must imagine an impossible scene, that of a body that has not yet been given social definition, a body that is, strictly speaking, not accessible to us, that nevertheless becomes accessible on the occasion of an address, a call, an interpellation that does not "discover" this body, but constitutes it fundamentally. . . . One comes to "exist" by virtue of this fundamental dependency on the address of the Other. . . . The terms that facilitate recognition are themselves conventional, the effects and instruments of a social ritual that decide, often through exclusion and violence, the linguistic conditions of survivable subjects.[5]

Butler's concern here is the queer body. Bodies with queer gender become socially recognizable once language has been created to describe them. To use a term developed in *Gender Trouble*, queer bodies become "intelligible" only through speech, once the categories of "boy" and "girl" become destabilized and other ways of thinking about gender proliferate.[6]

Butler brings together Althusserian social philosophy with the linguistic philosophy of J. L. Austin by foregrounding the performative function of naming. Using the example of hate speech, a type of naming that is typically harmful, she illustrates the positive potential of naming. She argues that while hate speech threatens the body by suggesting the possibility of physical violence, it can also become useful for increasing the types of gender that come into linguistic existence. The subject being named through hate speech may change its meaning by replicating, reiterating, and rearticulating it.[7] Furthermore, the interpellated subject replicates the system by naming others and thus performatively bringing others into linguistic and social existence (25–26).

Relational Gender in Antje Rávic Strubel's *Kältere Schichten der Luft*

The main theme of Antje Rávic Strubel's *Kältere Schichten der Luft* is the interpellation of a subject and his body. The story takes place over the course of a few weeks during which the narrator, Anja, a thirty-something woman from former East Germany, is employed at a summer camp in Sweden. While there she meets a mysterious young woman, also a German, who lives nearby. Upon their first encounter, the young woman (mis)recognizes Anja, calling her "Schmoll," an acquaintance, or perhaps lover, from her past. Although Anja initially protests, she soon begins to feel Schmoll emerging within her body when the young woman is present. Anja/Schmoll and the young woman engage in a love affair, but after a violent encounter between Schmoll and a fellow camp worker that leads to the coworker's death, the young woman disappears. Anja leaves the camp, returning to her home in Halberstadt and leaving Schmoll behind her.

The majority of secondary literature on Strubel's work focuses its discussion of queerness on her characters' lesbian relationships, female masculinities, and the coupling of gender and dislocation as themes following German unification. Susanne Kelley points out that in *Kältere Schichten der Luft*, Strubel distances her narrators from the physical geography of the nation that has disappeared, seeking neutral territory in Sweden (as she has in the Czech Republic and the United States in other novels) and thereby pairing the theme of dislocation with the main character's identity exploration.[8] Emily Jeremiah similarly links queer gender with geographical mobility, describing displacement in Strubel's work as a type of queer nomadism that "provides a useful way of going beyond ideas of Germanness as fixed and homogenous" and thereby challenging both nationalism and heterosexism.[9] Claudia Breger discusses the links between masculinity in crisis, displacement, and disorientation in the novel *Unter Schnee* (Snowed Under, 2001),[10] and Jeremiah points out that in Strubel's texts such destabilized men are set against queer women who represent transformative possibilities.[11] Finally, Helen Finch has connected dislocation in Strubel's texts to a need to work through memories of National Socialism and the East German past in order to "interrogate clichéd literary representations of Vergangenheitsbewältigung."[12]

In *Kältere Schichten der Luft*, Strubel develops a concept of gender and sexuality that is difficult to delimit. As Beret Norman has stated, Strubel's work attempts to push beyond the structured socialization of the GDR and explore "new ways of being, to expand the parameters of identity further than the limits of the binary language and social life."[13] Indeed, in *Kältere Schichten der Luft*, timelessness, tricks of the light, and the transitory space of the summer camp are motifs that support a reading of Anja/Schmoll's gender as ephemeral and situational. The category "transgendered" is perhaps the closest identity category available to us, but it is imprecise. Rather, Anja experiences a plurality of gender when Schmoll is present, since both she and Schmoll inhabit her body simultaneously. Moreover, Schmoll is purely relational. He is a discursive project whose social existence in the diegetic world depends upon interlocution between Anja and the young woman and whose embodiment depends upon the imagination of the reader.

Gender conceived as something relational derives in queer theory from Gilles Deleuze and Félix Guattari's concept of "becoming."[14] In the introduction to *A Thousand Plateaus*, Deleuze and Guattari repudiate the notion of stable identity in preference for relationships and interactions, illustrating their point with the example of the orchid and the wasp. The orchid mimics the wasp to attract it (and thus becomes a "becoming-wasp") and the wasp becomes part of the orchid's reproductive system by spreading its pollen (and thus becomes a "becoming-orchid"). The two entities become so entwined that they can no longer be conceived of as separate beings. Thus the parties in the system are always implicated in the "deterritorialization" of the self and the "reterritorialization" of the other, so that identity is lost in favor of interaction.[15] In terms of gender and sexual identity, "becoming" is a way of thinking about the fluidity of identity, interactions based on sexual object choice or sexual practice, and the transformative nature of desire. When paired with Butler's notion of interpellation, "becoming" emerges as a useful concept for understanding the ephemerality of Schmoll's existence, his surfacing through sexual desire, his reliance on speech between Anja and the young woman, and his quality of existing as part of Anja yet remaining separate from her sense of self.

Schmoll's interpellation occurs within the first three pages of the text and is the first event of the novel:

> Das Mädchen stieg langsam an Land.... "Schmoll," sagte sie und wandte sich zu mir um. "Sie sind ein kluger Junge. Sie haben die ganze Zeit gut aufgepaßt." ... "Ich heiße nicht Schmoll," sagte ich, "Und ich bin kein Junge." ... "Sehen Sie," sagte sie mir ins Ohr. "Ich habe Sie endlich gefunden. Ich wußte es."[16]

> [The girl came onto land slowly.... "Schmoll," she said and turned to me. "You are a clever boy. You were careful the whole time" ... "My name isn't Schmoll," I said, "and I'm not a boy" ... "You see," she said in my ear. "I finally found you. I knew it."]

The young woman's actions are as baffling to Anja as they are to the reader. She confounds social convention not only by insisting that Anja is Schmoll and ignoring Anja's subsequent objections, but also by using the formal pronoun "Sie" to address Schmoll, someone with whom she claims to share an intimate relationship.

Although Anja is initially unaware of her participation in the interpellation of Schmoll, it becomes evident in the next moment when she imagines herself and the young woman in an advertisement like the ones she has seen at Bahnhof Zoo in Berlin:

> Wir standen wie auf einer Werbetafel am Bahnhof Zoo. Auf einem dieser Hochglanzbilder. Anschmiegsame Mädchen, klein, in kräftige Schultern gekuschelt, und selbstsichere Jungs. Jungs, die auf ihr Mädchen und den Ku'damm hinuntersahen. Wir waren in dieses Bild eingepaßt. (*KSL*, 11)

> [We stood as though on an advertisement panel at Zoo train station. In one of those high gloss pictures. Affectionate girls, small, cuddled in strong shoulders, and self-assured boys who looked down at their girls and the Ku'damm. We had fitted ourselves into this picture.]

As Butler points out, the interpellation of a subject into linguistic and social existence relies on the preexistence of some convention, so that the individual is situated within structures already available through language. In this scene, the advertisement (literally a sign) provides Anja with that structure, allowing her to imagine herself as a boy. She both replicates the boy/girl binary offered up by the advertisement and queers it by using it to double her own gender.

To come to full social existence, however, Schmoll requires social validation in the wider community, and the young woman assures Schmoll's legitimacy by spreading the word about him around camp. Schmoll begins to develop a reputation, even though no one has actually seen him, and thus takes on an existence that is somewhat independent of Anja. Material evidence of his existence appears when the camp's soccer ball is vandalized with the words "no gays!" written on it in English. Anja is hurt by the hate speech, believing the words to be directed at her as a lesbian woman, and she interrogates her coworkers about it. The young woman, however, informs her that Schmoll is behind the act:

> "Das waren Sie doch selber. *Sie* haben das draufgeschrieben. . . . Das haben Sie gut gemacht. Sie waren glücklicherweise so klug, mir diese Botschaft zu hinterlassen. Sonst könnte es am Ende noch zu Verwechslungen kommen. Es könnte so aussehen, als wären Sie gar nicht Sie. Wenn man denen im Camp glaubte, gäbe es Sie nämlich nicht. Davor haben Sie mich beschützt. Uns beide." (*KSL*, 100; emphasis original)

["But that was you yourself. *You* wrote that. . . . You did well. You were clever enough, luckily, to leave me this message. Otherwise there could have been some confusion. It could have appeared as though you weren't you at all. If one were to believe the people at camp, you don't really exist. You protected me from that. Us both."]

The young woman's perplexing explanation can be understood in a number of ways. First, Schmoll could be writing himself into existence, calling on the ritual of hate speech to give intelligibility to queer identity. In *Excitable Speech*, Butler points out that hate speech is both hurtful and potentially creative: "We sometimes cling to the terms that pain us because, at a minimum, they offer us some form of social and discursive existence."[17] Or perhaps Schmoll is attempting to differentiate himself from Anja, lending himself currency in the camp community, which seems to harbor a latent homophobia and displays a general disregard for her. He is not the gay one; she is. Third, the young woman could have authored the offense in hopes of legitimizing her fantasy of Schmoll and further bringing him into existence. Whatever the case may be, the use of hate speech is effective. Schmoll is brought into social existence as a scapegoat for the camp's bad behavior.

Schmoll does not remain solely a linguistic project, however. Once he offers a new plausible gender for Anja, she begins to interpret the materiality of her body differently. The first time Anja sees Schmoll on her physical body, she is trying on a men's shirt alone in a dressing room:

Ich schloß den Vorhang und zog das Hemd über. . . . das Hemd paßte. Und die Veränderung war erstaunlich. Sie war nichts Großes, sie bestand nur in einer Verschiebung, als wären ein paar Details vertauscht oder zurechtgerückt oder als bilde sich ein Körper in mehreren Umrissen ab, von denen aber nur einer aktuell sichtbar wäre. . . . Ich stand in der provisorischen Umkleidekabine eines Kaufhauses, in dem sie alles verkauften, Klamotten und Gartenstühle und Lachs, und ich sah auf einmal tatsächlich wie ein Junge aus. Vierzehnjährig. Mitten in der Pubertät. (*KSL*, 86–87)

[I closed the curtain and put on the shirt. . . . the shirt fit. And the change was astonishing. It was nothing big, it consisted only in a slight shift, as though a couple of details were transposed or set straight or as though a body displayed itself in multiple contours, of which only one was visible at a time. . . . I stood in the provisional fitting room of a department store where they sold everything, clothes and lawn chairs and salmon, and suddenly I really looked like a boy. Fourteen. In the middle of puberty.]

The men's shirt fits her, but at the same time it changes her. Anja has already told us that she wears unisex clothing around camp, grew up imitating her brothers, and learned to love women from them, but she has always been intelligible as a woman. The shift, while small, is decisive. Anja sees multiple contours outlining her body and thus new possibilities for gender. In the context of this change, she sees the department store differently: as offering a multitude of instruments for everyday life, even those instruments that will make her new life as Schmoll possible, including the shirt. In the same breath she describes the changing room as "provisional," that is, transitional and temporary, an indication perhaps that Schmoll himself will not be permanent.

According to Butler, the interpellated subject has been brought fully into linguistic social existence once s/he can name others and thereby utilize his/her social agency to replicate the system.[18] The moment after Anja recognizes Schmoll in the mirror, Anja/Schmoll decides on a name for the young woman: Siri. As the novel progresses, Schmoll and Siri will emerge in those moments when Anja and the young woman spend time together. Schmoll and Siri rely on one another for interpellation and thereby exist in a relational system similar to Deleuze and Guattari's orchid and wasp.

This scene in which Anja sees Schmoll in the mirror is the first moment in which the reader imagines Schmoll's body as an overlay to Anja's. As the novel progresses, the reader continues to imagine (and thereby construct) Schmoll's body, but often only in parts. Schmoll's body emerges most completely in a final scene of the book when he and Siri dance:

> Er tanzte.... Er war ein Junge noch ganz ohne Vergangenheit bis auf die centgroße Narbe am Knie ... Er war ein Junge mit hellen Augen und einer Pigmentschwäche, eine kleine, weiße Flechte zog sich an seiner Schläfe hoch, ein Junge, der zum Beat den Kopf in den Nacken warf und dem die Hose ein bißchen zu tief auf der Hüfte hing.... Er tanzte zum ersten Mal und für sie. (*KSL*, 136)

> [He danced.... He was a boy still wholly without a history except for the penny-sized scar on his knee.... He was a boy with bright eyes and a weak pigmentation, a small white patch went up his temple, a boy who threw his head back to the beat and whose pants hung a bit too low around the hips.... He danced for the first time and for her.]

The young woman has called Schmoll into existence, but it is the reader who is ultimately responsible for Schmoll's embodiment. Although we as readers envision Schmoll dancing, Siri soon reminds us that Anja's physical transformation into Schmoll is not one that completes itself in the diegetic world. Later, in the novel's only sex scene, Siri remarks:

"Sie sind schön. Sie haben den Körper einer Frau." ... "Aber Sie sind ein Junge." ... "Ich kann ihn deutlich sehen." ... "Gucken Sie sich diese Arme an. Und die Augen! In Ihren Augen nehme ich ihn ganz deutlich wahr." (*KSL*, 167)

["You are beautiful. You have the body of a woman." ... "But you are a boy." ... "I can see him clearly." ... "Look at these arms. And the eyes! I see him quite clearly in your eyes."]

The reader is reminded of Anja's previous observation that she possesses "zwei Muskulaturen, zwei Schichten Haut" (*KSL*, 135; two muscular systems, two layers of skin). Anja never transforms completely into Schmoll. She narrates Schmoll even in those moments when he most takes over.

What is not fully possible in the diegetic world is thus possible for the reader. In certain moments—the scene with the mirror and later when Schmoll dances—we imagine Anja's transformation into Schmoll. In those moments in which Schmoll most consumes Anja, the reader goes one step further so that Schmoll is totally embodied. Schmoll has been called into social existence within the diegetic world through the act of interpellation. The final step of the transformation happens, even if only in moments, through the involvement of the reader's imagination. Yet this is a precarious kind of body construction—one that is easily hampered by the diegetic world. Schmoll's existence always relies on the cooperation of Anja, Siri, and the reader.

Anja contemplates the loss of Schmoll in the last pages of the text, as she sits on a bus heading home to Halberstadt. She must leave the summer camp after Schmoll and her coworker Ralf have engaged in a fight that led to Ralf's death. Both the young woman/Siri and Schmoll have disappeared as a result. In the last pages of the novel, Anja reflects on the impossibility of regaining the interpellated identity and the second body:

Ich werde in diesem Bus nach Halberstadt fahren, und in Halberstadt werden meine Brüder Anja zu mir sagen. ... Und vielleicht werden mich meine Brüder manchmal, verunsichert, *Schmoll* rufen, wenn ich sie darum bitte, und dann ihre Klappe halten, weil wir noch immer Geschwister sind. Sie werden *Schmoll* rufen, und es wird idiotisch sein. (*KSL*, 188, emphasis original)

[I will travel to Halberstadt in this bus, and in Halberstadt my brothers will say Anja to me. ... And maybe my brothers will sometimes call me *Schmoll*, bewildered, when I ask them to, and then keep their mouths shut because we're still siblings. They will say *Schmoll*, and it will be idiotic.]

Schmoll was a discursive project that was only possible between Anja and the young woman. Even though all witnesses to Schmoll's existence are gone, however, Anja realizes that she has proof that he physically existed. Schmoll had mustered the strength to defeat Ralf, who was much larger and had overpowered and sexually assaulted Anja earlier in the novel. Ralf's death is Anja's unsettling proof that Schmoll was real.

Reader Confusion/Gender Transformation in Judith Hermann's "Sonja"

In her short story "Sonja," from the collection *Sommerhaus, später* (1998; published in English as *Summerhouse, Later*, 2001), Judith Hermann similarly thematizes gender mutability by creating characters with differing degrees of gender intelligibility, and a first-person narrator whose gender is left undisclosed for the first half of the story. Whereas Strubel presents gender mutability and relational gender as major themes throughout *Kältere Schichten der Luft*, the moment of gender transition in Hermann's work is an effect of defying reader expectations. In the first half of the story, Hermann leaves the gender of her narrator open to the reader's imagination, and a first-time reader of this story may envision a female first-person narrator.[19] Nearly halfway through the story, however, any such reader expectation is defied when the narrator's lover, Sonja, utters the male pronoun "er" in reference to her/him and thus establishes that the narrator is male. The reader who has envisioned this narrator as a woman must reimagine the narrator as a man, and thus the protagonist is queered, paradoxically, by being oriented in what Judith Butler calls the "heterosexual matrix."[20] In this section, I examine the gender intelligibility of the three main characters in "Sonja," discuss the moment of female-to-male gender transformation initiated by Sonja's act of interpellation, and trace the implications for the narrator of being oriented in the heterosexual matrix.

Hermann's short story opens as the unnamed first-person narrator observes a strange young woman on a train from Hamburg to Berlin. Upon arriving in Berlin, the woman insists on following the narrator through the city. Over the course of the story, the narrator and Sonja develop an unconventional relationship that, if not exactly romantic, is erotically charged. The narrator finds Sonja alternately fascinating and irritating but does not commit to her because of a steady relationship with a woman named Verena in Hamburg. Ultimately, the narrator must choose between the eccentric Sonja and the more traditionally feminine Verena, and when the narrator chooses Verena, Sonja disappears. At the end of the story, the narrator is left with feelings of dissatisfaction and longing for the unintelligible Sonja.

In "Sonja," Hermann proposes a range of intelligibly female characters: Verena, who performs femininity easily and effectively; Sonja, who at times displays an almost parodic excess of femininity; and the lesbian narrator whom Hermann queers, or renders "unintelligible," later in the story.[21] A reading of the narrator as a lesbian at the beginning of the story is, of course, contingent upon the way in which the reader approaches the text. The story "Sonja" appears in a collection in which all other first-person narrators are (or at least are presumed to be) female.[22] Moreover, an initial reading of the narrator as female may also be affected by the reader's exposure to paratextual materials, especially the media publicity surrounding Judith Hermann's debut work.[23] Hermann was grouped with a number of female writers, characterized collectively as "das literarische Fräuleinwunder" (the literary wonder girls), who emerged in the late 1990s. These writers generally foregrounded women's perspectives in their works, and their book debuts were surrounded by a media spectacle that focused on the authors' femininity.[24]

Although Hermann could not have known in advance the degree of media attention that both her collection and her image would attract, her choice to conceal her narrator's gender in "Sonja" suggests a conscious play with gender. The narrator is not forthcoming with self-description, and thus the sparing details about the narrator hold value for interpreting gender. For example, on the first page, the narrator speaks of braiding Verena's hair—"[I]ch war sehr in sie verliebt. Verena hatte einen Kirschmund und rabenschwarzes Haar, das ich ihr jeden Morgen zu zwei dicken, schweren Zöpfen flocht . . ."; (I was very much in love with her. Verena had a cherry mouth and raven-black hair that I would plait into two thick, heavy braids every morning . . .)[25]—an activity that conjures images of sisterly affection rather than of masculine sexual or romantic attraction.[26]

In contrast to the narrator, whose femininity is implied by the narration, both Verena and Sonja represent more overt, yet different, expressions of femininity. Verena's femininity is anchored in cultural traditions. As Nancy Nobile points out, her "Kirschmund" (cherry mouth) and "zwei dicke schwere Zöpfe" (two thick, heavy braids) align Verena with the prototypical fairytale protagonist.[27] Verena's beauty is thus anchored in a genre that is often prescriptive of gender roles, behaviors, and beauty standards. Moreover, the narrator describes Verena as both adept at household matters and sexually available, thereby creating a domestic space of comfort and satisfaction for the narrator. Her territorialism over domestic space follows the nineteenth century "angel of the house" or more current "domestic goddess" model of femininity, brought up to date by her sexual attractiveness and availability.[28]

Sonja, by contrast, represents irritation rather than satisfaction, and her femininity is complicated by excesses and anachronisms in her body and gesture.²⁹ Sonja's tense posture on the train ("wie bei einem Bombenalarm"; as though there'd been a bomb alarm) is what initially draws the narrator's attention (*S*, 55). She unsettles the narrator, who describes her as "altmodisch" (old-fashioned), "biegsam" (pliable), and "seltsam" (strange) throughout the text. Despite the irritation that Sonja provokes, however, the narrator is also attracted to her, which causes a tension that becomes clear in a later scene in which the two meet at a bar for their first date:

> Sonja kam eine halbe Stunde zu spät. . . . Sie trug ein unglaublich altmodisches, rotes Samtkleid, und ich bemerkte irritiert, daß sie Aufsehen erregte. Sie stöckelte auf viel zu hohen Schuhen auf mich zu . . . und ich war kurz versucht ihr zu sagen, daß ich sie unmöglich fand, ihre Aufmachung, ihre Unpünktlichkeit, ihre ganze Person. Aber dann grinste sie, kletterte auf den Barhocker, kramte ihre Zigaretten aus einem winzigen Rucksack hervor, und mein Ärger löste sich in Belustigung auf. (*S*, 60)

> [Sonja arrived half an hour late. . . . She was wearing an unbelievably old-fashioned red velvet dress, and I noticed with irritation that she was attracting attention. She tottered toward me on heels that were much too high. . . and I was just about to tell her that I found her impossible—her style, her unpunctuality, her whole persona. But then she grinned, climbed onto the bar stool, dug her cigarettes out of a tiny backpack, and my anger turned into amusement.]

Not only is Sonja associated with anachronism in this scene—she arrives late and wears outdated clothing—but her appearance is loaded with an excess of femininity. She wears a red velvet dress, attire that is presumably too formal for a casual meeting at a bar, and "totters" on shoes with heels that are too high for her. Sonja's femininity in this scene verges on parody and conjures up the image of an inexperienced drag queen rather than someone who practices femininity easily.

For nearly half the story, Hermann draws out these themes of gender intelligibility and feminine excess, and the reader envisions the narrator entangled in two very different lesbian relationships. The moment of interpellation—that is, the moment in which Sonja calls forth a male narrator—is thus abrupt and surprising. The narrator describes arriving at a party to which Sonja has invited her:

> Die Wohnungstür stand offen, irgend jemand zog mich in den Flur, und dort stand Sonja. . . . sie lächelte mich an mit einem absolut siegesgewissen Gesichtsausdruck und ich fand sie zum ersten Mal schön. . . . Sonja deutete auf mich und sagte: "Das ist er." (*S*, 65)

[The apartment door stood open. Someone pulled me into the hallway, and there stood Sonja.... she smiled at me with an expression of absolute triumph and I found her beautiful for the first time.... Sonja pointed at me and said: "That's him."]

The masculine personal pronoun appears only this one time in the story. Its placement not only at the end of a paragraph, but marking the end of a text block, emphasizes its magnitude. The reader who has pictured a female narrator to this point has the space of a text break to reimagine the narrator as a man. Just as the mysterious young woman in *Kältere Schichten der Luft* calls Schmoll into existence, Sonja calls the narrator's male body into social existence in the mind of the reader. Paradoxically, by establishing that the narrator is a man and thereby orienting him intelligibly within the heterosexual matrix, Hermann queers the narrator. What is more, the reader must then grapple with the memory of this character—either attempting to reimagine the narrator as a man from the beginning of the story (and then harboring two memories of the narrator, one as female and one as male) or remembering a character who changes gender mid-text like Virginia Woolf's Orlando.

This gender transformation not only has an effect on the reader but also has implications for the narrator and Sonja in their diegetic world. After Sonja has effectively gendered the narrator male, a patriarchal power system rules their mode of engagement with one another. They attempt a private life in domestic space together, and their relationship, which at the beginning of the story took place in bars, parks, and streets, becomes uncomfortable and forced. Sonja visits the narrator every evening, once his workday is finished, and remains until well into the night. Rather than exhibiting the excessive personality that irritated and amused the narrator in the beginning of the story, Sonja has taken on the role of the passive and silent wife. The narrator describes Sonja in an infantilizing manner and, in one instance, compares her directly to a child. In these passages Sonja is not the excessive, over-the-top pseudo-drag queen in red velvet, but rather a small, silent child who patters around in stocking feet, following her husband/father around his apartment. Unlike Verena, she does not cook, clean, or sleep with the narrator, and the narrator's dismissive descriptions of her as silent and childlike contribute to a picture of her as small, unimportant, and asexual.[30] By making their relationship explicitly heterosexual and attempting to create a private domestic space with the narrator, Sonja has entered the heterosexual matrix, a place where she does not belong.

Butler argues in *Bodies That Matter* that heterosexuality can only maintain a sense of cohesion as an identity category if it keeps homosexuality at its constitutive border.[31] Hermann demonstrates this in her story as well. The narrator's heterosexuality is relational, having been conjured through interpellation, and he eventually picks Verena, the partner who he thinks will best perform the role of wife. The narrator believes he is choosing satisfaction (Verena) over irritation (Sonja), yet the narrator's sense of irritation does not vanish with Sonja. Just as queer identity remains on the constitutive border of heterosexuality, the narrator's sense of irritation returns time and again, reminding him that his choice of Verena also includes the loss of Sonja.

Paradoxically, the narrator's decision to be with Verena in many ways complicates the domestic ideal. Whereas Sonja had informed him, matter-of-factly, that they will live together, marry, and have children (despite the fact that she refused to sleep with him), Verena informs him that she will not take his name and will stay in Hamburg. The two will remain together institutionally, but not spatially or emotionally in the way that he and Sonja coexisted. While Verena's choice to live in separate spaces defies traditional notions of gender and domesticity, living separately is the only way she and the narrator can maintain a clearly intelligible heterosexual relationship according to the logic of the story. Hamburg has been the place in which, the reader imagines, Verena and the narrator have had a lesbian relationship. Berlin is the place of gender unintelligibility, performance of feminine excess, misrecognition, and only strained heterosexuality. The heterosexual matrix only works for the couple when Verena can visit intermittently, play the role of the domestic wife, and disappear again before the role loses its charm. Heterosexual marriage can only work for this couple when they have the distance to maintain their domestic ideal and when they have to perform it for only short periods of time.

The last sentence of the story indicates that the heterosexual matrix remains tenuous for the narrator:

> Manchmal habe ich auf der Straße das Gefühl, jemand liefe dicht hinter mir her, ich drehe mich dann um, und da ist niemand, aber das Gefühl der Irritation bleibt. (S, 84)

[Sometimes when I'm on the street I have the feeling that someone is walking right behind me. I turn around and no one's there, but the feeling of irritation remains.]

The narrator will continue to be reminded of Sonja in those transitional spaces outside the domestic sphere—the streets, bars, and parks—where they had been happy. Sonja is the interlocutor who had the power to queer the narrator through interpellation. Verena has no such power, because she represents conventionality and intelligibility—either a lesbian conventionality or a heterosexual one. The narrator has had the choice between convention or queerness. In these moments of movement and passage, the narrator is reminded that queerness is actually constitutive of his heterosexuality.

Conclusion

Strubel's and Hermann's texts that thematize the mutability of gender follow in a tradition of women's writing exemplified by Virginia Woolf's *Orlando* (1928), Ingeborg Bachmann's *Malina* (1971), and the collection of short stories on gender transformation, *Geschlechtertausch* (Sex Change, 1980), by Sara Kirsch, Irmtraud Morgner, and Christa Wolf. Strubel and Hermann depart from the tradition of such authors, however, in their depiction of gender and sex as relational. Rather than depicting gender transformation as drag, as a character's mysterious sex change, or as the narration of an alter ego, Hermann and Strubel write bodies that depend on an interlocutor to expose their gender potential. This writing follows on the heels of gender and queer theory since the 1990s, which has introduced new ways of thinking about gender and the body. Most notably, Judith Butler's works *Gender Trouble*, *Bodies That Matter*, and *Excitable Speech* have been influential in reconceptualizing both gender and sex as social constructions. Queer interpretations of Gilles Deleuze and Félix Guattari's concept of "becoming" have helped bring to light the relational nature of gender and identity as well. Moreover, both Strubel and Hermann utilize the scenario of a female-to-male transition to dismantle rigid gender binaries, a motif that is, no doubt, reflective of more visible female masculinities as outlined by Judith Halberstam.[32]

A particularly striking similarity between Hermann's and Strubel's work is that both texts produce moments of genderqueer by introducing elements of heteronormativity into a lesbian relationship. In Strubel's text, the heterosexual matrix provides a social and linguistic structure that makes Schmoll's interpellation possible. In Hermann's text, the heterosexual matrix is exposed to be an unnatural and uncomfortable fit for the characters forced into it in the interpellative moment. Both texts thereby destabilize the "naturalness" of heterosexuality and refute the rigidity of binary gender. Heterosexuality then becomes a tool for its ostensible opposite, "queer."

By depicting fluid sexuality and gender in their texts, Hermann and Strubel contribute to a larger trend in German literature of destabilizing the binary gender system that upholds patriarchy. Contemporary authors such as Julia Franck, Angela Krauss, Thomas Meinecke, and Emine Sevgi Özdamar, among others, thematize a free play of gender based on masquerade and performance.[33] My reading of Hermann's and Strubel's work draws attention to a new theoretical approach to gender in literature in the twenty-first century, one that involves the active participation of the reader in constructing bodies. Both Strubel and Hermann demonstrate literature's unique ability to construct queer bodies and variable gender. What is more, both authors demonstrate that such bodies rely on the active participation of the reader to help construct them. In some cases, the reader brings a gender transition into effect even more completely in his/her imagination than in the diegetic world. The reader may be informed only after the fact that the gender transition that occurred in his/her imagination did not take place in the world of the story. In these moments, the imagination becomes a third space apart from the world of the reader and the diegetic world of the text. This is a dynamic space for rethinking gender.

Notes

[1] I base my interpretation of gender in "Sonja" on my own reading experience, as well as on conversations I have had with others about this story. In several different instances, others have expressed to me their sense of embarrassment of having gotten the gender of the narrator "wrong." Rather than assuming that the reader has misunderstood something in the first half of the text—an assumption that has no support in Hermann's story—I find it more productive to think of this gender confusion as an effect of the text, and one that illustrates the active involvement of the reader in constructing bodies and gender in literature. See also Maria Katharina Wiedlack, who reports discussing a similar reading experience with peers in "Transgressing Genders—A Queer Reading of German Literature: Judith Hermann's 'Sonja' and Annemarie Schwarzenbach's *Lyric Novella*," in *Queering Paradigms*, ed. Burkhard Scherer (Bern: Peter Lang, 2010), 319.

[2] Butler introduces this argument in chapter 1 of *Gender Trouble* and explicates it further in *Bodies that Matter* with the example given. Judith Butler, *Gender Trouble: Feminism and the Subversion of Identity* (New York: Routledge, 1990), 6–9. Judith Butler, *Bodies that Matter: On the Discursive Limits of "Sex"* (New York: Routledge, 1993), 230–33.

[3] Louis Althusser, *Lenin and Philosophy and Other Essays*, trans. Ben Brewster (New York: Monthly Review, 1972), 176.

[4] Althusser makes a distinction between individuals and subjects. Individuals are subjects when they are aware of their place in the social world. Interpellation transforms individuals into subjects. Althusser, *Lenin and Philosophy*, 176–78.

[5] Judith Butler, *Excitable Speech: A Politics of the Performative* (New York: Routledge, 1997), 5.

[6] A body is "intelligible," according to Butler, when a person clearly expresses one gender through his/her clothing, gesture, and behaviors, and when this gender aligns with both that person's biological sex and sexual desire for members of the opposite sex. A person's gender intelligibility has direct implications for the ways in which that person is regarded, what choices are made available to that person, and whether that person is marginalized, accepted, or rejected socially. Butler, *Gender Trouble*, 151.

[7] Butler, *Excitable Speech*, 19–20.

[8] Susanne Kelley, "The Travel Motif in Post-*Wende* German Literature: Angela Krauß' *Die Überfliegerin* and Antje Rávic Strubel's *Offene Blende*," *South Atlantic Review* 74, no. 3 (2009): 12. Elizabeth Boa reads the Czech ski resort in *Unter*

Schnee as a backdrop for examining East-West German difference as it relates to historical memory. See Elizabeth Boa, "Labyrinths, Mazes, and Mosaics: Fiction by Christa Wolf, Ingo Schulze, Antje Rávic Strubel, and Jens Sparschuh," in *Debating German Cultural Identity since 1989*, ed. Anne Fuchs, Kathleen James, and Linda Shortt (Rochester, NY: Camden House, 2011), 146–47.

[9] Emily Jeremiah, "Disorienting Fictions: Antje Rávic Strubel and Post-Unification East German Identity," *German Life and Letters* 62, no. 2 (2009): 221.

[10] Claudia Breger, "Hegemony, Marginalization, and Feminine Masculinity: Antje Rávic Strubel's *Unter Schnee*," *Seminar* 44, no. 1 (2008): 154–73.

[11] Emily Jeremiah, *Nomadic Ethics in Contemporary Women's Writing in German: Strange Subjects* (Rochester, NY: Camden House, 2012), 115. See also: Jeremiah, "Disorienting Fictions," 226–27.

[12] Helen Finch, "Gender, Identity, and Memory in the Novels of Antje Rávic Strubel," *Women in German Yearbook* 28 (2012): 82.

[13] Beret Norman, "Antje Rávic Strubel's Ambiguities of Identity as Social Disruption," *Women in German Yearbook* 28 (2012): 66. In a 2008 interview with Anke Biendarra, Strubel asserts that by challenging the systemization of gender, one can push the boundaries of perceived reality: "Was mich stört und womit ich mich beschäftige, ist die Verengung der Realität durch verengte Wahrnehmung. . . . In Bezug auf Geschlechter beispielsweise wird jede kleine Abweichung sofort benannt, beschriftet und kann damit abgelegt werden in die Schublade, damit sie nicht mehr beunruhigt, damit es die immer perfektere Ordnung nicht durcheinanderbringt." Anke Biendarra, "'Schreiben verwandelt mich': Anke Biendarra im Gespräch mit Antje Rávic Strubel," *Glossen* 27 (2008): no pagination, accessed June 21, 2013, http://www2.dickinson.edu/glossen/Heft27/index.html.

[14] Noreen Giffney, "Introduction: The 'q' Word," in *The Ashgate Research Companion to Queer Theory*, ed. Noreen Giffney and Michael O'Rourke (Farnham, UK: Ashgate, 2009), 6.

[15] Gilles Deleuze and Félix Guattari, *A Thousand Plateaus: Capitalism and Schizophrenia*, trans. Brian Massumi (Minneapolis: University of Minnesota Press, 1987), 3–25.

[16] Antje Rávic Strubel, *Kältere Schichten der Luft* (Frankfurt am Main: S. Fischer Verlag, 2007), 10–11. All translations from *Kältere Schichten der Luft* are my own. Further references to this work are given in the text using the abbreviation *KSL*.

[17] Butler, *Excitable Speech*, 26.

[18] Ibid., 25–26.

[19] See Wiedlack, "Transgressing Genders," 319.

[20] The "heterosexual matrix" is the system of cultural expectations, institutions, and structures that create and maintain norms regarding gender and sexuality. The heterosexual matrix has direct implications for the ways in which bodies are interpreted and either accepted or rejected socially. See Butler, *Gender Trouble*, 151.

[21] Most of the scholarship on the story discusses a male narrator without addressing Hermann's choice to leave his/her gender open to interpretation. Only Mila

Ganeva attempts to resolve this gender ambiguity by stating: "The author endows the male narrator with almost feminine flexibility and softness, which allows him to tolerate the ambiguity and the ultimate futility of the mysterious erotic play initiated by Sonja." Mila Ganeva, "Female Flaneurs: Judith Hermann's *Sommerhaus, später* and *Nichts als Gespenster*," *Gegenwartsliteratur: Ein germanistisches Jahrbuch* 3 (2004): 268. Although Ganeva's assertion is plausible, I find that a queer reading of the character offers an opportunity to speak more broadly about the multiple ways in which gender operates in this text.

[22] The gender of the narrator-protagonist of the title story "Sommerhaus, später" is also left to the reader's interpretation, and the secondary literature on that story also assumes a female narrator.

[23] Jörg Döring, "Hinterhaus, jetzt—Jugend, augenblicklich—Hurrikan, später. Zum Paratext der Bücher von Judith Hermann," in *Fräuleinwunder literarisch: Literatur von Frauen zu Beginn des 21. Jahrhunderts*, ed. Christiane Caemmerer, Walter Delabar, and Helga Meise (Bern: Peter Lang, 2005), 13–35.

[24] Like many other members of the *Fräuleinwunder*, Hermann's likeness was familiar to potential readers before they had a chance to read her work. Hermann's famed PR photo takes up half a page in the original hard cover of *Sommerhaus, später* and features her in black and white with her hair swept back into a bun, her head leaning gently to the right, gazing off the page toward the reader. The photo is stylized to give Hermann a timeless, feminine look. Jörg Döring contends that the photo influenced not only who purchased the book but also how s/he read it. See Döring, "Hinterhaus, jetzt," 13. See also Ganeva, "Female Flaneurs," 255.

[25] Judith Hermann, "Sonja," in *Sommerhaus, später* (Frankfurt am Main: Fischer Verlag, 1998), 55. Further references to this work are given in the text using the abbreviation S.

[26] All translations of "Summerhouse, Later" are my own, in consultation with the translation by Margot Bettauer Dembo. Page number citations reference the German original. Judith Hermann, *Summerhouse, Later*, trans. Margot Bettauer Dembo (New York: Harper Collins, 2001).

[27] Nancy Nobile, "A Ring of Keys: Thresholds to the Past in Judith Hermann's *Sommerhaus, später*," *Gegenwartsliteratur: Ein germanistisches Jahrbuch* 9 (2010): 296.

[28] The "angel of the house" model of domestic femininity is based on the poem of the same title by Coventry Patmore from 1854. The poem was popularized in Europe and America in the late nineteenth century and became prescriptive of women's domestic roles.

[29] See Esther K. Bauer, "Narratives of Femininity in Judith Hermann's *Sommerhaus, Later*," *Women in German Yearbook* 25 (2009): 50–75. See also Nobile, "A Ring of Keys," 297.

[30] Scholarship on this story describes Sonja variously as a muse, a projection screen, and "auratic" rather than as a real woman. See Esther Bauer, "Narratives of Femininity," 61; Thomas Borgstedt, "Wunschwelten: Judith Hermann und die Neuromantik der Gegenwart," *Gegenwartsliteratur: Ein germanistisches*

Jahrbuch 5 (2006): 207–32; Katja Stopka, "Aus nächster Nähe so fern: Zu den Erzählungen von Terezia Mora und Judith Hermann," in *Bestandsaufnahmen: Deutschsprachige Literatur der neunziger Jahre aus interkultureller Sicht*, ed. Matthias Harder (Würzburg: Königshausen & Neumann, 2001), 164; and Brigitte Weingart, "Judith Hermann: *Sommerhaus, später*," in *Meisterwerke: Deutschsprachige Autorinnen im 20. Jahrhundert*, ed. Claudia Benthien und Inge Stephan (Cologne: Böhlau Verlag, 2005), 148–75.

[31] Butler, *Bodies that Matter*, 187–89.

[32] Judith Halberstam, *Female Masculinity* (Durham, NC: Duke University Press, 1998).

[33] See, for example: Necia Chronister, "'I Am Dismantling Everything Down to the Very Skeleton': Rupture, Multiplicity, and the 'Queer Encounter' in Angela Krauß's *Die Überfliegerin* (1995)," *Women in German Yearbook* 28 (Winter 2012): 42–64; and Alexandra Merley Hill, *Playing House: Motherhood, Intimacy, and Domestic Spaces in Julia Franck's Fiction* (Oxford: Peter Lang, 2012).

2: Matrilineal Narrative and the Feminist Family Romance

Valerie Heffernan

RECENT YEARS HAVE SEEN the publication in Germany of a vast number and array of multigenerational family narratives that look back to the turbulent history of the twentieth century. They look in particular to the family stories that are passed on from one generation to the next as a way of understanding and representing the past, and they also explore those that are kept secret or hidden from view and yet contribute to shaping the present. These narratives use the family as a prism through which to explore the residual impact of the historical events of the twentieth century, and in particular what Anne Fuchs has called the "agitated legacy" of the Second World War, as well as the concerns of contemporary society.[1] The fact that many such family novels have achieved commercial as well as critical success suggests that this genre is one that has secured its place on the German literary scene.

A particular concern with contemporary German family narratives is that they tend to be written from the point of view of the third postwar generation, a generation that has no firsthand experience of the war and is therefore inevitably dependent on the accounts of others for knowledge and understanding. Harald Welzer, Sabine Moller, and Karoline Tschuggnall have pointed to the discrepancies that can often emerge between what they term the "Lexikon" of objective, public knowledge about the National Socialist past and the subjective, private "Album" of stories and memories that are passed down through the family; this generation's understanding of past events is often based on secondhand knowledge gleaned from a number of different and often contradictory sources.[2]

The difficulties involved in piecing together the fragments of the family narrative, as well as the broader historical narrative, are often thematized in these texts themselves. Friederike Eigler points to the prevalence in contemporary German literature of generational novels, which she defines as "Romane, in denen Familiengeschichte erforscht oder mühsam rekonstruiert wird" (novels in which family history is examined or carefully reconstructed).[3] These generational novels do not confine themselves to merely telling the stories of various generations of a family but rather emphasize the constructive element that is an inevitable part of the process of reconstruction. Eigler's approach brings to the fore the difficult processes of remembering and reconstructing family history, and thus it also incorporates an examination of the formal practices of retelling:

> Viele der neueren Generationenromane sind durch zwei gegenläufige Tendenzen geprägt: In den Blick kommen zum einen die Brüche, Widersprüche und Diskontinuitäten familiärer Genealogien, die in den meisten Fällen direkt mit der deutschen Geschichte im 20. Jahrhundert verknüpft sind. Zum anderen sind diese Generationenromane von dem Bestreben geprägt, durch den Schreib- und Erinnerungsprozess, neue Verbindungen und Zusammenhänge, und in diesem Sinne Kontinuitäten herzustellen.
>
> [Many of the new generational novels are influenced by two opposing tendencies: On the one hand, they bring to light the fractures, contradictions, and discontinuities of familial genealogies, which are in most cases directly associated with German history of the twentieth century. On the other, these generational novels are characterized by an endeavor to create new connections and associations through the writing and remembering process, and in so doing to produce continuities.][4]

While the multigenerational narrative represents a significant tendency in German literature today, contemporary women writers often look at this question of family history from the point of view of a particularly female lineage; they explore how the family stories are communicated between and among women across generational lines. In exploring the relationships between female family members, and mothers and daughters in particular, they question the way in which the family narrative is interrupted, distorted, or skewed in the retelling.

In this chapter I consider three family narratives by contemporary female authors and examine the particular contribution of women writers to debates about representing German history through family history in twenty-first-century literature. I begin by questioning the extent to which the family stories they present offer an alternative vision of history that may be linked to a specifically female perspective, centered here on the figure of the mother. In focusing then on the way in which motherhood is engendered and envisioned in these novels, I also explore the way these writers speak to contemporary debates about the family in Germany. Finally, I will also investigate the particular narrative strategies employed by women writers to give voice to the maternal perspective, which has all too often been neglected in literary texts.

The three novels that are the focus of this chapter depict the family history of several generations of women through the twentieth century. Katharina Hagena's *Der Geschmack von Apfelkernen* (2008; published in English as *The Taste of Apple Seeds*, 2013) tells the story of the first-person narrator Iris's attempts to come to terms with her tragic family story and make peace with the female family members she has lost, as well as those she is left with; Anja Jonuleit's *Herbstvergessene* (Forgotten Ones of Autumn, 2010) uses the frame of a murder mystery to delve into the past and uncover the forgotten history of the Nazi *Lebensborn* homes; and Annette Pehnt's *Chronik der Nähe* (Chronicle of Closeness, 2012) considers the complex relationships between grandmother, mother, and daughter against a backdrop of wartime trauma and postwar hardship. Significantly, in all three novels the concept of motherhood is used as a prism through which to explore questions of a specifically female lineage, traits passed from one generation to the next, stories told from mother to daughter—and of some hidden by mothers and daughters—as well as the influence of the past on subsequent generations.

"Historia matria" of the Second World War

All three novels under analysis here begin with the death or impending death of a female family relative: Hagena's narrative opens with the funeral of the narrator's maternal grandmother, an event that obliges the narrator to return to her birthplace and confront her painful past. In Jonuleit's novel, it is the sudden death, ostensibly by suicide, of the narrator's mother that provokes her to delve into history as a way of understanding the circumstances of her mother's birth. Pehnt's novel is in some respects an account of what might have been and probably never will be, as a daughter sits at the bedside of her unconscious mother and sifts through the details of their shared past. All three narratives thus begin with the loss of a central maternal figure, an event that provides both the circumstances and the motive for a quest to understand the past.

Significantly, the narrators of the novels perceive the passing of their female relatives not only in terms of the immediate loss of the person who played such a central role in their lives but also as a rupture in the personal and family narrative. They feel a sense of sadness and disappointment that they no longer have access to the past through the stories of their mothers and grandmothers. Jonuleit's protagonist, Maja Starnberg, describes the "atemberaubende Wut" (breathtaking anger) that she feels toward her mother for failing to pass on her grandmother's story before her death, even as she acknowledges that her anger stems from her own regret that she was not closer to her mother during her lifetime.[5] The first-person narrator of Pehnt's novel expresses in very forceful terms her frustration that her comatose mother can no longer communicate with her:

Ich wollte deine Lippen auseinanderzerren und die Augenlider hochstemmen, einfach nichts zu sagen, das geht in unserer Familie nicht, vieles geht, aber nicht sprechen: nicht. Großmutter Mutter Kind: wortgewaltig, Lästermäuler, nicht auf den Mund gefallen, Quasselstrippen, Plaudertaschen, Zwitschermaschinen, redselig. Plötzlich schweigen gilt nicht.[6]

[I wanted to pull your lips apart and prop up your eyelids; to say nothing at all, that's not allowed in our family, a lot of things are allowed, but not talking is not. Grandmother mother child: chatterboxes, gossips, can't keep their mouths shut, windbags, blabbermouths, talkative, big mouths. To suddenly fall silent is unacceptable.]

The irony of this situation is that it is only through the loss of the maternal figure that each protagonist finally comes to appreciate the value of those stories and to recognize the part that they play in her understanding of her personal and family history as well as her present-day identity; Jonuleit's Maja describes this loss as an overwhelming feeling "dass ich etwas versäumt hatte, etwas Entscheidendes" (that I had missed out on something, something decisive).[7] Thus the three novels underline the importance of intergenerational storytelling in the reconstruction of history and the construction of identity, and they explore the problems that can arise when the family narrative is interrupted or severed in the retelling.

In their focus on the family and the domestic arena, all three novels present a very different perspective on the Second World War from that which is usually the subject of historical enquiry. The Mexican microhistorian Luis González has coined the term "historia matria" to describe this trend in contemporary historiography: where conventional historical accounts tend to focus their attention on great wars, great battles, and the great heroes that emerge triumphant from them—in other words, the history of the "patria" or fatherland—"historia matria" concerns itself with "the small, weak, feminine, sentimental world of the mother; that is to say, the family, the native soil, that which has until now been called the *patria chica* (home town or region)."[8] "Historia matria" contributes to the broader historical narrative by offering a view of historical events from the point of view of the mothers, sisters, daughters, and children who are also part of history but whose stories are seldom retold. Novels such as those that are the focus of this chapter could be seen as contributing in a similar way to our understanding of historical events, since they also offer an insight into the impact of those events on individuals and families. In telling the stories of grandmothers, mothers, and daughters, we might see the three writers as engaging in a type of maternal history or "historia matria" of the Second World War.

Hagena's *Der Geschmack von Apfelkernen* tells the story of three generations of the Lünschen family, all of whom were born and grew up in the fictional northern German town of Bootshaven. The narrative begins with the funeral of Bertha, an event that obliges her remaining family members to reunite in Bootshaven and compels them to rake over the ashes of the past. Bertha's death and in particular her legacy to her granddaughter Iris—the old stone house where she spent her childhood—provoke Iris to think back to days spent playing in the garden with her cousin Rosmarie or sitting at the heavy wooden kitchen table, listening to her grandmother's stories of her childhood and adolescence in Bootshaven. In sorting through her grandmother's belongings, however, Iris comes to the realization that there is a lot she does not know about her family history. Her efforts to piece together the events of the past and to understand the complex relationships between her family members meet with resistance, as her mother and aunts are unwilling to confront the painful memories of their shared past. A further complication is the fact that in the latter years of her life Bertha suffered from dementia and gradually retreated from the family into her memories, eventually falling silent. As Iris remarks, "Das Vergessen lag bei uns in der Familie" (Forgetting was a family trait).[9]

Since Iris no longer has access to her grandmother's stories and memories, she must look elsewhere for access to the past. It is her decision to accept the inheritance of the family house in Bootshaven that helps to her to fill some of the gaps in the family narrative. While tidying the overgrown garden, she is surprised to come across graffiti; someone had sprayed "Nazi" in red paint on the hen-house. This discovery causes Iris to question her grandfather Dr. Hinnerk Lünschen's wartime activities, and her questions are answered only in part when she also comes across Hinnerk's notebooks and the poems he wrote during the war years. Initially, Iris is surprised that her grandfather's poetry does not allude to his experiences of war or of his time spent in a denazification camp, but deals instead with the sights, sounds and smells of the countryside of his childhood:

> In Hinnerks grauem Buch war kein einziges Gedicht über den Krieg. Und auch keines, das darauf schließen ließ, dass die Verse in einem Lager geschrieben worden waren, das eigens dazu diente, die Insassen ihre eigenen und andere grauenvolle Taten der vergangenen Jahre ins Gedächtnis zu rufen. (170–71)

> [There wasn't a single poem in Hinnerk's grey book about the war. Nor were there any that suggested they had been written in a camp. In a camp whose purpose was to make the inmates recall gruesome deeds from recent years: their own and those of others. (157)]

However, Iris comes to recognize that her grandfather's traumatic experiences are expressed perhaps even more deeply in his silence on these subjects: "Ich stellte fest, das nicht nur das Vergessen eine Form des Erinnerns war, sondern das Erinnern eine Form des Vergessens" (171; I realized that not only was forgetting a form of remembering, but remembering was a form of forgetting, too, 157).

Iris also comes to an understanding of the impact of the war on the wives and mothers left at home, and a candid conversation with her grandmother's elderly neighbor, Carsten Lexow, causes her to look very differently on the grandmother she thought she knew so well. Through Lexow, Iris learns that her grandmother was not always the dutiful housewife that she had assumed she was; in fact, Bertha had a brief affair with this man during the war that raised questions about the paternity of her second daughter, Iris's beautiful aunt Inga. Iris is shaken by this new story that casts her grandmother in an entirely different light, and she ponders the manner in which it changes everything she understood about her family history: "So wurde Carsten Lexows Geschichte Teil meiner eigenen Geschichte und Teil meiner Geschichte über die Geschichte von meiner Großmutter" (72; Thus Carsten Lexow's story became part of my own story and part of my story about the story of my grandmother, 62).

Like Hagena's novel, Jonuleit's *Herbstvergessene* also recounts the tale of three generations of women: its main protagonist, Maja, discovers a secret about her grandmother that causes her to call into question everything she has taken for granted about her mother's and her own origin. The novel begins with a phone call from mother to daughter, when Maja's mother, Lilli, calls her daughter in London to ask her to come home, as she has something to tell her. However, when Maja arrives in Vienna, she discovers that her mother ostensibly committed suicide that morning. Among her mother's papers, Maja finds a photo of her grandmother Charlotte with a very young baby, and an inscription on the back of the photo indicates that it was taken two months before Lilli's birth. The strange circumstances of her mother's death, coupled with the incongruity of the photo, provoke Maja to embark on a search for the history of this photograph and of her mother's origins. This quest takes her on a journey to Northern Germany and back to the war years.

In describing Maja's exploration of her grandmother's past, Jonuleit's novel touches on one of the lesser-known aspects of German wartime history, namely the *Lebensborn* homes for unmarried mothers. *Lebensborn* was an SS agency established by Heinrich Himmler in 1935 with the aim of providing maternity care and assistance to unwed mothers who were pregnant with Aryan children, as long as the mothers could prove the racial purity of their children.[10] In *Herbstvergessene*, Maja gains insight into the past through the discovery of a memoir written by her grandmother, and she is shocked to discover that her grandmother, then called

Emmi, had entered a *Lebensborn* home called Hohehorst in 1943 and given birth to a son, Paul, in March 1944. In order to gain entry to the home, she had given evidence that her baby's father was her sister Ingeborg's husband, a German soldier; in fact, the child's father was her sister Leni's husband Paul, whose Jewish grandmother made him racially impure by National Socialist standards. After losing her son and her best friend Hanna to typhoid, Emmi steals Hanna's identification papers, takes Hanna's daughter, and runs away from Hohehorst. Thus Emmi becomes Hanna Charlotte Starnberg and brings up Hanna's daughter Lilli as her own. This newfound information leads Maja to the realization that the woman she had always believed to be her grandmother was in fact not a blood relative, and that her mother's origins were connected to one of the more secretive aspects of Nazi racial policy.

Where Jonuleit offers a "historia matria" of a very specific aspect of German wartime history, Pehnt's novel offers a broader insight into the struggles of women and children during this difficult time in German history. *Chronik der Nähe* again depicts three generations of women, and it uses the complex and difficult relationships between grandmother, mother, and daughter to point to the long-term impact of the Second World War on the third postwar generation. The novel shifts between two narrative perspectives: an unnamed first-person narrator tells her own story and describes her vain attempts to reach out to her mother in an effort to understand her, while a separate narrative recounts the experiences of Annie, her mother, in the third person. A third maternal figure is Annie's mother, the unnamed grandmother of the trio, who is presented from two different perspectives in these separate and at times contradictory narratives. It is clear from the outset, though, that Annie, as the only named character in the novel, is the central figure of the piece, and that she, as both daughter and mother, is the conduit between grandmother and daughter and between past and present.

Annie embodies in a very literal sense the traumatic aftereffects of the Second World War. Her experience of the final years of the war and the immediate postwar period is characterized by fear, insecurity, and solitariness. Her mother's frequent absences, sometimes for days on end, leave the child anxious and confused. Literally paralyzed by fear when the air raid sirens go off, she is forced to spend every night sleeping alone in a neighbor's cellar in case of an air raid, as her mother cannot carry her as far as the air raid shelters. More than anything else, Annie learns at an early age that she cannot rely on her mother to help her through her trauma; rather it is her responsibility to help her mother through the difficult years of shortage and instability by taking responsibility for the house and yard in her absence. Despite her mother's insistence that children were not affected by the war, since they do not remember things, the effects of the traumatic experience of war on Annie are evident throughout the narrative. Her acute fear of bells or sirens stays with her all her life; even the ring of the telephone causes her to stiffen with dread. She also suffers from intense and debilitating headaches, which she refuses to admit to, as though these were a failing on her part.

Through the account of the first-person narrator of the novel, Annie's daughter, we also find evidence that the traumatic legacy of the Second World War is passed on to the third generation. This daughter also grows up a very anxious child, an anxiety that necessitates psychological counseling at an early age. Annie, who has obviously been hardened by the difficulties she endured as a child, refuses to accept that there is any validity to her child's anxiety. She berates her daughter: "Woher hast du das bloß, also von mir hast du es nicht, ich hatte nie Angst, das durfte ich gar nicht. Im Krieg Angst haben, das ging nicht" (Where did you get that from, certainly not from me, I was never afraid, I wasn't allowed to be. To be afraid during the war, that just wasn't allowed).[11] Yet the distance between mother and daughter is obvious, as is its connection to the trauma that Annie went through as a child.

All three novels thus focus their attention on various aspects of female and maternal experience of the Second World War, a "historia matria" that serves as a useful counterfoil to more conventional historical accounts of the period. Hagena's and Pehnt's novels paint an alternative picture of wartime suffering by focusing on the experiences of the women and children working on the home front, whereas Jonuleit's focuses on a particular aspect of wartime maternal history often overlooked in the grand narrative of German history. In depicting the difficulties in the relationships of mothers and daughters within this context, the novels also touch upon the longer-term legacy of the Second World War.

Mothering and Motherhood

Women's writing often tends to focus its attention on the mother-daughter relationship, and women's writing in German is no exception.[12] At least since the 1970s, German-language novels by women have featured complex and oftentimes highly problematic relationships between mothers and daughters. These narratives, which almost always tend to be written from the perspective of the daughter, present mothers as caricatures, *Rabenmütter* who treat their daughters with disdain, neglect, and even violence.[13] Contemporary mother-daughter narratives offer what might be considered a more nuanced view of this complex relationship. The novels under scrutiny here make for a particularly fruitful examination of mother-daughter relationships, since they all feature three generations of women, thus mothers who are also daughters, daughters who are also mothers, and a multiplicity of female family relations. One might also argue that the relationships among the women are the driving force of the novels.

All three novels explore motherhood in an intergenerational context. While all three authors depict these relationships against the backdrop of the Second World War, their concern with motherhood, maternity, and practices of mothering has a very real relevance for current debates about the perceived crisis of motherhood in contemporary German society. The low birth rate in the country since at least the early 1990s has caused researchers and politicians alike to question the reasons behind current demographic trends and to try to counter them with new legislation intended to encourage German couples to produce more children. These debates have not been confined to the political arena, however; some more sensationalist media outlets have used the falling birth rate as evidence of the imminent demise of the German population.[14] The preoccupation in contemporary German literature, particularly in literature by women, with motherhood in all its forms is an indication of the centrality of this issue in contemporary German culture.

Hagena, Jonuleit, and Pehnt seek to explore motherhood within the context of Germany's wartime past and as part of Germany's intergenerational legacy. In this, it is noteworthy that all three novels present strong, determined female characters; all the female protagonists are compelled by family or historical circumstances to bring up their children alone, without the help of their children's fathers—and they do so admirably. At the same time, there is also a sense that each generation suffers the consequences of the mistakes of the previous generation; moreover, there is a tendency to repeat their mistakes. The novels thus present daughters as the image of their mothers, even as they fight against this.

In Hagena's *Der Geschmack von Apfelkernen* we encounter a number of mothers and daughters in a variety of constellations; in particular, the novel considers Bertha in her role of mother to her three daughters—Christa, Inga, and Harriet—and looks at Christa's and Harriet's mothering of their respective daughters, Iris (the narrator) and her cousin Rosmarie. Fathers play only a minor role in this female family romance; they are presented as emotionally distant, uninvolved, or entirely absent from their daughters' lives. Yet despite this fact, the mother-daughter relationships in the novel are depicted as anything but simple. Both Iris and Rosmarie favor their aunt Inga's company over that of their own mothers; while they pay little attention to their mothers, they are happy to sit at the kitchen table, accompanied by their friend Mira, and listen attentively to their grandmother's stories of the past. Iris's love for her grandmother is reflected in her fondness for the old house in Bootshaven, where Bertha grew up and where Iris spent many days during her childhood. Moreover, the fact that Bertha opts to leave her house to Iris, rather than one of her own daughters, indicates that her affection was appreciated and reciprocated.

The novel also explores questions of a particularly female legacy in the way that the daughters in the novel seem destined to repeat the mistakes of the previous generation. Rosmarie's death at fifteen after a fall in the garden harks back to the untimely death of her great-aunt Anna, Bertha's sister, at the age of sixteen. When Bertha begins to lose track of the present, this manifests itself in her confusing her daughters with each other:

> Bertha vergaß ihre Töchter der Reihe nach. Die älteste zuerst. . . . Sie nannte sie erst Inga, später Harriet. Inga war noch eine ganze Zeit Inga, dann wurde auch sie Harriet. Harriet blieb sehr lange Harriet, aber irgendwann, viel später, war selbst Harriet eine Fremde. (185)

> [Bertha forgot her daughters one by one. The eldest first. . . . First she called her Inga, then Harriet. Inga was still Inga for a while, then she became Harriet too. Harriet remained Harriet for ages, but one day, much later, even Harriet was a stranger. (171)]

In a poignant *volte-face*, by the end of the novel Christa is already beginning to show the first signs of the dementia that plagued her mother, suggesting that certain aspects of female legacy are unavoidable.

Jonuleit's narrative takes as its point of departure the ostensible suicide of Maja's mother, Lilli, with whom Maja had a very problematic relationship throughout her life. Lilli was a successful interpreter who traveled widely with her work, and she had little time or space in her life for her daughter. Maja spent the summer holidays with her grandmother, Charlotte, who did all she could to make up for Lilli's shortcomings as a mother. Maja initially studied for a career in interpreting and translating, but she disappointed and angered her mother by giving up her studies and moving to England to take up an apprenticeship as an interior decorator. Maja believes that Lilli took her daughter's decision as a personal affront:

> Meine Mutter hat mir nie verziehen, dass ich nicht die gleichen Träume habe, die gleichen Vorstellungen davon, was im Leben erstrebenswert ist. Sie hat mir nie verziehen, dass ich nicht wie sie bin.[15]

> [My mother never forgave me for not having the same dreams as her, the same idea of what is worth striving for in life. She never forgave me for not being like her.]

Before the phone call from her mother asking her to come to Vienna to visit her, Maja and Lilli had not spoken for almost ten years. However, Maja's hopes of reconciling with her mother are thwarted by her untimely death. Thus Maja's yearning to understand the past is in part motivated by a need to understand and reconnect with her mother.

Lilli's non-normative mothering has played a large part in Maja's own reluctance to become a mother. She never really understood why her boyfriend Wolf was so keen to have children, since she has never really known a family beyond her mother and her grandmother. However, it is only after losing her own mother and searching for her familial origins that she begins to appreciate the importance of family:

> Auf einmal erschien mir Wolfs Familie mit größerer Deutlichkeit und schärferen Konturen. . . . Ich hatte mich in ihrer Mitte immer entspannt, fast schon geborgen gefühlt. Doch seit Mutters Tod war eine andere Nuance hinzugekommen, eine Art Dankbarkeit, so kam es mir vor. Ich, das verlorene, elternlose Einzelkind, fühlte mich aufgehoben im Schoß einer anderen Familie. (163)

> [Suddenly I saw Wolf's family with greater clarity and in sharper focus. . . . I had always felt relaxed, almost safe in their midst. But since Mother's death, it had taken on another nuance, a sort of gratefulness, it seemed to me. I, the lost, orphaned child, felt protected in the bosom of another family.]

Maja's reaction to this realization is decisive: she takes her packet of contraceptive pills and throws them one by one into the toilet.

Pehnt's *Chronik der Nähe* is in part a chronicle of the first-person narrator's attempts to be close to her mother, Annie, but it also reveals much about the ambivalent relationship between Annie and her own mother and the impact that this has had on Annie's mothering. Initially, it is the child who seeks comfort from her mother, but the neglect and abandonment she experiences provoke an unwillingness or inability to trust others as an adult. When Annie reaches her teens, her mother repeatedly attempts to reconnect with her daughter, but her efforts come too late, as Annie has already distanced herself emotionally. Moreover, the ways in which her mother reaches out to Annie are awkward and have questionable outcomes. For example, her way of teaching Annie what it means to be a woman is to encourage her to go out to the park after dark and make use of her womanly wiles with the boys that hang around there. Although Annie soon becomes very popular with the local boys, this does not bring her lasting happiness and moreover causes her to be labeled a prostitute in the local area. Annie escapes from her mother through focusing on her education and gaining the college place that will ultimately allow her to move to another city.

The inadequate and inappropriate mothering that Annie received engenders a mistrust of others that ultimately drives a wedge between her and her own daughter. She is adamant that she does not want to have children and tries to convince her husband—referred to in the narrative only as "der Richtige" (Mr. Right)—that they do not need to have children to be happy. Her pregnancy and the birth of her daughter are thus not greeted as happy events, and the stories she tells her child of her early days of motherhood make it clear that she did not enjoy the experience: "Ich war, hast du immer wieder erzählt, ich war so ein anstrengendes Kind, so, so anstrengend, immer nur geschrien, ganz steif war ich vom vielen Schreien" (10; I was, you told me again and again, I was such a demanding baby, so, so demanding, all I did was cry, I was quite stiff from all the crying). Indeed, Annie is so traumatized by her memories of when her daughter was an infant that she cannot cope with looking after her granddaughter: when her daughter returns from the hairdresser, having left Annie to watch the baby for an hour, she finds the baby screaming and her mother nervously smoking in the next room.

It might be argued that in depicting a search for meaning in the past, each novel also narrates the very personal story of how the main female protagonist manages to move beyond the negative or inadequate mothering she received and make the transition to a new understanding of motherhood. In this respect, it is significant that all three narrators have had or are about to have children by the end of the novels, indicating that each protagonist's anxiety about becoming a mother has been overcome in the course of the narrative. In the epilogue of Hagena's *Der Geschmack von Apfelkernen*, we learn that Iris has accepted Bertha's legacy: we find her living in the house in Bootshaven with her husband and son. Maja, having pieced together the fragments of her grandmother's wartime past and come to terms with her mother's origin, is safely ensconced in her grandmother's holiday home in Italy and pregnant with her first child. Pehnt's *Chronik der Nähe* goes a step further in that it indicates that the "historia matria" will also be passed on to the next generation; by the end of her narrative, the first-person narrator has given up work to devote herself to bringing up her two daughters, "diese Weiber, eine Weiberfamilie" (132; these women, a family of women). Coming to terms with the past of their own mothers and grandmothers enables the protagonists of all three novels to take a step forward into the future as mothers.

Matrilineal Narrative Forms

In her seminal work, *The Mother/Daughter Plot*, Marianne Hirsch surveys a vast array of literary texts from Western Europe and North America since the beginning of the nineteenth century and focuses in particular on their depiction of mother-daughter relationships. While Hirsch observes the gradual emancipation of daughters in the course of the twentieth century, she remarks that with few exceptions, the maternal perspective is almost entirely disregarded. She finds it particularly problematic that most mother-daughter narratives tend to be written from the perspective of daughters, which means that mothers have traditionally been denied a voice, even in narratives in which they feature strongly. For women's writing to represent women in the fullest and most meaningful way, Hirsch argues, mothers must be allowed a voice in discourse, must be allowed to speak for themselves as subjects:

> The story of female development, both in fiction and theory, needs to be written in the voice of mothers as well as in that of daughters.... Only in combining both voices, in finding a double voice that would yield a multiple female consciousness, can we begin to envision ways to "live afresh."[16]

For Hirsch, it is not enough merely to present mothers in the literary text; rather, the text should give voice to the maternal perspective. Hirsch thus imagines "a feminist family romance of mothers *and* daughters, both subjects, speaking to each other and living in familial and communal contexts which enable the subjectivity of each member" (163).

Hagena, Jonuleit, and Pehnt employ various different formal strategies in an attempt to give voice to the maternal perspective on the German past. Through intergenerational storytelling, shifting narrative perspectives, and blending the voices of mothers and daughters, the novels analyzed in this chapter explore to varying degrees the potential for writing the maternal voice into the fabric of the literary text.

First, intergenerational storytelling is highlighted in all three of these narratives as crucial to the reconstruction of the family narrative and to the transmission of family history. In *Der Geschmack von Apfelkernen*, Iris comes to appreciate the stories passed down to her from her grandmother as a way of understanding her own position within the family line. In *Herbstvergessene*, Maja is thrilled to gain access to Emmi/Charlotte's memoir of her days in Hohehorst, an account that finally fills the gaps in her knowledge of her mother's origins. The daughter's entreaties to her mother Annie in *Chronik der Nähe* to tell her the stories of her childhood, and her repeated requests for her to record them in print or on tape, emphasize the value of storytelling both to the reconstruction of family history on the one hand and the reconstruction of broken relationships on the other. Moreover, the frequent references to "du" in the first-person narrative of Pehnt's novel indicates clearly that it should be understood as a story told from daughter to mother about their shared past as well as her hopes for a shared future.

Contemporary narratives such as those under analysis here emphasize the collaborative work done by generations of women in constructing and reconstructing the shared narratives of family and history. In *Der Geschmack von Apfelkernen* Hagena's Iris ponders the contribution of her various family members to the creation of their family story:

> Ich saß am Küchentisch in Berthas Haus und sah meine Großmutter als Kind und meine Großtante Anna, die nie anders dreinblickte als auf dieser Fotografie. Ich erinnerte mich bei einem Becher lauwarmer H-Milch an Dinge, die Bertha meiner Mutter und diese mir erzählt hatte, die Tante Harriet Rosmarie und Rosmarie Mira und mir erzählt hatte, an Dinge, die wir uns ausgedacht oder zumindest ausgemalt hatten. (64)
>
> [I was sitting at the kitchen table in Bertha's house, seeing my grandmother and great-aunt as children, although in my mind Anna never looked any different from how she did in the photograph. Sipping a mug of lukewarm UHT milk I recalled things that Bertha had told my mother and my mother had told me, or that Aunt Harriet had told Rosmarie and Rosmarie had told Mira and me, and things we had made up or at least imagined. (54)]

Through collaborative storytelling and imaginative investment, contemporary family narratives by women produce a rich tapestry of German maternal history that interrogates questions of familial legacy and offers new perspectives on the heritage of Germany's wartime past.

Jonuleit's and Pehnt's novels take this idea a step further by reflecting the collaborative efforts of the female family members in the formal structure of their narratives: both novels use multiple narrative perspectives to give voice to different members of the family and thereby emphasize the diversity of perspectives on the past. Throughout *Herbstvergessene*, the third-person account of Maja's search for the secrets of her family story are interspersed with chapters from Emmi's memoir of her days in Hohehorst; it is only when Maja pieces together the sequence of events that the reader realizes that Emmi is Charlotte, the woman that Maja has always believed to be her grandmother. However, the continuous passing of narrative authority back and forth between Maja and Emmi/Charlotte means that no one perspective is given precedence over the other. Moreover, given that Emmi's account is of her pregnancy and the birth of her son, a significant feature is that the maternal story is told from the point of view of the mother. In giving voice to the maternal subject in this way, Jonuleit's novel answers Hirsch's call for "the story of female development . . . to be written in the voice of mothers as well as in that of daughters."[17]

The shifting narrative perspective is arguably used to even greater effect in Pehnt's novel, which plays with the separation and fusion of narrative voices in interesting ways. Unlike Jonuleit's novel, Pehnt's *Chronik der Nähe* does not differentiate clearly between the maternal and filial perspectives; in fact, each of the two narrators, Annie and the unnamed first-person narrator, is both daughter and mother, and they speak simultaneously from both standpoints. Moreover, at times it is difficult to separate the two narrative voices in order to ascertain who is speaking: mother's and daughter's voices seem at times to blend into one another. As the past merges with the present, underlining the idea that the past is very much part of the present, the third-person story of Annie seems to echo the first-person narrative of her daughter; thus the novel emphasizes the similarities and parallels between their perspectives.

The perspectives of mother and daughter meet at the point where their experience overlaps, namely at the birth of Annie's daughter, the narrator: at this decisive moment, the third-person narrator discloses, "... ihre Tochter ist geboren, das bin ich" (211; ... her daughter is born, that's me). This is an interesting narrative dénouement, since it reveals the intricate involvement of the daughter in the maternal narrative; now that her mother has fallen silent, it is left to the daughter to pick up the threads of her mother's story. Crucially though, Annie's voice is in no way subsumed by her daughter's; rather, the maternal and filial perspectives go hand in hand and are presented as two sides of the same coin. One might even go so far as to argue that the dual voice of mother and daughter that runs the length of this narrative comes close to Hirsch's vision of a "double voice that would yield a multiple female consciousness" and that would seem to offer a way forward for contemporary renditions of the maternal perspective.[18]

Conclusion

On the threshold of the twenty-first century, contemporary writing in German is concerned with making sense of the past of the Second World War and its residual effects on the present, and this analysis of three contemporary novels by female authors demonstrates that women's writing has a particular part to play in this endeavor. Women writers often tend to write from a female perspective, to give voice to the experiences of the mothers, daughters, sisters, and wives, whose memory of the war is quite different from that of their male counterparts; the family stories that they tell narrate an alternative vision of the wartime past, one that tends to be neglected in the dominant historical narrative but nonetheless contributes to a fuller understanding of past events. In their work, these women writers give voice to "the small, weak, feminine, sentimental world of the mother," as González has defined "historia matria," but they move beyond essentializing discourses to call attention to the role of the marginal and the powerless in the broader narrative of history.[19] Family novels by women, such as those analyzed here, offer a more inclusive, multigenerational, and multiperspectival account of the history of the Second World War, and they indicate quite clearly the particular contribution of contemporary writing by women to ongoing questions and debates about the literary engagement with Germany's wartime past.

Furthermore, as this analysis has shown, the distinct formal and aesthetic strategies that contemporary women writers employ in their texts make possible the emergence of new voices, new literary forms, and new narrative structures. The particular strategies that Hagena, Jonuleit, and Pehnt employ to give voice to the maternal perspective in their writing certainly distinguish them from their male counterparts, but they also set them apart from their literary foremothers. Although German women writers of the twentieth century such as Elfriede Jelinek, Helga Novak, and Anna Mitgutsch depicted mother-daughter relationships in their work, Marianne Hirsch's observation that the stories of mothers are all too often told from the point of view of their daughters certainly rings true for their texts. Contemporary writers such as those featured in this chapter move beyond this to allow for a multiplicity of voices and subject positions in their narratives. Their emphasis on the collaborative work of intergenerational storytelling and their use of multilayered narrative perspectives could be seen as answering Marianne Hirsch's call for "a feminist family romance of mothers *and* daughters, both subjects, speaking to each other and living in familial and communal contexts which enable the subjectivity of each member."[20] What emerges in Hagena's, Jonuleit's and Pehnt's matrilineal narratives is a dialogue of equals, an interchange of narrative agency between mothers and daughters, and a blending of their voices in innovative and creative ways.

Notes

[1] Anne Fuchs, *Phantoms of War in Contemporary German Literature, Films and Discourse*, New Perspectives in German Political Studies (Basingstoke, UK: Palgrave Macmillan, 2010), 1.

[2] Harald Welzer, Sabine Moller, and Karoline Tschuggnall, *Opa war kein Nazi: Nationalsozialismus und Holocaust im Familiengedächtnis* (Frankfurt am Main: Fischer, 2002).

[3] Friederike Eigler, *Gedächtnis und Geschichte in Generationenromanen seit der Wende* (Berlin: Erich Schmidt, 2005), 24–25. Unless otherwise indicated, all translations are my own.

[4] Eigler, *Gedächtnis und Geschichte*, 26.

[5] Anja Jonuleit, *Herbstvergessene* (Munich: DTV, 2010), 219.

[6] Annette Pehnt, *Chronik der Nähe* (Munich: Piper, 2012), 7.

[7] Jonuleit, *Herbstvergessene*, 26.

[8] Luis González y González, "El arte de la microhistoria," *Invitación a la microhistoria* (Mexico: Edición Clío, 1997), 16. On "historia matria" see also Katherine Stone's essay in this volume.

[9] Katharina Hagena, *Der Geschmack von Apfelkernen* (Cologne: Kiepenheuer & Witsch, 2008), 113. In English, *The Taste of Apple Seeds*, trans. Jamie Bulloch (London: Atlantic, 2013), 103.

[10] For a comprehensive guide to the *Lebensborn* Association, see Georg Lilienthal, *Der "Lebensborn e. V.": Ein Instrument nationalsozialistischer Rassenpolitik* (Stuttgart: Fischer, 1985).

[11] Pehnt, *Chronik der Nähe*, 14.

[12] Norgard Klages, *Look Back in Anger: Mother-Daughter and Father-Daughter Relationships in Women's Autobiographical Writings of the 1970s and 1980s* (New York: Peter Lang, 1995), 14.

[13] Some of the more prominent examples of this type of literature are Helga M. Novak's *Die Eisheiligen* (Frost Saints, 1979); Elfriede Jelinek's *Die Klavierspielerin* (1983; The Pianist, published in English as *The Piano Teacher*, 1988); and Waltraud Anna Mitgutsch's *Die Züchtigung* (1985; The Chastisement; published in English as *Three Daughters*, 1987). For a comparative analysis of these three novels, see Ricarda Schmidt, "Die böse Mutter: Zur Ästhetik sadomasochistischer Mutter-Tochter-Beziehungen in literarischen Texten aus dem Kontext der Frauenbewegung," in *Mutter und Mütterlichkeit: Wandel und Wirksamkeit einer Phantasie in der deutschen Literatur*, ed. Irmgard Roebling and Wolfram Mauser (Würzburg: Königshausen & Neumann, 1996), 347–58. For a broader analysis of the depiction of mothers and motherhood in German women's writing of the 1970s and 1980s, see Emily Jeremiah, *Troubling Maternity: Mothering, Agency, and Ethics in Women's Writing in German of the 1970s and 1980s* (London: Maney, 2003).

[14] For example, the German tabloid *Bild-Zeitung* ran the headline, "Baby shock: We Germans are dying out!" on 15 March 2006.

[15] Jonuleit, *Herbstvergessene*, 17–18.

[16] Marianne Hirsch, *The Mother/Daughter Plot: Narrative, Psychoanalysis, Feminism* (Bloomington: Indiana University Press, 1989), 161.

[17] Hirsch, *Mother/Daughter Plot*, 161.

[18] Ibid.

[19] González, "El arte de la microhistoria," 16.

[20] Hirsch, *Mother/Daughter Plot*, 161. Italics in original.

3: The Pitfalls of Constructing a Female Genealogy: Cultural Memory of National Socialism in Recent Family Narratives

Katherine Stone

WRITING WOMEN'S LIVES has always been central to the feminist project. In the 1970s confessional and autobiographical writing by women contributed to and popularized a feminist politics of self-discovery, autonomy, and solidarity.[1] Questioning the relationship between language and the subject, the body and culture, female authors asserted the social and historical import of their experiences. Notably, women's writing provided insight into women's experiences of war and the Third Reich at a stage when feminist history of the period was still in its infancy.[2] And now, in the twenty-first century, women writers are continuing to revisit the National Socialist past and its psychological legacy from a female perspective. The recent proliferation of autobiographical and fictional family narratives, written by women about women, suggests that there remain important stories to be told about the women who lived through the Nazi period in Germany.[3] The female narratives that are typically sidelined in family and cultural memory are a pivotal concern in the memoirs *Das endlose Jahr* (The Endless Year, 2002) by Gisela Heidenreich, *Stille Post* (Chinese Whispers, 2007) by Christina von Braun, and *Schweigen tut weh* (The Pain of Silence, 2007) by Alexandra Senfft. These authors believe that autobiography can fill in the gaps of "official" narratives regarding women's subjective experience of history. Reflecting on the processes through which family and cultural memory are produced and gendered in the German context, they expose the exclusionary structures of cultural memory. Their works enable us to trace the social and political processes through which memory becomes inflected by gender. Recent memory narratives by women thus shed light on a question that has guided feminist interventions into memory studies: "Who wants whom to remember what and why?"[4]

Moreover, each author treated in this chapter reflects on what it means for her, as a mother and a daughter, to confront the family past.

The authors structure their narratives around the testimonial objects—diaries, photographs, and letters—through which they have gained access to the past. Integrating these objects into their writing, Heidenreich, Senfft, and von Braun unfold in front of the reader gendered forms of memory transfer. They raise important questions about how women mediate memory from one generation to the next, via various mnemonic practices such as mourning and diary-writing, but also through acts of repression. To different degrees all three imply that gender inflects not only *what* is remembered, but also *how* it is remembered. They share the suspicion that psychosomatic illnesses, such as depression and eating disorders, are symptoms of repressed or ignored female histories. They feel out the repressed emotions and traumatic reactions that are an important form of memory transfer. In these matrilineal narratives generations of women appear to be united by their feminine responses to history. Implicitly or explicitly, then, these authors suggest that there is something unique, and indeed particularly authentic, about the way that women experience the past, psychologically and corporeally.[5] As a matter of fact, they largely exclude men from their reflections on memory.

As Joan Wallach Scott compellingly argues, however, a critical practice that relates the epistemological and social value of women's experience to their difference has a limited capacity to examine the assumptions that "excluded considerations of difference in the first place."[6] An unreflective emphasis on women's difference may well naturalize gender roles, concealing the political and discursive operations that produce subjectivity and circumscribe agency on the basis of gender. Making reductive claims about the singular nature of women's experience of history may then reproduce the terms that have caused certain types of experience to be undervalued in cultural memory. Since certain values and attributes are codified as "masculine" and "feminine" within the cultural field of gender hierarchy, the capacity of cultural memory to represent a history that unfolds outside these imaginary parameters is restricted. This in turn limits our understanding of the agency and experience of real men and women now. In this article I consider how Heidenreich, von Braun, and Senfft negotiate the potential pitfalls of an exclusive focus on women as the subjects and objects of memory. In the first section I discuss their valuable engagements with female experiences that are all too often excluded from family and cultural memory. In the second part of this essay I turn to the various ways that Heidenreich, Senfft, and von Braun understand women as subjects and mediators of memory. Finally, I argue that the authors most successfully do justice to the specificities of female experience and memory practices, without falling back on unhelpful clichés about the otherness of femininity, when they reconstruct the mnemonic processes through which gendered identity is performed.

Judith Butler argues that there is no substrate of gender identity behind expressions of gender; "identity is performatively constituted by the very 'expressions' that are said to be its results."[7] Building on implicit references to the iterative nature of cultural memory in authoritative social-constructivist theories of memory, we could describe cultural memory, with Judith Butler, as a "construction that regularly conceals its genesis."[8] A certain version of the past is produced in conformity with hegemonic social values and is sustained by commemorative rituals that are performed by individuals and groups. Theories of performativity have proven instrumental to those interested in exploring the processes whereby cultural memory becomes gendered and rearticulated.[9] Sabine Müller and Anja Schwarz thus encourage further consideration of how "Gedächtnis und Geschlecht sich gegenseitig hervorbringen, stützen oder aber vielleicht in Frage stellen" (memory and gender produce and sustain each other, or perhaps even challenge each other).[10] In this article I suggest that memoir is uniquely positioned not just to elucidate the relationship between cultural memory and gender but also, as an important medium of cultural memory, to challenge the very gendered norms that it enshrines and perpetuates.

Remembering Women

Heidenreich, Senfft, and von Braun scrutinize aspects of female experience previously overlooked in family memory and public discussions about the Nazi past. The untold stories of mothers and grandmothers lay the groundwork for their explorations of the transgenerational effect of the unsaid. This endeavor is necessarily gendered in Gisela Heidenreich's best-selling *Das endlose Jahr*, since the author was raised by the women on her mother's side of the family.[11] While working as an administrator at an SS officers' training school, Heidenreich's mother, Antonie, became pregnant with the child of a married SS Commandant. She traveled to German-occupied Norway to give birth anonymously in a *Lebensborn* maternity home, where she continued to be employed afterward. Across Germany and occupied territories the SS established welfare and maternity homes for unmarried, "racially valuable" women who wished to give birth in secret. Designed to raise the birth rate in the Aryan population, the *Lebensborn* scheme fell under the auspices of the *Rasse- und Siedlungshauptamt* (Race and Settlement Main Office), which was charged with safeguarding the racial purity of the SS and the "Germanization" of occupied territories.[12] Heidenreich struggles to discover the facts about her mother's work as an administrator in these SS institutions. Her psychological need to know the truth about her family conflicts with a filial desire to protect her aged mother from a painful confrontation with uncomfortable aspects of the past.

In the appendix to her auto/biography, Heidenreich condemns the persisting lack of rigorous historical research into the *Lebensborn* program, a state of affairs that frustrates her desire to understand her personal history. This may be one reason why her relationship with her father, whom Heidenreich finally meets in her late teens, barely features in the narrative. The nature of his work in the SS is never in doubt. The history books cannot, however, help Heidenreich to fill in the gaps in her mother's version of her past. Nor can historical narratives, focused on objective truths, give an adequate account of the impact of history and memory on private identity formation. In her auto/biography Heidenreich constructs a narrative of lived memory, organized around female experiences that would not conventionally be deemed worth telling. As she begins associatively to piece together the memories, imagined dialogues, and fantasies that define her own memories and sense of self, she shows subjective memory to be as important as cultural memory with regard to how an individual orients herself as a gendered subject in society.

Like Heidenreich, Alexandra Senfft uses historical, literary, and family sources to produce a case study of female family memory in her book *Schweigen tut weh*.[13] She tries to find a site of knowledge where history and subjective memory overlap, and hopes to gain insight into the lives of both her mother and her grandmother and into the way her own subjectivity has been formed in reaction to family history. An obvious springboard for Senfft's exploration of her mother's depression and alcoholism are the actions of her maternal grandfather, Hanns Ludin, Hitler's ambassador to Slovakia, who was executed in 1947. Erika, Senfft's mother, was traumatized by his arrest and hanging. Psychological issues resulting from her failure to come to terms with his death were exacerbated by unresolved questions of historical guilt. Senfft describes her narrative as "eine Art Tabubruch" (*STW*, 11; a sort of breach of taboo). Yet the taboo at stake is not the image of the honest, upstanding Hanns Ludin perpetuated by her grandmother, Erla. This had already been publicly challenged by her uncle, Malte Ludin, in his documentary film *2 oder 3 Dinge, die ich von ihm weiß* (2 or 3 Things I Know about Him, 2005). Instead, Senfft breaches female family taboos: Erika's mental-health problems and Erla's political failings. Like Heidenreich, Senfft thus confronts an internalized taboo against criticizing beloved maternal figures. She notes that while men like her grandfather ensured the success of the Third Reich, so too did many women,

> angefangen mit den Ehefrauen. Sie alle waren Komplizen, gemeinsam der Sache verpflichtet—und sie sind auch nach dem Krieg eine kameradschaftliche, solidarisch verbundene, eingeschworene Gemeinschaft geblieben, in der ihre Kinder und Kindeskinder aufwuchsen. (*STW*, 338)

[beginning with the wives. They were all complicit, dedicated to the cause—and even after the war they maintained a community, bound together in comradeship and solidarity, in which their children and grandchildren grew up.]

Senfft's narrative corroborates the findings of sociologists Gabriele Rosenthal and Margit Reiter, who have argued that a growing body of historical research about women's participation in the Third Reich has not filtered down to the level of family memory. Family confrontations with National Socialism appear to be highly gendered: "Wenden sich Kinder und Enkel dem Thema einer möglichen Täterschaft in ihrer Familie zu, dann stehen meist die Väter oder Großväter unter Verdacht" (if children and grandchildren broach the possibility of guilt in their family, then it is mostly fathers and grandfathers who come under suspicion).[14] Breaking the mold and foregrounding female relatives, Senfft seeks to bring family memory into alignment with history.

Senfft realizes that she cannot hope to understand the destructive effects of repressed knowledge and guilt while still protecting Erika and Erla from critique. Reading between the lines of Erika's letters, she unravels the psychological causes of a distress that others attributed to somatic disorders. Erika's inexplicable weight gain in the immediate postwar years was repeatedly misdiagnosed as an endocrine disorder. This diagnosis becomes a byword for her symptoms. Just as "resettlement," "fatigue duty," and "deportation" are hermeneutic loopholes for her family when dealing with the Nazi crimes, the diagnosis "hormonal issues" is a euphemism that normalizes Erika's feelings of guilt. It allows the rest of the family to continue to repress the past. Senfft hopes that by belatedly responding to Erika's disguised cries for help she will be able to work through her own guilt toward her mother and check the unconscious power of transgenerational legacies. In retrospect Senfft understands her own tomboyish behavior as a child as an attempt to draw attention to her difficulty coping with this troubled family history. She interprets the eating disorder and sleeping issues that plague her as an adult as an extension of Erika's problems. Through her writing Senfft wishes to protect her daughter from this negative inheritance.

In *Stille Post* Christina von Braun explicitly describes the generational continuity of psychological problems as female reactions to repressed history.[15] By excavating her female family history she aims to unearth remaining family secrets and to master destructive psychological legacies such as the manic episodes of her mother, Hilde. Von Braun focuses on Hilde's ambivalent memories of her own mother, Hildegard, who died in prison in September 1944 after being arrested by the Gestapo for her involvement with a Communist resistance group. Von Braun believes that the anti-communist and anti-Jewish sentiments of the Federal Republic prevented Hilde from embracing her mother's past and their shared Jewish heritage. Given von Braun's prominence as a feminist scholar and filmmaker, it is unsurprising that she styles her narrative as a corrective to the androcentrism of both cultural and family memory. In the 1920s Hildegard Margis had risen to prominence in political and business lobbies after establishing a successful firm advising women on consumer affairs. Like many early feminist activists and writers, however, she was forgotten until the advent of feminist history in the 1970s. The men in von Braun's family, diplomats, politicians, and scientists, suffered no such fate. Their lives are recorded in biographies and memoirs both published and unpublished.

Von Braun is suspicious of traditional memoirs that, "aus dem Rückblick verfasst, verführen dazu, die eigene Geschichte mit 'der Geschichte' in Einklang zu bringen. Sie treten in jedem Sinne des Wortes die Herrschaft über die Vergangenheit" (*SP*, 14; tempt the individual to reconcile their own story with "history" because they are composed retrospectively. They exercise mastery, quite literally, over the past). She uses the same language to discuss the genealogical research of her grandfather. She perceives traditional autobiography and genealogy as indicating the prejudices of a patriarchal society that, passing wealth and the family name from one male generation to the next, devalues women and expunges them from history. She sees this mastery at work when she compares the published autobiography of her paternal grandfather, Magnus, with the unpublished diary of his wife, Emmy. In many instances Magnus had simply transferred Emmy's observations into his own authoritative voice and deleted nearly all traces of her in the process.

It is no coincidence, von Braun muses, that her brother comes into possession of the official family memories, like the family tree, while she is charged with sorting through the diaries and photographs. She demonstrates that contributions to public memory and acts of private memory transfer belong to highly gendered traditions of authorship and inheritance. The diaries of Emmy and her mother thus form the basis of *Stille Post*'s matrilineal narrative. They allow von Braun to trace the exclusionary practices through which historical narratives are consolidated and, by implication, gendered. Favoring these female sources, she implicitly rejects the value judgments associated with generic auto/biography in which the public positioning of the writing subject, traditionally male, reflects wider social assumptions. The diaries that interest von Braun are composed in the present and without an audience in mind. They do not conform to dominant notions of what is historically relevant or to established interpretations of the past. They thus suit well her feminist genealogical project: "Ich möchte mich gern in ihre Zeit versetzen. Ich möchte etwas von dem aufspüren, was nicht in die offizielle Geschichtsschreibung eingeflossen ist" (*SP*, 14; I would like to imagine myself in their times. I would like to ferret out some of what has not flowed into official historiography).

Like *Das endlose Jahr*, *Stille Post* blurs traditional boundaries between the apparently objective form of the biography and the more self-reflexive style of the autobiography. Von Braun's research into the lives of her relatives is presented in short, chronologically ordered sections, which are framed by fictional letters that she writes to her deceased grandmother, Hildegard Margis. In these letters von Braun considers how the events that she relates in that section either impacted Hildegard or might have been impacted by her. She then probes her own relationship to this emotional history. Although her mother and grandmothers are the apparent focus of her narrative, she thus reminds her readers that, in fact, "es ist *meine* Geschichte, und sie erzählt davon, wie die 'stille Post,' die sie aufgegeben haben, bei mir angekommen ist" (*SP*, 16; it is *my* story, and it recounts how I received the "Chinese whispers" that they passed on). "Stille Post" is a children's game in which messages are whispered from one person to the next, and often distorted in the process of transmission. It is known as "Chinese whispers" in the British context and as "telephone" in the United States. The authors of the widely read sociological study *"Opa war kein Nazi": Nationalsozialismus und Holocaust im Familiengedächtnis* ("Grandpa Wasn't a Nazi": The Holocaust in German Family Remembrance, 2002) use this game as a model to explain how memory is passed from one generation to the next. They thereby emphasize the subjective factor in the transmission of family memory. The perspective of each individual determines "welche Geschichten vom 'Dritten Reich' in den einzelnen Generationen erzählt werden, wie diese Geschichten gemeinsam im Familiengespräch verfertigt werden, welche Versatzstücke und Einzelelemente weitergegeben werden und welche nicht" (which stories about the "Third Reich" are told in different generations, how they are collectively produced in family discussions, which clichés and individual elements are passed on and which ones are not).[16]

For von Braun, the image of this children's game particularly conveys the unpredictable and unarticulated effects of history on the individual psyche. She believes that latent messages or memories are primarily passed from mother to daughter. Von Braun attributes her academic interest in the women's movement and Jewish culture to the "unerledigte Aufträge" (*SP*, 15; unfinished assignments) that she has unconsciously taken on from Hildegard. Under the pressure of repression, she suggests, this inheritance can also take on warped forms such as her mother's depression and her own eating disorder. For von Braun, then, the history books are not the only sign that women's memories have been overlooked. This history of repression can be read "am eigenen Leib" (*SP*, 191; on one's own body), effectively meaning the bodies of women. Combining their reconstructions of female family history with an exploration of the psychological impact of repression on generations of mothers and daughters, Heidenreich, Senfft, and von Braun's works go further than many recent examinations of women and memory.[17] They direct the reader's attention to important social and psychological questions about women as subjects and agents of memory.

Women Remember

The subtitle of *Stille Post* is "eine andere Familiengeschichte" (a different family history). The difference that it evokes refers not merely to the stories of female relatives but to the medium in which they are communicated. At the heart of *Stille Post* are the intimate and embodied forms of experience not usually acknowledged by academic history. Von Braun traces the operations of history on the female subject in order to understand better how non-canonized forms of historical knowledge are generated and imparted. She senses that women like her mother "'die Geschichte' oft in einer ganz spezifischen Weise 'am eigenen Leib' erfahren und sich nur mit Verzweiflungstaten—oder eben durch Krankheiten—dagegen zu wehren vermöchten" (*SP*, 109; often experience "history" in a very specific manner "on the body" and can only offer resistance through acts of desperation—or even through maladies). She draws out a connection between the way that women experience history and the reasons why their stories remain untold. Von Braun argues that women have been forced to channel their feelings into non-linguistic forms because the phallogocentric order is hostile to expressions of affect. This has sent women's memories underground. In a literary extension of her decade-long academic research into women's position in phallogocentric Western culture, von Braun reads her mother's depressive episodes and fits of anger as expressions of hysteria.[18] She sets up an implicit opposition between women, who are associated with the body and truth, and men, who are related to the distorting discourses of logic. This understanding of the hysteric is common among second-wave feminists influenced by Lacanian psychoanalysis and its understanding of woman's position as non-subject in the phallogocentric order.[19]

The imprint of history on Hilde can be seen in the bouts of depression and self-destructive behavior, to which "sie *als Frau* wiederholt ausgesetzt worden ist" (*SP*, 394; she is repeatedly exposed *as a woman*).[20] Von Braun seems unwilling to consider embodied reactions to history as anything other than feminine. The fact that her uncle, Hans, has obviously been touched by Hildegard's legacy is an exception to the rule rather than a reason for von Braun to expand her theory beyond binary notions of gender. The final pages of *Stille Post* extend the notion of corporeal semiotics beyond Hilde to the readers of the autobiography, who, von Braun believes, share "eine Sprache, die zu einem Teil unseres Denkens, Fühlens, der Leidenschaften und damit auch unserer Geschichten wird" (*SP*, 405–6; a language that becomes part of our thoughts, feelings, passions, and therefore also of our history). The use of the first-person plural presupposes a common (female) identity between the author and her readers. Reifying gender as a primary constituent of historical experience, von Braun risks naturalizing the very experiences and feminine identities that she recovers from patriarchal reductionism. Her conception of female historical experience may be regarded as falsely homogenizing, as repeating the gestures of a sexual politics that justifies its operations on the basis of an assumed difference between men and women. As Marianne Hirsch and Valerie Smith have argued, "experience, as well as its recollection and transmission, is subject to gendered paradigms. But gender, like memory, must be grounded in context if it is not to remain an abstract binary structure."[21]

Furthermore, there is something deeply problematic about von Braun's claim that she is less interested in the content of paternal grandmother Emmy's diaries than in the language that she uses. She senses that Emmy was not truly writing in her own name, having internalized the expectations of her husband. Emmy's comportment also bears traces of male determination; she is, unlike Hilde, a paragon of female fortitude. Her behavior shows no signs of rebellion against prevailing circumstances. This explains to von Braun why Emmy seems to have had less of an impact on her sense of self than Hilde or even Hildegard Margis, whom she never met. The lasting impression of von Braun's narrative is that the most valuable female memories are those expressed in forms that cannot be subsumed by the phallogocentric logic of official cultural memory. It would certainly be valid to ask whether this idealized conception of authentic female experience is capable of furthering our understanding of the relationship between memory and gender performance. In her eagerness to appropriate resistance as part of a female genealogy, von Braun downplays the extent to which women, as active agents, participate in existing power hierarchies and the shaping of hegemonic cultural memory. Indeed, von Braun glosses over the fact that the achievements of Hildegard Margis are silenced in family memory because Hilde is unwilling to talk about them. It will not be possible to understand fully the normative logic and repressive mechanisms of cultural memory until we are willing to acknowledge that women are not always passive or resisting participants in hegemonic culture.

In comparison to von Braun, Senfft and Heidenreich enrich our understanding of women as agents of memory by reconstructing the practices and evolution of family memory. While Senfft depicts her grandmother as arbiter of family memory, Heidenreich critically reflects on her mother's status as custodian of family memory. Throughout her entire adult life her mother, Antonie, constructed various lies in order to obviate the shame of being an unmarried mother. After the war Heidenreich was led to believe that her father was presumed dead when, in fact, he was living happily with his other family. Antonie had forbidden him from contacting their daughter. In this family, men, and not women, are expunged from the family tree. Outside the home Antonie denies her daughter's existence. Her former role as the mistress of an SS officer, and the daughter who resulted from this relationship, are not compatible with her postwar social identity. The lengths to which Antonie, in partnership with her mother and sister, goes in order to construct a different version of the past are an extreme manifestation of Maurice Halbwachs's recognition that "it is in society that people normally acquire their memories. It is also in society that they recall, recognize, and localize their memories."[22]

Only the taunts of Heidenreich's malicious uncles inject an element of historical reality into the fallacious family story perpetuated by the women. Unlike von Braun, Heidenreich does not divide notions of historical authenticity along the demarcation line of gender. Even when Heidenreich finally learns what her uncles had meant with their spiteful remarks about the "SS bastard," she is never fully convinced that her mother has told her everything about their past. Heidenreich's doubts are reinforced by a phone call from a Mr. Moser, a man who claims that his biological parents had been involved in the resistance movement within the German army. Moser believes that he was taken from his family by the SS and placed in an adoptive home by Antonie and her colleagues. Heidenreich is disturbed by Moser's speculation that her mother might be part of a conspiracy of former *Lebensborn* personnel who guard remaining secrets about the program.[23] She nonetheless offers tentative evidence in support of this hypothesis. Heidenreich is haunted by the memory of a collection of old files hidden away in their home. She also battles with the knowledge that her mother is still in contact with *Lebensborn* colleagues and acquaintances, including Hitler's secretary, from her time in Allied captivity. For Heidenreich, as for Senfft, then, women are complicit in the construction of dominant and repressive historical narratives. Moreover, she suggests that there is no simple dividing line between "official" cultural memory and "unofficial" family memory. In the case of Antonie they overlap in a particular object of repression. The exchange between different forms of memory is shown to be dynamic. It is as distorted by personal investments as by cultural edicts.

It follows that for Heidenreich trauma is not a constituent characteristic of *women's* relationship to repressed memory. Heidenreich does believe in the existence of a "law of transmission" that causes mistakes to be repeated over generations. The fact that she had, as a teenage mother, considered giving her child up for adoption makes her wonder how deeply her mother's shame had been ingrained in her own psyche. Unlike von Braun, however, Heidenreich does not suggest that this law of transmission is gendered, that is to say, that it primarily passes between mothers and daughters. Looking back on the first meeting with her father when she was a teenager, Heidenreich is shocked to remember that he had reacted to a photograph of her then boyfriend, blue-eyed and blonde-haired, with the remark "wie schön, dass du auch so ganz in unserer Art bleibst" (*EJ*, 278; how nice that you are sticking with our sort, too). She asks "ob ich nicht bei dieser ersten Begegnung von meinem Vater so etwas wie einem 'Auftrag' übernommen und die 'Lebensborn'-Ideologie verinnerlicht habe" (*EJ*, 279; whether I had taken on something like a "mandate" from my father at this first meeting and internalized the "Lebensborn" ideology). For Heidenreich, a trained family therapist, psychological inheritance and historical trauma are clinical, not cultural or feminist issues. She thus feels no need to distinguish her own attempts to deal with the legacy of the past from her husband's engagement with National Socialism in his journalistic work or her son's attempts to work through the family past by writing a comedy, although these outlets for personal expression are arguably in themselves gendered.

Similarly, Alexandra Senfft's understanding of trauma is framed by empirical studies of transgenerational guilt. In this respect she is heavily influenced by her friendship and professional collaboration with Dan Bar-On, whose trailblazing *Legacy of Silence: Encounters with Children of the Third Reich* (1989) investigated the moral and psychological legacy of guilt. The trauma that von Braun regards as part of the feminine tradition is interpreted by Senfft as the individual's reaction to a specific personal history. She interprets her own eating disorder as an attempt to gain control over her life in the face of her demanding and deeply troubled mother. One should bear this in mind when reading some of Senfft's most rhetorically striking comments about female genealogy. She memorably describes the photographs of herself, her mother Erika, and her grandmother Erla that hang in her hallway: "Irgendwann sollten wir auch ein Bild meiner Tochter hinzufügen, schließlich gehört sie zur nächsten Generation von Frauen in unserer Familie" (*STW*, 264; one day we should add a picture of my daughter; after all, she belongs to the next generation of women in our family). She implies that if their complicated family past is not confronted, her daughter will feel its burden more acutely than her son. The symbolic power of such images overshadows other references in *Schweigen tut weh* to the impact of the troubled family past on male relatives. For example, Senfft informs her reader that Erika's brothers, too, acted out after the death of their father, clearly feeling the lack of a male figure of authority in the home. She also powerfully describes her younger brother's reaction to Erika's depression and alcoholism.

On several occasions Senfft implies that women, as mothers, constitute the emotional core of the family and therefore have a particular relationship to memory. Erika's brothers stay well out of the conflict between

Erika and their mother and largely leave worries about her well-being to their sisters. Similarly, Senfft, and not her brother, appears to be primarily responsible for supporting Erika. For Senfft, women do not physically remember, that is to say, experience, the past differently than men. They are, however, perhaps more likely to experience it as a burden because they engage in different processes of transmitting memory. For example, Senfft explains the urgency of her project by stating:

> Nach meiner Großmutter und meiner Mutter, die kurz hintereinander starben, bin nun ich die Nächste in der weiblichen Linie. Ich fühle mich verantwortlich, meinen Kindern meine Perspektive zu vermitteln. (*STW*, 16)

> [I am the next in the female family line after my grandmother and my mother, who died in short succession. I feel responsible for conveying my perspective to my children.]

Women appear closely connected to history through their traditional roles as educators and caregivers.

The home appears to define the parameters of female memory practice in the narratives discussed here. Certain memory practices are gendered because they are tied to women's conventional relationship to the domestic sphere. Von Braun and Senfft come into possession of their mothers' diaries and letters because it is their duty, as daughters, to clear out the homes of deceased family members. Furthermore, the act of collecting connects the three generations of women in *Schweigen tut weh* to repressed memories: Senfft keeps her mother's letters, Erla keeps a secret box of mementos from the Nazi era, and Erika has an almost fetishistic relationship to her father's letters and possessions. According to Australian historian Tanja Luckins, collecting may form the basis of a "poetics of female memory" since, traditionally, "household and personal possessions were under the eye and care of women who, because they were less likely to control property and land, were more likely to place greater emotional investment into personal and household things."[24] In the aftermath of war, Luckins continues, this investment is increased as collecting and preserving memory objects becomes integral to the process of mourning. After war, women, left behind on the home front, are then more likely than ever to be assigned the cultural task of mourning, as the matrilineal narratives of von Braun, Senfft, and Heidenreich demonstrate. As a wealth of feminist criticism has argued, however, these gendered practices are not natural or immutable. One learns and internalizes certain gender identities, performing the roles attached to them, in so far as one remembers and iterates observed behaviors and norms. Memorial practices are therefore not just gendered: they gender.[25]

Remembering Gendered Identity

Narrating the mental processes and physical practices whereby different individuals remember and respond to the past, the family narratives treated here tease out the ways in which gender and memory are reciprocally related in the construction of historical meaning and gendered identity. The authors intimate that both *doing gender* and *doing memory* are performative processes.[26] Like gender, as Judith Butler conceives it in *Gender Trouble*, cultural memory can be considered a regulatory fiction with temporal, collective, and public dimensions. The repeated performances inherent to both gender and memory sustain the social discourses of which they are effects. Relying on repetition and internalization for their normative effect, both are therefore open to resignification. The failure to repeat will expose as tenuous political constructs the historical interpretations and social norms enshrined in cultural memory.[27] At its most perceptive, Christina von Braun's metaphor of the game Chinese whispers or telephone attests to the doubly subversive potential of memory practices. The hysterical female reactions to history that she admires can be read as a refusal to remember, perform, and validate hegemonic gender and historical norms. Furthermore, von Braun explicitly acknowledges that remembering is therefore an act of both recovery and creation, remarking that "über die Botschaften, die weitergegeben werden, bestimmt jeder Teilnehmer neu" (*SP*, 51; each participant determines anew the messages that are passed on). Individual acts of remembrance can overturn the hegemonic mandate of repression. The possibility of social transformation is therefore located in the arbitrary relation between individual and cultural memory.

For von Braun this discontinuity is the key to social innovation; she believes that there is a cultural exchange between subjective and objective forms of knowledge and that "die Gesellschaft einen Gutteil ihrer Erinnerungen dieser 'stillen Post' anvertraut, vielleicht sogar die wichtigsten: all das, was verschwiegen wird, aber nicht verloren gehen darf" (*SP*, 15; society commits the bulk of its memories to these Chinese whispers, perhaps even the most important memories: all that is kept silent but that must not be lost). She focuses primarily on the implications of this process of exchange for cultural memory. The mechanisms of individual, family, and cultural memory are, however, also intertwined with the psychological and social processes through which individuals come to understand themselves as gendered subjects in history. After all, the regulatory fiction of binary gender identity and heterosexuality is sustained by cultural memory. Telling different stories about history, performing a different memory, or a different kind of memory, from that sanctioned by official memory culture thus also challenges the binary gender positions produced by that culture. The particular achievements of Alexandra Senfft and Gisela Heidenreich lie in the light that they shed on this dynamic.

In *Das endlose Jahr* Heidenreich demonstrates that the gendered norms inscribed in cultural memory influence an individual's interpretation of his or her relationships and the past. Culturally ingrained ideas about motherhood, and therefore feminine identity, affect Heidenreich's personal ability to process her mother's past. When Heidenreich visits her birthplace in Oslo, she is struck by a statue of a mother with her newborn baby displayed in the Vigeland park. Heidenreich struggles to associate Antonie with this archetypal image of motherhood. She believes that her mother was anaesthetized by Nazi ideology and that her detached approach to her work has left traces in their relationship. Heidenreich thus implies that the characteristics that led her mother to make politically and morally troubling decisions during the Third Reich also explain her deficiency as a parent.[28] In her reflections on the *Lebensborn* program, Heidenreich reproduces an ideology that reifies motherhood as moral identity. This ideal of motherhood explains why Heidenreich holds Antonie to a higher standard than her father. She finds it easier to understand why her father might have joined the SS, even though he is hardly the stereotypical Nazi sadist, than to imagine that her mother, or more accurately, any mother, could join the racist organization. On an intellectual level, however, Heidenreich recognizes that the gender ideals preserved in cultural memory do not measure up to the manifold experiences of real women. The circumstances of her birth make clear that the ideals she projects onto her mother are historically contingent. While Antonie was regarded as an honorable German mother within the context of the *Lebensborn* system, for instance, after the war she was subjected to opprobrium. The juxtaposition of three generations of mothers shows how feminine and motherly identity is renegotiated in line with changing social frameworks and in reaction to the experiences of previous generations. Antonie, for example, became involved with National Socialism as a way to avoid the sort of restrictive and exhausting life led by her mother. In turn Heidenreich's identity as mother is performed as a determined break from *her* mother's style of parenting.

The narrative draws to a close with a series of rhetorical questions that stage the reflexive processes through which individuals make sense of history and gendered identity over time. Heidenreich's newly won understanding of the reciprocal and dynamic relationship between memory and identity finally allows her to find peace. Reflecting on her mother's postwar identity, Heidenreich accepts that

> sie glaubt an das Lebenskostüm, in das sie geschlüpft ist, sie kann es nicht noch einmal vertauschen gegen das alte. Damals hat sie das alte Leben abgelegt wie ein gebrauchtes Kleidungsstück, das sie nun nicht mehr findet. Sie wäre nackt, wenn sie nach fünfzig Jahre das heutige Kostüm abstreifen würde. (*EJ*, 300–301)

[she believes in the life costume that she has slipped into, she can no longer exchange it for the old one. Back then she discarded her old life like a piece of clothing that she had worn out and has now lost. She would be naked if she were to strip off the costume that she wears nowadays.]

Heidenreich's allusions to costume evoke the performative processes through which individual memory is refashioned in conformity with evolving individual and collective parameters of remembrance, not least gender norms. For Judith Butler, identity is neither coherent nor stable but a "constituted social temporality," tenuously constructed in time and space through a stylized repetition of acts. Identity is ultimately a "performative accomplishment which the mundane social audience, including the actors themselves, come to believe and to perform in the mode of belief."[29] Just as identity is a constantly evolving expression of individual and social value systems, memory of an event cannot be definitively separated out from the diachronic investments, norms, and external discourses in which it is implicated.

In a similar manner, in the process of writing *Schweigen tut weh* it becomes clear to Alexandra Senfft that her mother's memories of her father shifted as her sense of self changed and with it her understanding of his impact on her life choices. As a young woman Erika strived to embody the traditional Germanic ideal of femininity that her father had exhorted her to follow in his letters from prison:

Er mahnt sie "anständig und nützlich" zu sein . . . Sie solle Sport treiben und habe als Frau "geradezu die Pflicht, hübsch zu sein"— wobei er vor allem die innere Selbstdisziplin und ein gepflegtes Äußeres meint. (*STW*, 163)

[He admonishes her to be "respectable and dutiful" . . . She ought to keep fit and, as a woman, has "well-nigh the duty to be handsome"—by which he means, above all, inner self-discipline and a groomed appearance.]

Erika obsessively rereads her father's letters in times of crisis in order to find a source of personal orientation. She also refashions his old clothes, literally styling herself on him. These practices provide as much insight into Erika's psychology as the artifacts themselves. Reading and rereading her father's letters enacts a mnemonic process through which Erika reinforces her memories of her father. Intimately connected to a memory praxis encoded as feminine, that is, mourning, this rereading is a negotiation of family and collective history into identity. If to remember is to situate one's life in meaningful narratives that conform to established social codes regarding gender, nationality, and race, then *Schweigen tut weh* conveys the inextricability of gendered identity formation from memory construction and recall. The letters sustain a feminine ideal with roots in the Third Reich, which is internalized by Erika as she reads and rereads them. The letters are initially Erika's primary frame of reference for interpreting her place, as a woman, in society and history. This reflects Judith Butler's contention that gender identity is never "fully self-styled, for styles have a history."[30] Erika's constant desire to reinvent herself, as Eri or Erica, the softer, less Germanic variants of her name, and eventually Nora, nevertheless implies her discomfort with this ideal of femininity.

Integrating excerpts from Hanns's letters into the narrative, Senfft reconstructs the manner in which Erika, in the process of remembering her father, positioned herself as gendered subject in society. "Hausfrau und Mutter will Eri sein," Senfft describes; "sie stürzt sich mit Wucht in diese Rolle und spielt sie für ihre Außenwelt perfekt" (*STW*, 219; Eri wants to be a housewife and mother; she throws herself wholeheartedly into this role, which she plays perfectly to the outside world). This language of performance characterizes Senfft's descriptions of her mother. Just as Heidenreich senses that her mother created a false identity for herself in public in order to repress her feelings of shame, Senfft suggests that her mother disguised debilitating feelings of guilt and abnormality behind a performance of ideal femininity. Indeed, this performance was most successful when she was confronted with the left-wing friends of her husband who would have been most likely to judge her family history negatively.

In an article on gender and memory in contemporary memoirs, Susanne Luhmann obliquely suggests that Erika's alcoholism and affective outbursts are a sign that she has refused gendered normalcy, "so fully does she inhabit the negative affective legacy of her father's role in the death of thousands of Slovakian Jews."[31] In other words, her unhappy performance of the role of dutiful housewife and responsible mother expresses the traumatic knowledge of familial guilt. Erika's outbursts indicate the fundamental conflict between her wish to live up to her father's expectations and the subconscious desire to refuse their ideological foundations and to reject him for his crimes. Senfft perceptively unfolds the rituals through which her mother remembered her family past and in so doing re-membered herself as a woman in West German society. As she reassesses her image of her father, in line with changing attitudes to the Nazi past in West Germany, Erika's performance of traditional feminine identity is destabilized more and more frequently.

In comparison to von Braun, who equates trauma with femininity, Senfft shows how trauma can produce certain stylizations of gender. Laying bare these moments of trauma to the reader, without forcing them into a mythologizing explanatory framework, Senfft refuses to perpetuate a family legend that has denied the effects of guilt and naturalized her mother's illness as a "hormonal disorder," as a feminine condition. She insists on the iterative nature of memory, writing: "wir alle sind Komplizen ihrer Krankheit und Komplizen beim Tradieren einer Familiensaga, die wir glauben wie Kinder ein Märchen" (*STW*, 289; we are all accessories to her illness and complicit in handing down a family saga. We believe in it just as children believe in fairy tales). Breaking from this script, Senfft implies, would expand the parameters of family and cultural memory and liberate the individual from the gendered norms that they perpetuate.

Conclusion

Today, as during the heyday of the feminist movement, women's memoirs remind us of the specific contours of gendered experience. What is more, Gisela Heidenreich, Christina von Braun, and Alexandra Senfft redress the selective inscription of women's experience into cultural memory. In this chapter I have argued that we can and should look to memoirs in order to understand better the relationship between gendered identity formation and cultural memory, notably their common regulative fictions and performative practices. Memoir is one site among many where the ideological construction of memory is orchestrated. It stages the private processes through which individuals become aware of and renegotiate the gender and conventional norms through which "history" is publicly remembered and integrated into long-term cultural memory. The memoirs analyzed here also deepen our understanding of the reciprocal relationship between acts of remembrance and identity performance. Indicating that both memory and gendered identity are constructions, they largely obviate the pitfalls of early feminist writing on women and memory that naturalized women's otherness.[32] At their most innovative, the memoirs discussed in this article suggest that the repetition central to rituals of remembrance opens up possibilities for contesting the cultural script of remembrance through a reinterpretation of established historical and social norms. Moreover, since memoirs enrich and expand the archive of cultural memory, they facilitate a potential renegotiation of the hegemonic narrative that constitutes cultural memory and the mapping of gender within it. A powerful critical and political tool, memoir can stage important feminist interventions in cultural memory by reminding us, in the words of Marianne Hirsch and Valerie Smith, "that forgetting and suppressing must be contested by active remembering and that the practice and analysis of cultural memory can in itself be a form of political activism."[33]

Notes

[1] Seminal examples of politicized autobiographical writing include *Häutungen* (Shedding, 1975) by Verena Stefan and *Klassenliebe* (Class Love, 1973) by Karin Struck. For a thoughtful discussion of many more examples see Angelika Bammer, "Feminism, *Frauenliteratur*, and Women's Writing of the 1970s and 1980s," in *A History of Women's Writing in Germany, Austria and Switzerland*, ed. Jo Catling (Cambridge: Cambridge University Press, 2000).

[2] Iconic texts include the anonymous diary *Eine Frau in Berlin* (A Woman in Berlin, 1959); Melita Maschmann's account of her work in the League of German Girls, *Fazit: Kein Rechtfertigungsversuch* (1963; published in English as *Account Rendered: A Dossier on my Former Self,* 1964); and Marie-Thérèse Kerschbaumer's fictional documentary *Der weibliche Name des Widerstands* (The Female Name of Resistance, 1980). For more on this trend consult Cordula Mahr, *Kriegsliteratur von Frauen? Zur Darstellung des Zweiten Weltkriegs in Autobiographien nach 1960* (Herbolzheim, Germany: Centaurus Verlag, 2006).

[3] A selection of recent fictional family narratives includes Melitta Breznik's *Das Umstellformat* (The Reversal Format, 2002), Tanja Dückers's *Himmelskörper* (Heavenly Bodies, 2003), Anna Mitgutsch's *Familienfest* (Family Celebration, 2003), Viola Roggenkamp's *Familienleben* (Family Life, 2004), Sabine Schiffner's *Kindbettfieber* (Childbed Fever, 2005), Larissa Boehning's *Lichte Stoffe* (Light Materials, 2007), Katharina Hagena's *Der Geschmack von Apfelkernen* (The Taste of Apple Seeds, 2008), and Annette Pehnt's *Chronik der Nähe* (Chronicle of Closeness, 2012). On female family narratives, see also Valerie Heffernan's contribution to this volume.

[4] Peter Burke, "History as Social Memory," in *Memory: History, Culture and the Mind*, ed. Thomas Butler (New York: Blackwell, 1989), 107.

[5] This is an established motif in German women's writing. In her uncompleted prose cycle *Todesarten* (Ways of Death), Ingeborg Bachmann related the anxiety of her female protagonists to widespread social amnesia, on the one hand, and to aspects of the self incompatible with the values of hegemonic culture, on the other. Other examples include Christa Wolf's *Nachdenken über Christa T.* (The Quest for Christa T., 1968) and Helma Sanders-Brahms's film *Deutschland bleiche Mutter* (Germany Pale Mother, 1980). For more on this see chapter 4 in Sigrid Weigel, *Die Stimme der Medusa: Schreibweisen in der Gegenwartsliteratur von Frauen* (Dülmen-Hiddingsel, Germany: Tende, 1987), and Claudia Öhlschläger, "Gender/Körper, Gedächtnis und Literatur," in *Gedächtniskonzepte der Literaturwissenschaft: Theoretische Grundlegung und Anwendungsperspektive*, ed. Astrid Erll and Ansgar Nünning (Berlin: Walter de Gruyter, 2005), 227–48. On somatic memory more generally see Aleida Assmann, *Der lange Schatten der Vergangeheit: Erinnerungskultur und Geschichtspolitik* (Munich: C. H. Beck, 2006), 119–37.

[6] Joan Wallach Scott, "The Evidence of Experience," *Critical Inquiry* 17 (1991): 777.

[7] Judith Butler, *Gender Trouble: Feminism and the Subversion of Identity*, 3rd ed. (New York: Routledge Classics, 2006), 34.

[8] Ibid., 190. Aleida Assmann writes, for example, "das Gedächtnis festigt sich durch Elaboration und Wiederholung" (memory is consolidated through elaboration and repetition) in *Der lange Schatten der Vergangenheit*, 128. She and Jan Assmann primarily consider the iterative nature of commemorative rituals.

[9] Jennifer Moos and Meike Penkwitt, eds., "Erinnern und Geschlecht," special issues, *Freiburger Frauenstudien* 19 (2006) and 20 (2007). See also Sabine Lucia Müller and Anja Schwarz, eds., "Iterationen: Geschlecht im kulturellen Gedächtnis," special issue, *Querelles: Jahrbuch für Frauen- und Geschlechterforschung* 13 (2008).

[10] Sabine Müller and Anja Schwarz, "Einleitung," in "Iterationen: Geschlecht im kulturellen Gedächtnis," *Querelles: Jahrbuch für Frauen- und Geschlechterforschung*, 18.

[11] Gisela Heidenreich, *Das endlose Jahr: Die langsame Entdeckung der eigenen Biographie—ein Lebensborn-Schicksal* (Frankfurt am Main: Fischer, 2004). Further references to this work are given in the text using the abbreviation *EJ*.

[12] The *Lebensborn* program is a topic of contemporary literary interest. See Karina Berger, "Children of the Lebensborn: The Search for Identity in Selected Literary Texts of the Berlin Republic," *Focus on German Studies* 15 (2008): 105–20.

[13] Alexandra Senfft, *Schweigen tut weh: Eine deutsche Familiengeschichte* (Berlin: List, 2008). Further references to this work are given in the text using the abbreviation *STW*.

[14] Gabriele Rosenthal, ed., *Der Holocaust im Leben von drei Generationen: Familien von Überlebenden der Shoah und von Nazi-Tätern* (Gießen: Psychosozial Verlag, 1997), 354. See also Margit Reiter, *Die Generation danach: Der Nationalsozialismus im Familiengedächtnis* (Innsbruck: Studienverlag, 2006).

[15] Christina von Braun, *Stille Post: Eine andere Familiengeschichte*, 3rd ed. (Berlin: List, 2011). Further references to this work are given in the text using the abbreviation *SP*.

[16] Harald Welzer, Sabine Moller, and Karoline Tschuggnall, *"Opa war kein Nazi": Nationalsozialismus und Holocaust im Familiengedächtnis*, 8th ed. (Frankfurt: Fischer, 2012), 14.

[17] Feminist studies of cultural memory still frequently emphasize the ways in which women have been excluded from cultural memory without thought for their participation in its production and transmission. See for example the introduction to *The Gender of Memory: Cultures of Remembrance in Nineteenth- and Twentieth-Century Europe*, ed. Sylvia Palatschek and Sylvia Schraut (Frankfurt: Campus, 2007), 7–28. The aforementioned special issues of *Freiburger Frauenstudien*, edited by Penkwitt and Moos, and *Querelles: Jahrbuch für Frauen- und Geschlechterforschung*, edited by Müller and Schwarz, represent initial but significant attempts to grasp women's participation in and influence by memory culture.

[18] See Christina von Braun, "Fort da: Die Wiedergänger des kulturellen Gedächtnisses," in *[Auslassungen]: Leerstellen als Movens der Kulturwissenschaft*, ed. Natascha Adamowsky and Peter Matussek (Würzburg: Königshausen & Neumann, 2004): 265–70, and *Nicht Ich: Logik—Lüge—Libido* (Frankfurt: Neue Kritik, 1985).

[19] See Mark Micale, *Approaching Hysteria: Disease and Its Interpretations* (Princeton, NJ: Princeton University Press, 1995).

[20] My emphasis.

[21] Marianne Hirsch and Valerie Smith, "Feminism and Cultural Memory: An Introduction," special issue on "Gender and Memory," *Signs* 28, no. 1 (2002): 7.

[22] Maurice Halbwachs, *On Collective Memory*, trans. Lewis Coser (Chicago: University of Chicago Press, 1992), 38.

[23] On the extent to which women from the highest echelons of the Third Reich seem to have closed ranks after the war, see Margarete Dörr, *Wer die Zeit nicht miterlebt hat: Frauenerfahrungen im Zweiten Weltkrieg und in den Jahren danach*, 3 vols. (Frankfurt am Main: Campus, 1998), 1:23.

[24] Tanja Luckins, "Collecting Women's Memories: The Australian War Memorial, the Next of Kin and Great War Soldiers' Diaries and Letters as Objects of Memory in the 1920s and 1930s," *Women's History Review* 19, no. 1 (2010): 31.

[25] The performative element of memory is implied by the reflexive pronoun that accompanies the verb "to remember" in languages such as French ("se souvenir") or German ("sich erinnern"). As Paul Ricoeur notes, "in remembering something (*se souvenant de quelque chose*), one remembers oneself (*on se souvient de soi*)." In other words, both the past and the subject who remembers it are produced when an individual remembers. See Ricoeur, *Memory, History, Forgetting*, trans. Kathleen Blamey and David Pellauer (Chicago: University of Chicago Press, 2004), 96.

[26] On the performative dimensions of memory see the contributions to *Performing Memory in Art and Popular Culture*, ed. Liedeke Plate and Anneke Smelik (New York: Routledge, 2013). See also Müller and Schwarz, "Einleitung," 11–22.

[27] Butler, *Gender Trouble*, 190–92.

[28] A similar suggestion is made in other *Lebensborn* narratives, such as Birgit Bauer's *Im Federhaus der Zeit* (2003), and in Helga Schneider's autobiography, *Lass mich gehen* (2004), about her estranged mother who worked as a concentration-camp guard.

[29] Butler, *Gender Trouble*, 191.

[30] Ibid., 190.

[31] Susanne Luhmann, "Gender and the Generations of Difficult Knowledge: Recent Responses to Familial Legacies of Nazi Perpetration," *Women in German Yearbook* 25 (2009): 187.

[32] See the contributions to "Women and Memory," ed. Margaret Louri, Donna Stanton, and Martha Vicinus, a special issue of *Michigan Quarterly Review* 26, no. 1 (1987). Selma Leydesdorff reassesses this tendency in the foreword to a revised edition of *Gender and Memory*, ed. Selma Leydesdorff, Luisa Passerini, and Paul Richard Thompson (New Brunswick, NJ: Transaction, 2005).

[33] Hirsch and Smith, "Feminism and Cultural Memory," 11.

4: Reckoning with God: Attitudes toward Religion in German-Language Women's Writing in the Twenty-First Century

Sheridan Marshall

IN THIS ARTICLE I EXAMINE the place of religious beliefs, and the interrelation between religion and gender, in a selection of twenty-first-century German-language prose fiction written by women. In line with the widespread recognition of a "religious turn"[1] or "(re)sacralization"[2] that is transforming political and cultural discourse in the "post-secular society"[3] in which we live, the role of religion in contemporary German-language literature is subject to increasing scrutiny. In German literary studies the depiction of Islam in Germanic culture and the history of German-Jewish identity currently receive much more explicit attention than the place of Christian faith.[4] Julian Preece and Frank Finlay discuss this bias in their edited volume *Religion and Identity in Germany Today*. They speculate that the non-religious backgrounds of most "white" German-language authors and the academics who analyze their texts—who nonetheless belong to national traditions that have been strongly influenced by Christianity—mean that they have to rediscover a conceptual apparatus in order to address the Christian God. The same critics are more at ease when discussing Muslim and Jewish religious beliefs, which, arguably, do not have the same disconcerting relation to their own intellectual heritage.[5] It is precisely this capacity of religious beliefs to unsettle and disconcert—their demand for a reckoning with or without God—that interests me in the literary texts here, and I follow this process of reckoning in relation to Jewish and Christian conceptions of God.

Nicolas Boyle has described how twentieth-century writers' recurring engagement with the confrontation between religion and secularity is one of the means by which they are able to conceptualize some of the most profound changes in notions of personal and collective identity entailed by modern life.[6] Boyle's assessment remains true for writers in the twenty-first century, and for the female novelists whose work I consider here, religious identity is a key aspect of characterization and frequently serves as a means of exploring other aspects of identity, including their gender, because of the ways in which experiences of religion intersect with and impinge upon other means of self-understanding. In the portrayal of attitudes toward religion in contemporary literature, the gender of the characters is shown to be integral to the experiences that have shaped those attitudes.

Sociological accounts of secularization in industrialized Western societies describe how the more pronounced demarcation between people's public and private lives entailed by the advent of industrial working relations corresponds with a decline in the Christian church's influence over public life and its increasing association with the domestic sphere. The habitual division of male and female responsibilities along the same public/private lines meant that while men's attendance at church began to decline, women's involvement in church activities initially did not. Secularization then accelerated during the 1960s as female emancipation and other social changes provided women with ways of exploring identities other than through their roles at home and in the church, resulting in many women choosing to move away from the church. Despite these kinds of historical differences between men and women's experiences of religion, accounts of secularization all too often originate from a male standpoint that excludes female perspectives.[7] In its exploration of the continuing confrontation between religious faith and secularity throughout twentieth-century European history, German-language women's writing in the twenty-first century works to redress the historical under-representation of women's experiences of religious faith.

Of the four books considered in this article, three—those by Ursula Krechel, Jenny Erpenbeck, and Sibylle Berg—have protagonists who live through either the period of the Second World War or the Communist regime in East Germany, or both of these. Bettina Balàka's novel has a contemporary setting, although key scenes refer back to one character's experiences during the Second World War. While it is certainly the case, as Katharina Gerstenberger writes in an article on the intergenerational memory of the Holocaust in contemporary women's writing, that "by the twenty-first century, memory of the Nazi period has lost some of the collective identity-forming power it held for the first two generations of postwar Germans,"[8] it remains a cornerstone of contemporary German-language writing. Literary responses to the Holocaust in particular—as a defining part of twentieth-century history in which religious identity could be a matter of life and death—tend to generate important insights into evolving attitudes toward religion during the twentieth century. The fact that during the Nazi period Jewish identity came to signify a death sentence under laws that were tolerated and even instituted by people defining themselves as Christians has given rise to an intense examination of both the Jewish and Christian faiths since the Second World War. The

Holocaust has generated a new context for the skepticism toward and questioning of God that was already well established during the twentieth century, and the reexamination of religious faith continues into the twenty-first century. The Holocaust also raises fundamental questions about attitudes to religion that stem from women's experiences during this time; the novels considered here by Ursula Krechel and Jenny Erpenbeck examine the extraordinary strains placed upon mothers of Jewish children under the Nazi regime and the consequences for these women's attitudes toward religious identity.

"God was asleep; he was resting after allowing so much chaos."[9]—Ursula Krechel's *Landgericht*

The second of the two epigraphs in Ursula Krechel's novel *Landgericht* (State Justice, 2012), winner of the 2012 German Book Prize, points to the complicated status of religious identity in the book: "Er kam in sein Eigentum, aber die Seinen nahmen ihn nicht auf. (*Joh.1, 11*)." The quotation is taken from the New Testament Gospel of John (1:11) and describes how Jesus was rejected by his own Jewish people during his time on earth: "He came unto his own, and his own received him not." Krechel's protagonist, Richard Kornitzer, is a German Jew who is forced into exile in Cuba in 1939. When he returns to postwar Germany in 1948 and attempts to resume his career in the judiciary, aspiring to use his legal expertise to contribute to the rebuilding of the country, he makes the painful discovery that his colleagues in the legal profession include many former Nazis who supported the anti-Semitic policies that had forced him to flee. Despite his apparent success, he is plagued by his sense of remaining an outsider among the professional equals who should count as "his own." So the biblical epigraph in some sense helps to characterize the secular insecurity that defines Kornitzer's return to postwar Germany. The epigraph is relevant to his professional situation rather than to his relationship with the Jewish faith, and the professional alienation he experiences occurs as a result of his Jewish ethnicity, irrespective of his religious affiliation with Judaism. Kornitzer's situation illustrates one way in which religious frameworks remain relevant for people's postwar experiences and identities, even if they do not practice their religion.

Ursula Krechel's novel shows the impact of Jewish and Christian identities on those born in Germany in the first half of the twentieth century and their continuing importance for those who are rebuilding their lives in postwar Germany. Most of the action in Krechel's novel is influenced by the Jewish or Christian heritage of its protagonists, and yet for the characters themselves such categories are initially unimportant. Richard and Claire Kornitzer marry in 1931, as Richard is embarking on a promising legal career and Claire is running a successful company producing cinema advertising. Even though Richard's mother would rather have seen her son marry a Jewish girl than the Protestant Claire, the couple's different religious backgrounds at first seem inconsequential. But then in April 1933 Richard Kornitzer is barred from the legal profession for being a Jew. As the Nazi regime makes itself felt in all aspects of their lives, Richard and Claire are made painfully aware of their differing religious identities. For assimilated German Jews such as Richard, who did not grow up with a strong sense of Jewish identity, the successive rulings against Jews under National Socialism and the institution of the Nuremberg Laws in 1935 meant that their religious background all at once assumed a new and devastating significance. While the Nuremberg Laws were introduced to enable the Nazis to classify Jews according to their racial origins, regardless of their religious observance, they nonetheless had an impact on the way non-religious Jewish individuals perceived their religious identity. For many members of 1930s Germany's large assimilated Jewish population who had not necessarily thought of themselves as Jewish prior to the Nazis' institutionalized anti-Semitism, being labeled as Jewish gave rise to a reevaluation of their attitudes toward the Jewish religion, even if only as something practiced by their parents or grandparents. Krechel's novel demonstrates how for non-practicing Jews in Nazi Germany, any residual sense of spiritual identification with the Jewish religion was overtaken by the disturbing social and political implications of Jewish ethnicity for the individual concerned. The way in which spiritual aspects of religious identity are overshadowed by its ramifications for people's social and political existence is reinforced by the few references to God in *Landgericht*. Having presided over the wartime chaos, God is apparently now asleep. Unlike the other texts I will consider here, in which characters invoke God or address him accusingly, even if ironically, in the course of their daily lives, Richard and Claire Kornitzer do not address God except on the occasions when they engage in Protestant worship.

The absurdity by which many German Jews gained a sense of themselves as Jewish only through the Nazis' persecution of them as such has an additional twist in the case of Richard Kornitzer, who converts to Christianity during the 1930s and experiences a closer connection with his wife's Protestant faith through his own experiences of persecution: "Seit er verfolgt war, verstand er besser das Zusammenscharen unter den Bildnissen, den Statuen des Gekreuzigten, die Religion, die den gemarterten Judenkönig in ihren Mittelpunkt gerückt hatte" (*L*, 255; Since being persecuted he was better able to understand the coming together under the effigies, the statues of Christ on the cross, the religion that had placed the martyred King of the Jews at its center). The paradoxical effect of the persecution experienced by Kornitzer as a non-practicing Jew is to strengthen his capacity for spiritual identification with the Christian faith. Krechel makes it clear that Kornitzer's conversion to Protestantism is not part of a calculation to derive benefit for himself or for his children—which in any case is impossible under the National Socialists' interpretation of the effects of Christian conversion upon Jewish racial identity—but rather an indefinable feeling that he is not able to explain rationally. Kornitzer muses on the effects of his conversion but is not able to draw a conclusion: "war denn Religion zufällig oder austauschbar? Neutralisierte die Taufe, machte der Religionswechsel zu einem Sowohl-als-auch?" (*L*, 256; so was religion coincidental or interchangeable? Did baptism have a neutralizing effect or did changing one's religion enable both to exist alongside each other?) These questions are not answered directly, but Kornitzer's ambiguity toward religious experience is highlighted in the mixed emotions he continues to have both during his wartime exile to Cuba and in the postwar period. While he identifies strongly with other Jews and experiences a powerful sense of connection when reading about others' experiences of anti-Semitic prejudice, his period in exile also makes him feel disconnected from his own Jewishness, which is described as "eine lose Hülle, in der er steckte; schon der Zwischenraum schmerzte" (*L*, 374; a loose shell which he was inside; even the in-between space was painful). Kornitzer's Jewish identity is by no means altogether cast off after his conversion, nor does Christian identity become a substitute for it.

Richard Kornitzer's professional achievements, including his rapid promotion to the role of director of the District Court in Mainz, are overshadowed by the way in which the anti-Semitic prejudice and persecution that he has suffered in the past persists in the present. The far-reaching implications of Nazi persecution of the Jews include the fact that they continue to be denied the opportunity to participate fully in Germany's legal system even beyond 1945. Krechel's historically accurate articulation of Richard Kornitzer's fraught position, in which as a victim of Nazi persecution he is barred from being involved in the judicial process of reparation for other victims, demonstrates the enduring legacy of Nazi anti-Semitism for the lives of Jews in postwar Germany.

Alongside her documentation of the persistence of anti-Semitism in Germany after 1945, Krechel describes how the reassertion of Christian values shapes postwar German society. Upon arriving in Mainz to take up the position he is offered at the District Court, Kornitzer observes the return of Mainz's church bells, an event that is of momentous importance for the local people. Bells were removed from church buildings throughout Germany so that the metal could be used to serve the war effort, but after the war many were found to be intact and could be returned to the churches. The bells are brought up the river by ship, and a crowd of people gather on the quayside to welcome them home: "Sie waren willkommen, sie wurden erwartet und geliebt. Die Glocken gaben

Orientierung, auch wenn diese auf vielen anderen Gebieten fehlte" (*L*, 126; They were welcomed, they were eagerly anticipated and beloved. The bells provided orientation, even if this was lacking in many other areas). The sentimental reports in the local newspaper that accompany the return of the church bells convey an understandable delight in the restoration of a part of the city of Mainz's architectural and spiritual heritage in the face of the widespread destruction wreaked on the city during the Allied bombing campaign. Yet these reports also signify the potential for an unquestioning reinstatement of the institutions that had guided the moral life of Germany prior to 1933 and had largely failed to oppose the persecution of the Jews and other minority social groups under National Socialism. This is reinforced by the way in which references to church buildings recur in the novel as a means of orientation both in Germany's bombed-out cities and in its largely unspoiled villages.[10] While virtually all traces of Jewish heritage have been permanently erased from the postwar German townscapes, places of Christian worship abound. From Richard Kornitzer's point of view, most of the types of orientation that Mainz's church bells and other ecclesiastical buildings might be capable of providing are thoroughly unwelcome, since the majority of Germany's Christian community did little to oppose the Nazi policies of Jewish persecution that led to the Holocaust. Furthermore, the centuries of Christian anti-Semitism that preceded the Holocaust arguably helped to create conditions under which it was possible for it to happen. As the bells are received at the quayside, a priest greets them with a prayer and the hope "daß mit den alten Glocken ein neuer Ton angeschlagen würde" (*L*, 128; that the old bells might strike a new tone). Kornitzer's experiences of continuing prejudice and of the ubiquity of former Nazis within the judicial system suggest that such hopes are in vain.

The lives of the female characters in Krechel's novel are also indelibly marked by questions of religious identity, in ways that are related to their gender-specific roles as wives, mothers, and daughters. When the Kornitzers' children leave Germany for England on a Kindertransport, aged just four and seven, they are saved from death at the hands of the Nazis, but the Kornitzers' family life is irrevocably damaged. Claire Kornitzer's position as a frustrated and disappointed mother of absent children is brought about by the Nazis' persecution of her husband and children as Jews. Throughout the novel it is the loss of her children—who, even when she is reunited with them, remain permanently estranged from her—rather than the loss of her career or damage to her relationship with her husband that counts as the defining aspect of the multifaceted suffering inflicted by the Nazis. Claire experiences the loss of maternal responsibility as a primal disappointment—an unspeakably great pain: "Der Schmerz war zu groß, war übergroß, eine riesige, unheilbare Wundfläche, ein unstillbares Schweigen" (*L*, 426; The pain was too great, exceedingly great, a vast wound that would never heal, an unending silence). Krechel shows how the collapse of Claire's maternal identity—an experience common to many women who lived through the Second World War, and the Holocaust in particular—is inseparable from the Nazi categorizations of Jewish identity that affect Claire's husband and children.

The ongoing importance of identity based on religious tradition for generations living after the Second World War is illustrated by their daughter Selma's desire to marry a Jewish man. Richard Kornitzer does not understand why the Jewish identity of Selma's future husband should matter so much to her—this is one of the principal reasons why she is attracted to him—and his lack of understanding irritates her. Her father's failure to see why Jewishness matters at this point may seem to her to perpetuate the sense of rejection and betrayal that she still feels at her parents' decision to send her away from them. For Selma, marrying a Jewish man is a way of recuperating some of what she has lost through an upbringing that was so negatively determined by her father's Jewishness. It is as if, through her philo-Semitic marriage, she were trying to undo some of the consequences of Nazi anti-Semitism, although the novel ultimately gives us little sense of gauging the success of this measure. In common with other literature written after the Holocaust, *Landgericht* exemplifies both the widespread erosion of religious faith that occurred as a consequence of the desolation of the Holocaust and the continuing significance of questions of religious identity afterward. These questions necessarily remain unresolved, and in their very unresolvability they help—in literature and elsewhere—in the task of formulating a memorial response to the Holocaust, a response sensitive to the need to ensure that it cannot happen again.

"The Lord giveth, and the Lord taketh away."[11] —Jenny Erpenbeck's *Aller Tage Abend*

Like Krechel's *Landgericht*, Jenny Erpenbeck's novel *Aller Tage Abend* (2012; published in English as *The End of Days*, 2014) is concerned with the historical significance of Jewish identity in Germany, and in common with Erpenbeck's earlier work, *Heimsuchung* (2008; published in English as *Visitation*, 2011), *Aller Tage Abend* also focuses on the ways in which the lives of individuals—and those of women in particular—are bound up with large-scale historical events.[12] The novel opens in Galicia in 1901, as a young Jewish woman is grieving for her baby daughter. The novel's conceptual framework is expressed in religious terms in its opening lines:

> Der Herr hat's gegeben, der Herr hat's genommen, hatte die Großmutter am Rand der Grube zu ihr gesagt. Aber das stimmte

nicht, denn der Herr hatte viel mehr genommen, als da war—auch
alles, was aus dem Kind hätte werden können, lag jetzt da unten und
sollte unter die Erde. (*ATA*, 7)

[The Lord giveth, and the Lord taketh away, the grandmother had
said to her at the graveside. But that wasn't true, because the Lord
had taken away a lot more than what had been there—all the things
that might have become of the child were now lying down there and
had to go under the earth.]

While the woman's grandmother, a religious Jew, rationalizes the loss
of the child in theological terms, in which God is answerable for all the
good and ill that befalls humankind, the woman's attempts to fathom her
unbearable loss involve envisaging that God does not wield this ultimate
power over humanity: "Schön wäre es, denkt sie, wenn der Zufall regieren würde, und nicht ein Gott" (*ATA*, 6; It would be nice, she thinks, if
things were governed by chance and not by a god). This thought reflects
the woman's religious upbringing and her difficulty even so in comprehending how God could possibly have presided over her daughter's death.
As the child is dying, the woman attempts to bargain with God, offering
her own life in exchange for her daughter's, "Aber der Gott, wenn es
ihn gab, hatte das Geschenk nicht angenommen" (*ATA*, 7; But God, if
he existed, had not accepted the gift). In contrast to her grandmother's
stoical acceptance of God's actions, the young woman imagines a world
without God, attempts to reason with him, and then doubts his existence,
but God nonetheless remains the dominant ordering principle in her life.

In *Aller Tage Abend* Erpenbeck imagines that the baby girl for whom
the woman is grieving in the opening scene had gone on living, and in
each of the novel's different sections she tells the story of the girl's life—
"all the things that might have become of the child"—up until various
other possible times that she might have died. The question of the extent
to which characters from different generations rely upon faith in a metaphysical reality to provide orientation in the material realities of their
daily lives persists throughout the novel. As in Krechel's *Landgericht*,
however, because of the historical period in which the novel is set, the
inherited religious identity of the characters plays a defining role in their
lives in any case, independent of their personal religious beliefs. Many
of Erpenbeck's characters remain unnamed and therefore familial designations like daughter, mother, and grandmother are used more frequently, serving to highlight the intergenerational bonds and the ways
in which the characters' identities are defined by their relationships to
other family members. The dominance of the matriarchal relationships
within the novel is one of the ways in which Erpenbeck achieves what
Katharina Gerstenberger aptly describes as foregrounding "gender as a

determining factor in a character's experiences as victim, as perpetrator, or both."[13] Erpenbeck's narrative highlights the resourcefulness of the female family members in adapting to the continually evolving sociopolitical environment of the twentieth century. Petra Bagley's discussion of what she terms "Großmütterliteratur" (grandmother literature) in relation to Erpenbeck's short story "Tand"—emphasizing the significance of the relationship between granddaughters and grandmothers in contemporary German literature, particularly in relation to portrayals of the Nazi period—is also relevant here, where the successive granddaughter-grandmother relationships play a critical role in the transmission of religious identity to the younger generation.[14]

The first section of the novel describes the circumstances of the grieving woman's family. To her grandfather's lasting disappointment the young woman made an early marriage to a Christian man. Her own mother was instrumental in organizing this marriage, however, having tempted her daughter's suitor with the offer of a dowry that would pay off his considerable debts. Having witnessed the murder of her husband in their own home at the hands of a mob of local people during an anti-Semitic attack, she is eager to furnish her daughter with a way of leaving her potentially fatal Jewish identity behind. The account of the attack in which the father of the young woman—then still a baby, concealed elsewhere in the house with her nanny—loses his life includes the two final lines of Psalm 39: "Hear my prayer, O Lord, and give ear unto my cry; hold not thy peace at my tears: for I *am* a stranger with thee, *and* a sojourner, as all my fathers *were*. O spare me, that I may recover strength, before I go hence, and be no more." This plea to God is a striking demonstration of faith in the midst of murderous anti-Semitic brutality: just as the couple are subjected to fatal violence as a consequence of their religious identity, they assert their faith in God, quoting from a psalm that speaks of faith as a certainty in the midst of human strife and sorrow, and even of human troubles as a path to faith. Their unwavering faith is not shared by subsequent generations of the family.

The evolution of the family members' mixed religious identities is explored with the passing of the twentieth century, as each section, or "book," of Erpenbeck's novel imagines a successively longer life for the child who has died before she is six months old. In the first book the child's early death divides the family, as the mother follows Jewish mourning customs and the father grieves separately, praying in church and drinking at an inn, increasingly unable to imagine returning to his wife in their family home. After a chance encounter at the inn he makes the decision to travel to America and leaves his old life behind completely. A short section entitled "Intermezzo I" envisages a possible intervention that would have saved the baby girl's life and kept her family living together, before book 2 begins, describing how the girl's life would have gone on following the family's emigration to Vienna. Book 2 opens shortly after the end of the First World War, by which time the daughter is a teenager and has a younger sister, and Erpenbeck describes in detail the miserable living conditions of the inhabitants of Vienna, who are subsisting on the edge of starvation. We are told how the girl's Jewish mother continues the efforts made by her own mother, the girl's grandmother, to suppress her Jewish heritage by strengthening the family's Christian identity, to the extent of limiting contact with her grandmother when she flees Galicia for Vienna in the first year of the war. The grandmother stays with the family for a short time after her arrival in Vienna until her daughter finds her another apartment and forbids her granddaughters to visit her there. Yet even this brief time in her grandmother's company has lasting consequences for the girl's sense of religious identity: "Erst damals war ihr klar geworden, dass auch sie selbst eigentlich jüdischer Herkunft war, der Vater aber ging Sonntag für Sonntag mit ihr und der Schwester zum christlichen Gottesdienst, um mit den anderen Beamten und deren Familien in der Beamtebank zu sitzen" (*ATA*, 56–57; It only became clear to her then for the first time that she too was of Jewish descent, although her father went to the Christian church service with her and her sister Sunday after Sunday, in order to sit with the other officials and their families in their designated pew.) Her upbringing away from Galicia in Vienna, where her father strives to prosper in his civil service career—explaining his wife's absence from church by claiming that she has difficulty walking and therefore attends another service nearer to their home—have ensured that the girl has remained ignorant of her Jewish heritage, and yet the reencounter with her grandmother is enough to restore that connection with her Jewishness. Later in the novel, in book 3, the familial division caused by the different religious identities is reinforced as the girl—now grown-up and living in Russia—reflects on her Viennese childhood in which she, "the Christian daughter," attended church while "her Jewish grandmother" was spat at while out shopping the next day (*ATA*, 94).

During her short stay with the family in Vienna, the grandmother talks to her granddaughter about the story of Lot in Genesis, telling her of the beauty of the two angels to whom Lot offered hospitality in Sodom and who went on to save him and his family when God destroyed the city. This is the second time in the novel in which the grandmother recalls Lot: in the description of the anti-Semitic attack in which her husband was killed in book 1, which includes the quotation from Psalm 39, she also thinks of Lot's angelic visitors who save him from the angry mob of Sodomites outside his house, pulling him inside to safety "mit ihren Engelhänden" (*ATA*, 12; with their angel hands). She cannot match the angels' strength and is unable to pull her husband up onto the roof with her so that he is hacked to death by the villagers while still holding onto her hand. The grandmother's faith does not serve her with an immediate life-saving intervention in the manner of Lot's faith; in spite of, and even because of her faith, she loses her husband and must surrender her daughter and grandchildren to a life in which they suppress their Jewish identity, including cutting themselves off from her, in order to avoid persecution and survive. The grandmother remains thankful for her own survival and for her daughter's marriage to the non-Jewish man, which has guaranteed her and the two granddaughters a measure of security that would not have been possible had they remained in Galicia, the location of renewed anti-Semitic violence and murder that has prompted her own flight to Vienna.

Book 2 concludes with the girl's suicide, the culmination of her despair at the prevailing misery of everyday life in Vienna, the mistrust between her and the rest of her family, and her unrequited love for a friend's fiancé. During her funeral the girl's mother looks over to the Jewish section of the cemetery and muses: "Jetzt könnte die Großmutter sehen, dass die Enkelin es wenigstens bis auf den katholischen Friedhof geschafft hat" (*ATA*, 67; Now the grandmother could see that her granddaughter had at least made it as far as the Catholic cemetery). This bitter summation of a life lived in the shadow of a potentially lethal religious identity demeans the considerable efforts and sacrifices made by the girl's mother and grandmother to protect their daughters from anti-Semitic persecution. Crucially, in this version of the family's history, the girl's mother has never been told what happened to her own father and grows up believing that he left home. The grandmother keeps silent about her husband's unspeakable death out of a desire to protect her daughter from the truth. This leads to misunderstandings, however, as her unwillingness to discuss what may have become of her husband is liable to be interpreted as a weakness or an insufficiency of marital love, in addition to making it more difficult for her daughter to understand the precise motivation for some of the decisions about her upbringing. The secret, although motivated by the best of intentions, creates a divide between the two generations of women.

The novel's different books present not parallel lives but extended variations on the lives of a woman—the dead baby girl of its opening scene—and members of her family. The course of each of the novel's subsections hinges on the choices made or actions taken at a series of key moments in the woman's life. The intermezzo that precedes the opening of each new book explores the ramifications of these moments and postulates how things might have happened differently, thus setting up the circumstances with which the next book opens. The third and fourth books of the novel imagine that the woman goes on living in Vienna, where she becomes progressively involved with the activities of the Austrian Communist Party before emigrating to Russia in 1935 with her husband, also a communist activist. While the third book ends with the woman's miserable death in a Soviet labor camp, where she digs her own grave, by the time of her death in the novel's fourth and final book the woman has become a celebrated author, playwright, and cultural commentator in the GDR and is being mourned by her teenage son. Among her final thoughts as she trips down the stairs in her home and falls to her death is a conversation she had with her grandmother about the rights and wrongs of receiving letters on Shabbat: "Wenn ihr jetzt einfiele, was die Großmutter auf dieser Frage geantwortet hat, würde alles noch einmal gut. Aber es fällt ihr nicht ein. Sie stürzt" (*ATA*, 118; If she could remember how her grandmother had answered this question, everything would be good again. But she can't remember. She falls). At the point of death her sense of well-being depends upon her ability to remember her grandmother's answer to a question about the observance of Jewish law. Although her adult life appears to have been dedicated to the decidedly secular ambition of furthering the Communist cause, it is her sense of religious identity—which, in spite of her mother's determination for her to have a Christian upbringing, is mediated through her grandmother's profound Jewish faith—that proves critical to her sense of reconciliation at the end of her life. Religious identity is a key theme in this novel; it feeds into the novel's central concern with the range of possibilities open to women in the course of their lives—"all the things that might have become of the child"—within the context of the historical circumstances in which they find themselves.

"God just would not allow himself to be provoked."[15] —Bettina Balàka's *Kassiopeia*

Bettina Balàka's 2012 novel *Kassiopeia* (Cassiopeia) has a contemporary setting within which religion initially seems to play no part. Balàka's protagonist, Judit Kalman, is obsessed with a Viennese novelist, tracking his every move and following him to Venice, where she attempts to seduce him. Judit is the daughter of wealthy parents and, now in her mid-forties, has never needed to work to earn a living. Her indulgent parents have always given her everything she wanted, yet without ever taking an interest in the sorts of things she liked. Judit's father, Franz Kalman (born Ferenc Kálmán) comes to Vienna from Hungary before the end of the Second World War and eventually establishes himself as a highly successful property developer in Salzburg, where he marries Judit's mother. Throughout Judit's childhood he sidesteps any serious conversations about his past and falls back on vague generalities and jokes. The only occasion when Judit hears her father reflect upon his experiences during the 1940s is during a speech he gives to a chamber of commerce following his election as a councillor in recognition of his business achievements. In what for the most part is a light-hearted and humorous novel, the sections dealing with Franz Kalman's time in Austria during and immediately after the Second World War introduce an emphatically different mood as they reckon with the persecution and injustices of National Socialism.

Whereas in the first part of the novel, in which we are introduced to Judit Kalman's family circumstances and made familiar with some of their history, there are no references to God or religious belief, the confusion experienced by Franz Kalman in Vienna at the end of the war, during the period after the Nazis' withdrawal but before the appearance of the Russians, is characterized as a Godless time: "Man lebte in einem Zwischenreich, am Anfang der Zeit. Als hätte Gott eben erst die Welt geschaffen und sei dann schlafen gegangen" (*K*, 65; It was an in-between world, at the beginning of time. As though God had just created the world and then gone to sleep). It is as if God's presence is immaterial as long as there is some sort of normal order in the world, but in order to conceptualize the extremes of human experience when social norms collapse, God becomes a reference point again, even by virtue of his perceived absence.

Franz Kalman tells how, in postwar Vienna, passers-by were often recruited by the occupying Russian soldiers to assist with clearing rubble from the bombed-out streets. On one such occasion Franz is helping to clear away the remains of what was once an apartment building when two bodies are uncovered in the rubble. The bodies of a man and a woman are entombed in the upper layer of rubble from the highest floor of the former building and are presumed to be Jews who were in hiding and therefore could not have taken refuge in the communal air-raid shelters. Franz then discovers the body of a small girl of around three or four years old. Painfully, he imagines the child's life—born in hiding to a mother unable to make a sound during labor, the infant's cries suppressed by her parents so that their hiding place was not betrayed; a life of whispering and stale air imbued with her parents' fear. Shattered by his painful discovery, Franz Kalman makes a vow to live the rest of his life in a way that will do justice to the dead girl's memory:

> Er würde sein Leben nützen, und er würde es für das tote jüdische Mädchen tun, das sein Leben nicht mehr nützen konnte. Er würde nicht eine Sekunde seines Lebens verschwenden. Es war unmöglich, ihrem Tod einen Sinn zuzuschreiben, er konnte sie nur in seinen Gedanken aufheben und sich von ihr sagen lassen, wie kostbar das Leben war. (*K*, 72)

> [He would do something with his life, and he would do it for the dead Jewish girl who could no longer do anything with her life. He wouldn't waste a second of his life. It was impossible to find

meaning in her death; he could only keep her in his thoughts and have her remind him how precious life was.]

Through his insight into the wasted lives and premature deaths of the persecuted Jewish family, Kalman puts his desire for a family of his own and his dedication to their well-being at the center of his life's plan.

While Franz Kalman's decision to live a good life in order to do justice to the memory of a dead Jewish girl bears some resemblance to the Christian model for a life that honors the crucified Christ, the framework for the Kalman family's life does not include religion. Judit recounts her reaction to her father's revelation in terms that show how the dead Jewish girl has become a substitute for a source of religious authority: "Solange Judit lebte, war dieses Mädchen dagewesen, hatte Einfluss genommen und gelenkt—nicht Gott, nicht Jesus, keine Schutzengel oder Dämonen—, und erst jetzt hatte sie von ihm erfahren" (*K*, 74; This girl had been there Judit's whole life, influencing and guiding—not God, not Jesus, no guardian angels or demons—and she had only just found out about her.) There is little place for adherence to religious belief in the lives of any of Bettina Balàka's cast of contemporary characters, and Franz Kalman is unusual for having found an alternative means of structuring his life that nonetheless echoes religious inspiration. Balàka sketches the life of a Viennese woman who offers Franz Kalman lodging during his time in Vienna and who manages to be grateful that she has been raped by Russian soldiers, in the belief that this will mean her daughter is spared the same fate:

> Sie sagte immer, sie danke Gott dafür, dass es sie erwischt habe, so sicher war sie sich, dass Gott zum Ausgleich ihre Tochter verschonen würde. Zum Glück wurde sie zumindest in diesem Punkt von Gott nicht enttäuscht. (*K*, 67)

[She always said she thanked God for the fact that she was the one it happened to, as she was so sure that God would compensate her by sparing her daughter. Happily God did not disappoint her, at least in this regard.]

Balàka shows just how low people's expectations of God are in the aftermath of the Second World War: people's faith in God—and humanity—has been reduced to the hope that one person might be raped rather than another.

Despite their Roman Catholic baptisms, which take place only for form's sake, Judit and her sister Katalin grow up in a religious vacuum, a "Glaubensvakuum" (*K*, 159). This term is coined by their maternal grandmother who, like the grandmother figure in Erpenbeck's *Aller Tage*

Abend, is religious, although her Catholic faith is not as integral to her characterization as Jewish faith is with Erpenbeck's grandmother, and unlike her she does not discuss her faith with her granddaughters. There is no reckoning with God during Judit's childhood, in which "Gott ließ sich grundsätzlich überhaupt nicht provozieren.... Engel ließen sich nicht blicken, die Muttergottes auch nicht" (*K*, 159; God just would not allow himself to be provoked.... Angels did not show their faces, and neither did the Mother of God). Judit describes how the absence of religious influences in her life leads to a situation in which she believes in nothing and her sister believes in everything. Balàka charts how both these positions result in profoundly disorienting experiences for Judit and her sister, which are portrayed as characteristic of women's social experiences in general during the twenty-first century.

"no God who had made a world out of the void"[16] —Sibylle Berg's *Vielen Dank für das Leben*

Sibylle Berg's novel, *Vielen Dank für das Leben* (Thank You for Life, 2012) describes the desolate and tormented life of a hermaphrodite called Toto, who is born to an alcoholic mother in the GDR during the 1960s. Toto's mother's fraught existence and limited horizons are presented as failings of the socialist state. Berg suggests that the absence of any source of spiritual or religious authority makes life even harder for citizens of the GDR: "Es war ein schwieriges Leben, in dem kleinen sozialistischen Land, ohne Götter, die die Welt in Geschichten gefasst hätten. Götter, die eine übergreifende Ordnung in Millionen parallele Leben gebracht hätten und einen Sinn erzeugt" (*VD*, 33–34; It was a difficult life in the small socialist country, without gods to collect the world together into stories. Gods who would have imposed a comprehensive order on millions of parallel lives and divined a purpose for them). Barely surviving herself, and unable to give her existence meaning—either through her role as a mother or through any sense of theological authority—Toto's mother cannot cope with looking after her baby and, following a devastating period of maternal neglect, Toto is committed to a children's home, where he continues to receive appalling treatment at the hands of the caregivers and the other children. After being sold to a pair of violent alcoholic farmers, he escapes to West Germany, where he fares little better. Toto eventually adopts a female identity that suits her better, although she continues to be treated brutally by everyone with whom she comes into contact.[17]

Utterly different in tone to Balàka's light-hearted novel, Berg's darkly humorous text is also more relentlessly bleak than those by Krechel and Erpenbeck, and this is partly expressed through an increased sense of religious disorientation. In spite of the anti-Semitic persecution and genocide suffered by previous generations of their families, which have had profound consequences for their own lives, the children and grandchildren in *Landgericht* and *Aller Tage Abend* all continue to identify with or be drawn to the Jewish tradition. This is not to say that they claim to believe in God, but the Jewish religion nevertheless has a residual capacity to provide orientation in their lives, as in Selma Kornitzer's choice of a Jewish husband in *Landgericht*, for example, or in the death of Erpenbeck's protagonist in book 4, when her last thought is of a question surrounding the observance of the Shabbat laws. Berg's novel is more explicit in its characters' rejection both of theological possibilities and the religious identities that would be associated with these. Whenever appeals are made to God in Berg's novel, he is found absent or wanting. Toto, seeking comfort after yet another experience of rejection, reflects that in the absence of God there is no one who can provide it.

In the Christian men's home in which Toto briefly finds sanctuary in West Germany there is a requirement to engage in daily worship that gives rise to some highly skeptical reflection: "Wo soll der sein, der Gott? Das höhere Wesen. Keiner der Anwesenden überlegte sich die metaphorische Bedeutung einer übergeordneten moralischen Instanz, wenn schon, dann glaubten sie an einen Mann mit Bart, und den konnte man nirgends besichtigen" (*VD*, 152; Where is he supposed to be, this God? The higher being. None of those present gave any consideration to the metaphorical significance of an overarching moral authority. If anything, they believed in a man with a beard, and he was nowhere to be seen). The book's particularly bleak quality is derived from the utter absence of any source of "overarching moral authority"—religion, the political regimes in East or West Germany, and individual human beings are all deemed incapable of acting as sources of moral guidance. God has lost his divinity and become just another man with a beard. This de-sacralization is exemplified by the figure of the priest in the Christian refuge who turned to Christianity to try to transcend his revulsion toward his pubescent body and burgeoning sexual desire, and who might just as easily have sought out a cult or political organization. His sense of shame only intensifies after he first has sexual intercourse with a girl, and he converts to Catholicism in order to distance himself further from his corporeal embarrassment: "Evangelisch ist für Versager" (*VD*, 154; Protestantism is for losers). The priest goes on to deride Toto in his sermon at the refuge, stirring up resentment toward him among the other residents, for whom religion consists of praying to a God they do not believe in and being receptive to the priest's highly questionable moral authority.

Berg's novel spans the last third of the twentieth century and the first third of the twenty-first. There is a hiatus in the narrative action in the middle of the book that also marks the midpoint of the chronological period of the narration, that is, the beginning of the twenty-first century, where Berg gives a satirical and pessimistic overview of the social and political state of affairs in Western Europe. In the near future, civilization will be in decline, and humanity is rapidly heading toward a new stone age in which each individual will be fighting for survival. Religion here is placed alongside science as one of the last bastions of patriarchal dominance, in a world in which male participation in human reproduction is being rendered increasingly redundant. In Berg's dystopian future, religion and science are initially obstinately defended by a male minority who are resisting the encroachment of a bland form of social equality where human personalities are superseded by computers and which, rather than signifying any sort of victory for women's rights, is presented as the dreadful apotheosis of contemporary impulses toward political correctness. The tone in this section is reminiscent of that of Berg's weekly column for *Spiegel Online*, "Fragen Sie Frau Sibylle," in which she takes issue with aspects of contemporary life—like ubiquitous advertising and the pervasiveness of the Internet—which tend to be taken for granted. In her column from 22 June 2013, for example, she writes about the frenetic pace of modern existence that reduces people to overstressed workaholics, and she laments "es gibt keine Orte mehr für Freaks, für Menschen, die langsamer sind oder anders, kurz—nicht wettbewerbsfähig" (there are no longer any places for freaks, for people who are slower or different, or, in a word: uncompetitive).[18] This sort of attitude is embodied by the figure of Toto in *Vielen Dank für das Leben*, whose physical differences continually provoke revulsion and violence in those he encounters, so that his life is measured from one experience of rejection to the next. Despite feeling more comfortable after swapping his male identity for a female one, Toto is never at ease in the world and dies without ever having found her place in life. The remarkably bleak perspective of Berg's novel is derived from its utter lack of faith in the possibility of any form of consolation for Toto, or for human society more generally, be it religious, political, or human.

The "fortdauernde Krisezeit" (*VD*, 315; continuous crisis period) prophesied by the narrator of Berg's novel between 2010 and 2030 ends in an unexpected period of calm, in which there are no more wars and no more religions. This is not an idyllic peacetime, however, but one in which people are too preoccupied with the daily business of survival to concern themselves with religion. The new world is populated by politically correct, gym-obsessed over-achievers who epitomize the contemporary tendencies toward social conformity that Berg critiques in her *Spiegel Online* column. In this social milieu Toto's lifelong experiences of other people's disgust toward him/her would have been tempered by virtue of the extraordinary self-discipline that people are suddenly able to exercise over their thoughts and behavior, and their restrained, over-polite communication with one another. The base brutality of the world into which Toto was born, in which people drank themselves to death in squalid poverty, has been replaced by a sanitized nightmare typified by Toto's death in a care institution without corners in which dirt might be allowed to accumulate, and where the bars on the window are painted pink to match the walls. The clean and pleasant surroundings of the institution and the polite concern of its staff mask the moral equivocation toward elderly and vulnerable people that prevails in many twenty-first century societies. As Toto nears death the narrator reflects that Toto "konnte nicht wissen, wie es gewesen wäre, hätte sie von einem geliebt werden können" (*VD*, 392–93; could not know how it would have been if she could have been loved by someone). Toto has lived for nearly sixty years without ever having been loved. Toto's life, like her mother's, has had no meaning. The dearth of loving contact with other human beings and the absence of any metaphysical meaning for her life, which might have been conferred by religious belief, mean that she dies without leaving anything behind.

Conclusion

In the four contemporary German-language novels considered here, attitudes toward religion and gender are developed alongside an appraisal of recent European history. Reckoning with God—at least in the Jewish and Christian contexts of these novels—is shown to be a matter of diminishing significance for successive generations. Within each generation, however, the female characters' particular attitudes to and experiences of religion remain bound up with their gendered identities. Gendered experiences of religion are foregrounded in Erpenbeck's novel, which focuses on the experiences of successive generations of women in one family, and in which the intergenerational relationships are particularly significant for both the transmission of religious identity and its suppression. The older women's unquestioning faith in God's divine purpose, expressed through the supposedly comforting epithet "The Lord giveth, and the Lord taketh away," is set against the context of the ongoing struggles of the younger generations of women to lead fulfilling lives—to realize "all the things that might have become of the [female] child." In Berg's novel, religion is presented as a male-dominated system that has radically failed in its task of giving meaning to human lives, both through the flawed figure of the priest in the Christian refuge and in Berg's description of religion and science in the twenty-first century as the last bastions of doomed masculine claims to epistemological supremacy. In the context of the world into which Berg's hermaphroditic protagonist Toto is born, religious faith is only ever couched in negative terms: "no God who had made a world out of the void." Toto's religious experiences, defined by negativity, absence, and rejection, are mirrored in his more profoundly disorienting experiences in relation to both male and female gender positions. Although in each of the novels the youngest generation of characters no longer has faith in any theological authority, they are still obliged to take account of the religious labels that applied to their grandparents.

Both Krechel and Erpenbeck underline the historical importance of religious tradition in determining women's fates in twentieth-century Europe, showing how anti-Semitic persecution and prejudice had devastating consequences for practicing and assimilated Jews alike. The female characters in *Landgericht* and *Aller Tage Abend* come from families whose lives have been variously disrupted by the actual or threatened murder of their Jewish relations, and both novels explore how the women's familial and professional roles are shaped by their experiences of religion. Balàka's protagonist grows up in a religious vacuum in which "God just would not allow himself to be provoked," only to discover that her father has, in Christian fashion, dedicated his adult life to the memory of a dead Jewish girl. In Berg's novel the uncertainty of the protagonist's gender is central to this character's recurrent experiences of rejection, including rejection by a priest who ostensibly embodies Christian compassion. Berg's characters are generally too cynical to countenance any kind of religious faith, and they no longer have faith even in their fellow human beings. Yet in her portrayal of the morally bankrupt societies on either side of the Berlin Wall, there is a lingering sense of nostalgia for the capacity of religion to offer a source of collective identity. In all four novels, reckoning with God cannot entirely do without God; living without theological authority still makes reference to a notion of that authority in order to define itself.

In his analysis of the religious positions in postmodern texts by contemporary German-language writers, Stefan Neuhaus observes that religion is now only "zitiert" (quoted):[19] whereas religions once claimed to offer transcendental meaning, in the texts discussed by Neuhaus they have become interchangeable with various material means of understanding the world. Because of their engagement with twentieth-century European history and the fatal significance of Jewish identity during the Holocaust in particular, the novels I consider by Ursula Krechel, Jenny Erpenbeck, Bettina Balàka, and Sibylle Berg present a slightly different view of religion. God is not an empty signifier in their texts, in the postmodern sense. He is more like a once-respected figure of diminishing relevance to contemporary lives, a figure whose former significance (or the nostalgia for that sense of significance) cannot be relinquished—like an ageing ruler who has succumbed to Alzheimer's disease and who remains in the room although no longer able to take a meaningful part in the conversation. As Krechel puts it: "God was asleep, he was resting after allowing so much chaos." So while God is variously found to be sleeping, inattentive, impotent, or absent in these texts, a notion of God—albeit one far removed from the Jewish or Christian ideal—nonetheless finds its way into the lives of female characters who have little or no faith; thus for these characters theological authority remains a force to be reckoned with.

Notes

[1] See Stanley Fish's assertion that religion is "where the action is" in "One University under God?" *Chronicle of Higher Education*, 7 January 2005. http://chronicle.com/article/One-University-Under-God-/45077/.

[2] Kristin Aune, Sonya Sharma, and Giselle Vincent, eds., *Women and Religion in the West: Challenging Secularization* (Aldershot, UK: Ashgate, 2008), 2.

[3] Jürgen Habermas, "Notes on Post-Secular Society," *New Perspectives Quarterly* 25 (2008): 17–29. British philosopher Simon Critchley corroborates Habermas's definition of society as post-secular with his observation: "The return to religion has become perhaps the dominant cliché of contemporary theory. . . . Somehow we seem to have passed from a secular age, which we were ceaselessly told was post-metaphysical, to a new situation in which political action seems to flow directly from metaphysical conflict." Simon Critchley, *The Faith of the Faithless: Experiments in Political Theology* (London: Verso, 2012), 13.

[4] For discussions of Islam and German culture and literature see Ala Al-Hamarneh and Jörn Thielmann, eds., *Islam and Muslims in Germany* (Leiden, Netherlands: Brill, 2008); James Hodkinson and Jeffrey Morrison, eds., *Encounters with Islam in German Literature and Culture* (Rochester, NY: Camden House, 2009); and Beverly M. Weber, *Violence and Gender in the "New" Europe: Islam in German Culture* (New York: Palgrave Macmillan, 2013). Recent discussions of German-Jewish literary identity include Jonathan Hess, *Middlebrow Literature and the Making of German-Jewish Identity* (Palo Alto, CA: Stanford University Press, 2013); William Collins Donahue and Martha B. Helfer, eds., *Nexus: Essays in German Jewish Studies*, vol. 1 (Rochester, NY: Camden House, 2011); and Pól Ó Dochartaigh, ed., *Jews in German Literature since 1945: German-Jewish Literature?* (Amsterdam: Rodopi, 2000).

[5] Julian Preece and Frank Finlay, eds., *Religion and Identity in Germany Today* (Oxford: Peter Lang, 2010), 1, 3.

[6] Nicolas Boyle, *Who Are We Now? Christian Humanism and the Global Market from Hegel to Heaney* (London: Continuum, 2000), 305.

[7] Aune, Sharma, and Vincent, *Women and Religion in the West*, 4–6.

[8] Katharina Gerstenberger, "Fictionalizations: Holocaust Memory and the Generational Construct in the Works of Contemporary Women Writers," in *Generational Shifts in Contemporary German Culture*, ed. Laurel Cohen-Pfister and Susanne Vees-Gulani (Rochester, NY: Camden House: 2010), 111.

[9] Ursula Krechel, *Landgericht* (Salzburg: Jung & Jung, 2012), 23. Original German: "Gott schlief, Gott ruhte aus, nachdem er so viel Chaos zugelassen hatte." Further references to this work are given in the text using the abbreviation *L*. All translations from the German in this chapter are my own, unless otherwise stated.

[10] See, for example, 90, 198.

[11] Jenny Erpenbeck, *Aller Tage Abend* (Munich: Knaus, 2012), 7. Original German: "Der Herr hat's gegeben, der Herr hat's genommen." Further references to this work are given in the text using the abbreviation *ATA*.

[12] Gerstenberger, "Fictionalizations," 108.

[13] Ibid., 111.

[14] Petra M. Bagley, "Granny Knows Best: The Voice of the Granddaughter in 'Grossmütterliteratur,'" in *Pushing at Boundaries—Approaches to Contemporary German Women Writers from Karen Duve to Jenny Erpenbeck*, ed. Heike Bartel and Elizabeth Boa (Amsterdam: Rodopi, 2006), 151–66.

[15] Bettina Balàka, *Kassiopeia* (Innsbruck: Haymon, 2012), 159. Original German: "Gott ließ sich grundsätzlich überhaupt nicht provozieren." Further references to this work are given in the text using the abbreviation *K*.

[16] Sibylle Berg, *Vielen Dank für das Leben* (Munich: Carl Hanser Verlag: 2012), 34. Original German: "kein Gott, der aus dem Nichts eine Welt geformt hätte." Further references to this work are given in the text using the abbreviation *VD*.

[17] I refer to Toto as "he" when I am writing about events that took place during the period in which Toto identifies as male, and as "she" thereafter.

[18] See Sybille Berg, "Wir schweißnassen Selbstausbeuter," *Spiegel Online*, June 22, 2013, http://www.spiegel.de/kultur/gesellschaft/sibylle-berg-ueber-stress-und-wettbewerb-a-906629.html.

[19] Stefan Neuhaus, "'In dieser Gegend gibt es keinen Gott.': Religion in der 'postmodernen' Literatur am Beispiel von Helmut Krausser, Hape Kerkeling und Felicitas Hoppe," in *Religion and Identity in Germany Today*, ed. Julian Preece and Frank Finlay (Oxford: Peter Lang, 2010), 83.

5: Muslim Writing, Women's Writing

Lindsay Lawton

WOMEN'S MEMOIRS THAT SHARE common themes of forced marriage, honor killing, or "crimes of honor" and detail the cruelty and violence to which the protagonist is subjected during her quest to pursue a "Western" lifestyle have been a part of the German-language literary landscape for decades. As they are increasingly tied to Islam, however, these memoirs have become especially visible in the twenty-first century.[1] The similarity of these works is reinforced by marketing conventions, including sensational titles like *Ich wollte nur frei sein: Meine Flucht vor der Zwangsehe* (I Only Wanted to be Free: My Flight from Forced Marriage, 2005), *Mein Schmerz trägt deinen Namen: Ein Ehrenmord in Deutschland* (My Pain Carries Your Name: An Honor Killing in Germany, 2005), or *Mich hat keiner gefragt: Zur Ehe gezwungen—eine Türkin in Deutschland erzählt* (No One Asked Me: Forced into Marriage—a Turkish Woman in Germany Explains, 2007). Such texts are also linked by similar cover designs featuring portraits of distraught and veiled, or defiant and bareheaded women, many of whom are the author-narrators using obvious pseudonyms like Ayşe, Leila, or Inci Y.[2] Many of these memoirs have been bestsellers, have been printed in multiple editions, and are available in translation throughout much of Europe and North America. They are often framed as critiques or exposés of Islam, cited together as evidence of various problems with Islam in Europe, and categorized together by booksellers.[3] Some of the most polemical author-narrators of such works have successfully published second books and developed careers as public speakers and activists.

Yet few categories of writing seem so immediately and obviously problematic as that of Muslim women's memoirs: after all, the impact of an author's faith and gender on a text is inextricably linked to linguistic, cultural, socioeconomic, and many other factors that are obscured by the use of the label "Muslim women's memoir," as is the participation of those who are neither Muslim nor women in the writing of the texts. The label appears to connect certain kinds of violence with religious faith and to support the continued racialization of Islam; the very existence of the genre indicates a standardization of diverse experiences and opinions, while its profitability suggests the potential exploitation of author-narrators, the trivialization of gender violence, and the reinforcement of destructive stereotypes about women and about Islam.

These books tend to generate one of two reactions from audiences: shock and outrage (that such things happen in a given time and place), or disdain and suspicion (that the stories are greed-driven exaggerations or complete fictions). Their ubiquity, their low cultural status, their high profit margins, and the controversial positions of their most prominent author-narrators color any reading. The stories about these memoirs, from marketing to activism to scholarship, have come to overshadow much of what is contained within them, including author-narrators' critical responses to the role of the German state, its agents, and its citizens in their suffering. The categories of Muslim, woman, and victim are so closely connected around these texts that the author-narrators are prone to disappear as individual women writers, a situation complicated by the fact that many of them do not actually do the writing themselves but work with (often unacknowledged) coauthors or ghost writers. But read carefully and separated from the stories *about* them, Muslim women's memoirs can offer complex portrayals of faith and gender, as well as of discrimination, sexuality, motherhood, the body, and labor. While the author-narrators of the works are not always practicing Muslims, they and their experiences are indelibly marked as other. As such, Muslim women's writing can have strategic value as a way of bringing minority women's experiences into dialogue with nonminority women's writing, and by complicating our understanding of the latter as an analytical category.

While the details, the author-narrators' responses, and the role of Islam vary from story to story, the basic plot points and characters in these memoirs are similar enough to map onto a very general narrative framework. In broad strokes, some of these include the heroine's growing sense of gendered oppression and exploitation, often coinciding with puberty and resulting in resistance to gender norms and expectations; escalating physical, emotional, and usually sexual violence at the hands of a tyrannical figure (typically the heroine's father, mother-in-law, or husband); and the heroine's break with her family and community. The implication that family and community groups pose a continued threat to the author-narrator's safety serves as a bridge between the conclusion of the central text and the public story about the memoir. Many author-narrators publish their stories under pseudonyms for their own protection, but their photos are often featured on the covers of their books, and they participate actively in publicizing and marketing their work, making the exposed woman as much a commodity as her story.

At the same time, there is significant variation among these works. *Sterben sollst du für dein Glück: Gefangen zwischen zwei Welten* (You

Should Die for Your Happiness: Trapped between Two Worlds, 2004), for example, was written by a Pakistani-Austrian woman under the pseudonym Sabatina James.[4] This story of James's childhood in Pakistan and Austria, her family's attempt to force her to marry her cousin, her time in strict Muslim boarding schools in Pakistan, and her conversion to Christianity quickly reached bestseller status even as (or perhaps because) several scandals involving nude photos leaked to the press by her former coauthor Rupert Leutgeb landed James on tabloid covers. Religion—particularly in the form of conflict between Islam and Christianity—played an important role in James's memoir and in the career she has developed as an outspoken critic of Islam, a public speaker, and head of a non-profit organization dedicated to helping women who are victims of forced marriage or so-called crimes of honor. Her second book, *Nur die Wahrheit macht uns frei: Mein Leben zwischen Islam und Christentum* (Only the Truth Makes Us Free: My Life between Islam and Christianity), was published in late 2011 and heavily promoted during an international publicity tour that included interviews with CNN and *Newsweek*.

By contrast, in the best-selling 2005 memoir *Mich hat keiner gefragt: Zur Ehe gezwungen—eine Türkin in Deutschland erzählt*, a woman writing under the pseudonym Ayşe recounts her journey via forced marriage from a small Anatolian village in eastern Turkey to a city somewhere in southern Germany, where she spent twenty years suffering the physical, sexual, and psychological abuse of her husband and in-laws.[5] Ayşe also describes how, after finally separating from her husband, she arranged her own teenage daughter's marriage and later helped her get a divorce. Ayşe writes explicitly in her memoir that Islam hardly played a role in her family, but Islam was still prominent in the book's marketing and especially its reception. Although Ayşe publicized her memoir by attending readings and giving interviews and even appeared in a documentary about forced marriage, she did not capitalize on her memoir's bestseller status to the same extent as James. According to Ayşe's coauthor, Renate Eder, Ayşe remarried not long after the book was published and moved back to Turkey.

Muslim women's memoirs are technically categorized as non-fiction, but because of their thematic focus as well as the role of their author-narrators, they do not have the same status as many other non-fiction genres. Instead, they have been described as "Schleierliteratur" (literature of the veil),[6] "Betroffenheitsliteratur" (literature of the affected),[7] and "Schundromane" (trashy novels).[8] Beverly Weber refers to them as "victim narratives,"[9] Fatima El-Tayeb calls them "escape narratives,"[10] and Lila Abu-Lughod describes them as "popular memoirs sold in airport bookstores and instantly recognizable by the veiled women stamped on their covers."[11] Most of these designations imply "essentialism, inauthenticity, and a lack of artistic merit"[12] and mark the entire genre as lesser:

less significant, less literary, less respectable; in a word, trivial—a label frequently applied to women's writing. The relatively low cultural status of this set of texts goes hand in hand with a tendency to regard author-narrators as interchangeable figureheads, icons, or, in Abu-Lughod's formulation, "stamps."[13]

The impression of uniformity among author-narrators is strengthened by the tendency to focus on the most famous and most polemical of them, such as the widely criticized and frequently quoted Necla Kelek.[14] Kelek and a few other prominent anti-Islam activists are sought-after reviewers of these memoirs, and their own books have been widely discussed in popular and academic coverage of the genre. Their prominence as anti-Islam activists in Germany plays a major role in the assumption that their experiences and opinions, as well as their books, are representative of those of other author-narrators writing in this genre. The differences among the author-narrators and their stories are also overshadowed by the idea of a monolithic and violent Islam as the source of women's suffering and the belief that they must reject this religion as well as their families and communities in order to live a life free of abuse.[15] Both standpoints are fundamental to the complex cultural context in which these books are produced and promoted.

In this essay, I begin to tease apart the discursive knots that have formed around Muslim women's memoirs by examining different facets of their production and promotion and attempting a reading that is open to what Gayatri Spivak calls the "imagined agency of the other."[16] Such a reading entails not only an awareness of author-narrators as individual, active participants in the production of their books, rather than as victims in need of rescue (that is, from the abuse of Muslim men or from the exploitation of greedy capitalists), but also a caution against the impulse to align the publication of their memoirs with the granting of agency. This sort of reading requires an openness to the possibility of the author-narrators as agents prior to the writing of their memoirs—prior even to their flight from abusive families. This approach also entails imagining author-narrators as agents during and after publication. Imagining even their participation in publicity, activism, or other projects that arguably exacerbate the very problems they claim to combat as coherent with their understanding of agency could prevent the dismissal of their works on the grounds that they do not "properly" advocate for themselves or for groups to which readers, from positions of relative privilege, might want or believe them to belong.

Distinguishing between the central narratives of these memoirs and their accompanying paratexts reveals a wide range of attitudes and experiences that destabilize dominant understandings of these author-narrators as representative of female Muslim victimhood. This kind of reading also reveals that Muslim women's memoirs share many of the same concerns addressed by other women's writing, such as family relationships, the body, sexuality, labor, and discrimination. We can understand women's writing as strategically drawing attention to the intersection of gender with these themes. While the category of Muslim women's memoirs holds the possibility of a similar strategic engagement with intersectional difference, this is too often hindered by popular conceptions (and presentations) of such texts shaped by the familiar script of the Muslim woman victim.

Muslim/Woman/Victim

"A virgin shall not be married without her consent. And sufficient as (sign of) consent shall be **her silence** (due to her natural modesty)."[17]

"Islam actually did not play a very big role in our family."[18]

Despite the important similarities that allow these books to be understood as a genre, there is substantial variation in author-narrators' experiences with regard to family, integration, the state, and especially religion. Here the label "Muslim," its connection to Islam, and its application to these memoirs and their author-narrators merits further discussion. In the twenty-first century, the label "Muslim" has multiple and fluid meanings, referring to adherents of Islam as well as to a range of practices, cultural identities, and ethnic and national heritage. The changes to German citizenship laws that went into effect in 2000 and the resulting crisis of language when referring to those previously (not always accurately) categorized as guest workers, Turks, migrants, or foreigners; the advent of the global war on terror; and the growing boundaries of and identification with the European Union have resulted in the increasing use of the term "Muslim" to refer to a range of visible minority groups, from Turkish women in headscarves to the descendants of Portuguese immigrants to Indian tourists.[19] As Fatima El-Tayeb and many others have pointed out, this shift has coincided with hyperbolic discourse on national and transnational belonging informed by conservatives like Thilo Sarrazin and characterized by a growing Islamophobia that threatens to define Europe in the twenty-first century.[20] In the discursive context that shaped (and has been shaped by) these memoirs, "Muslim" signifies a convergence of race, class, and national and cultural heritage in a monolithic category of otherness that is tied to a notion of a single, global, and equally monolithic Islam. As visible minorities and as (presumed) members of a transnational community that demands primary loyalty and opposes European values, those labeled "Muslim" are thus doubly marked as non-European.[21]

My use of the term "Muslim" in the pages that follow is meant to highlight some of the problems and contradictions that emerge when the label is applied to texts such as those considered here and to their author-narrators. These women are publicly defined by their gender, victim status, and a perceived connection with and expertise on Islam, so they are widely referred to as Muslim. This happens even though they are assumed and expected to have rejected the religion and community as part of their quest for freedom. The story of the Muslim woman victim is so old and familiar in German-language literature, going back at least to Novalis's *Heinrich von Ofterdingen*, that it constitutes a sort of paratext that Jonathan Gray describes as a filter through which audiences pass on their way to the text itself.[22] The label "Muslim," when applied to an abused woman, carries with it enough history that it can distract audiences from how a particular text deviates from the script they know and anticipate, or how it connects to other "serious" literature. Another consequence of this labeling is that author-narrators' participation in public discourse does not extend beyond "Muslim" issues, such as forced marriage, to other topics that arguably have greater impact on them, such as education or economic policies. This creates a double bind: they must reject Islam and the affiliated community for their speech to be heard, but their contributions are marginalized because of their perceived connection to Islam.

The quotations at the start of this section provide a useful point of departure for examining the relationship between the label and the text. As Çileli's foreword indicates, these memoirs are framed as condemnations of Islam and the moral culture associated with it, while the author-narrators are understood as *Islamkritikerinnen* (critics of Islam, a term popularized by public figures like Çileli). Ayşe's insistence that Islam did not play a big role in her family calls into question who is really behind the figure of the Muslim woman victim (and the Muslim tyrant who torments her). Yasemin Yildiz has argued that "the figures that these stories [about abused young women in Germany] create are ultimately made up of generic features and stock characteristics that show only slight variation" despite the fact that they "seemingly" refer to "actual women and their lives."[23] This is very often the case, particularly when it comes to news reporting and other narratives not created by formerly abused women. But the central figure—both the narrative "I" and the public figure—created by each memoir does, in fact, refer to an *actual* individual woman and her life. The author-narrator's actual existence is emphasized when she is pictured on the cover, attends readings, and gives interviews. How can we make sense of the "artificial, yet affectively charged,"[24] overdetermined *figure* of the Muslim woman victim as well as and in relation to the *actual* women participating in the creation of such figures and appearing in the public sphere?

In the familiar script, it is necessary for the heroine to totally reject Islam, her family, and "the" Muslim community in order to protect herself. But the women's roles in marginalized families and communities described in many of these memoirs deviate from that script. For example, Hülya Kalkan ends her memoir by describing how she repaired her relationship with her mother, who had tried to force both Kalkan and another daughter to marry, and who had been cast as the primary villain throughout most of the text.[25] Kalkan offers a sober (rather than sensational) exploration of this complicated relationship, and of her struggle to understand and accept both her mother's and her sister's faith, even as she rejects the possibility of a relationship with the aunts who participated in Kalkan's abuse.

In another example, after leaving the first marriage into which her family forced her, Inci Y. agreed to her family's plan for her second marriage to a German Muslim man she had never met.[26] This decision, like many others described in her memoir, is tied to her struggle to provide for her children. In both her memoirs, written with coauthor Jochen Faust, Inci examines her role as a mother and a daughter and describes her efforts to shift the dynamics of her relationship with her parents without cutting them out of her life altogether. Like Kalkan, Inci describes changing, often ambivalent family relationships and illustrates a range of gender roles, aspects of her memoir that conflict with the way her work is marketed and categorized. In another example, Ayşe, who escaped her abusive husband and in-laws after nearly twenty years, also grapples with her role as a mother and a daughter, describing generations of difficult family relationships, her efforts to care for children conceived as a result of rape, and her decision to push her own teenage daughter to marry the son of her coworker while they were on vacation in Turkey. The complex relationships between author-narrators and their families and communities in these examples illustrate just one gap between these memoirs and their paratexts.

Sexuality is another important theme, and, like the family relationships discussed above, suggests the influence of (anticipated) audience expectations. The sexual freedom of Muslim women is at the heart of current liberatory discourse, even as it is shaped by deeply conservative and heteronormative judgments about sexual morality. While most author-narrators decline to include much information about their own sexuality in their memoirs, keeping the focus primarily on the men who sexually abused them, Ayşe describes her romantic relationship with a man who helped her leave her husband and later became her lover. Her account of the relationship is anything but sexually explicit, which presents quite a contrast to the vivid physical descriptions of her husband's abuse. The tendency in these works to downplay or omit positive sexual interactions is not surprising, given the harsh public reactions to "scandals" involving the sexuality of Sabatina James, Hatun Sürücü, and Sibel Kekilli.[27] Such scandals evidence audiences' desire for Muslim women to have the sexual freedom that their oppressors wish to regulate or deny. At the same time, these scandals demonstrate audiences' expectation that Muslim women exercise this freedom within the boundaries of a "Western" kind of chaste, heteronormative sexual morality.

The familiar narrative of the Muslim woman victim positions the Western state or its representatives as heroic. Yet many of these memoirs challenge this expectation by including critiques of the same state that, as Weber puts it, "asserts national (German) and transnational (European) identity by claiming to be the proper guardian of (immigrant) women's rights."[28] Author-narrators' accounts of how public services such as consulates, hospitals, shelters, social workers, and others failed to protect their rights (or even to inform them of such) are common in these memoirs. Ayşe comments that she should have attended school after arriving in Germany, but that she did not know about the law and authorities never followed up with her mother-in-law. Sabatina James, whose memoir is otherwise a very close fit to the familiar script of female Muslim victimhood, wrote that her story

> mag übertrieben klingen. . . . Und genauso reagierten die Behörden, als ich zum ersten Mal zur Polizei ging. . . . Wahrscheinlich hielten sie mich für einen Teenager, der zu viele schlechte Filme gesehen und noch mehr Schundromane gelesen hatte.[29]
>
> [might sound exaggerated. . . . And that's exactly how the authorities reacted when I went to the police for the first time. . . . They probably thought I was a teenager who had seen too many bad films and read even more trashy novels.]

Such deviations from the standard narrative of the oppressed Muslim woman call into question the impression of a stable and autonomous "I" in which the narrator, the creative subject, and the author-narrator's public images cohere, and cast doubt on the extent to which this "I" correlates with that of other author-narrators.

Producers/Promoters/Consumers

Muslim women's memoirs are marketed as courageous works by women who heroically risk their own safety to bring their suffering and oppression to light as a way of raising awareness of "crimes of honor," yet the books are not uniformly the products of individual conviction or altruism. The networks that support their creation and production are dense and complex; the participation of coauthors or ghost writers, editors, designers, activists, and publishers in the creation of a commodity and in the cultivation of an audience of consumers is often obscured by the marketing emphasis on the Muslim woman victim "speaking for herself." The contributions of many of these professionals are a given for the production of most any literature, but their role in producing these narratives in particular deserves a second look because of the extent to which Muslim women's memoirs depend on the perception of a single, coherent "schreibende Suleika" (writing Suleika) for their success.[30]

It is clear that the authenticity of these stories, while often called into question, is also critically important for their success. An impression of authenticity happens at several different points: in the story itself, in the story about the memoir's creation, and in the aftermath of publication. The central texts of these memoirs are held to complex standards, wherein they must be similar to one another and fit audiences' preconceived ideas about what such stories are like, while also withstanding the scrutiny of publishers anxious to avoid publishing false memoirs. The stories need to be familiar enough to be recognized and sensational enough to make a profit, but not so familiar or sensational that they appear to be fabricated.

Contributing writers occupy a unique facilitating role here insofar as their primary purpose is to make the experiences of the author-narrator comprehensible to audiences, a task that includes thoroughly understanding the author-narrator's experiences and anticipating the expectations of multiple audiences. At the same time, they participate in fact-checking the claims of author-narrators in order to maintain the integrity of the project and serve as a liaison between author-narrators and other producers. It is perhaps no surprise that both Faust and Eder, who worked with Inci and Ayşe, respectively, have described their work in negative or even violent terms, emphasizing how difficult the projects were for them.[31] Interestingly, both writers felt that gender contributed to the burden: Eder explained that she had to overcome assumptions (her own and others') that her gender would grant her an innate understanding of Ayşe's experiences;[32] in addition to the suspicion that his relationship with Inci was sexual (as in the case of Rupert Leutgeb, who leaked photos of James),[33] Faust understood his gender as an obstacle to fully grasping and accurately representing Inci's experiences.[34]

Activists also play an important role in the industry surrounding these stories. Most activists involved with the memoirs are women engaged in (Muslim) women's-rights work. Some, like Necla Kelek and Seyran Ateş, are also authors and prominent contributors to public debates about Islam in Europe as well as invited participants at the German Islam Conference (*Deutsche Islam-Konferenz*).[35] Others, such as Serap Çileli and Sabatina James, head their own non-profit organizations in addition to their work as author-narrators. The involvement of celebrity activists can overwhelm or drown out the voices of less famous individual author-narrators, a point to which I will return in the next section. The women's aid organization Terre des Femmes is one of the most prominent activist contributors and supporters. This network of women (membership is not open to men) has worked extensively to raise awareness of forced marriage and "crimes of honor." As part of this work, the group has contributed extensively to the production and promotion of memoirs by writing afterwords, promoting and selling books on their website, helping to organize readings, and even managing publicity on behalf of at least one author-narrator. The organization engaged Sabatina James as an "ambassador," and lists Seyran Ateş among its prominent supporters.[36]

The lack of involvement by immigrant or minority women's groups in the production and promotion of the genre is especially noteworthy given the high-profile support from individual women like Kelek and Ateş. Weber has suggested that the popularity of Muslim women's memoirs actually prevents activists of immigrant background from being heard unless their experiences and attitudes fit with the dominant discourse (also shaped in part by the memoirs themselves) about the oppression of Muslim women.[37] I argue that this dynamic is further complicated by the fact that, in many instances, memoirs are molded to fit the dominant discourse at the expense of the author-narrator's understanding of her experiences. Minor author-narrators are not exactly silenced by this discourse, but the fact that some of them share their experiences of victimhood while also rejecting aspects of the dominant narrative or complicating the figure of the Muslim woman victim is eclipsed by their connection to more prominent—and predictable—works such as Kelek's *Die fremde Braut* (The Foreign Bride, 2005).

Socioeconomics/Profit/Fraud

> "The dreams of many Turkish women who believed they could break free from forced marriage and mental oppression fail. . . . In order to survive, in the end they sell the only capital that their parents gave them to take on their way: their femininity."[38]

> "To idealize feminine traits is to remain oblivious to the intense pressures of class on gender; the vision of a nurturing, noncompetitive femininity presumes a certain distance from the grubby reality of economic hierarchies."[39]

While the proliferation of Muslim women's memoirs suggests a concomitant increase of concern for oppressed Muslim women, if not a proliferation of oppressed Muslim women themselves, the socioeconomics of the genre tell a different story. The first quote above refers to women forced into sex work after fleeing abusive marriages, but because femininity (*Weiblichkeit*) in these narratives is synonymous with victimhood as well as sexuality, Inci Y.'s assessment of how (and why) women fleeing forced marriages end up as sex workers also extends to the women who leave forced marriages and become best-selling authors. They—and, significantly, the economy in which they operate—may understand the story of their victimization to be the most valuable thing they possess, and trading on this victimization may prove more immediately effective than other methods of improving their situation. There is much to be gained from the transformation of these experiences into marketable commodities. In addition to the benefit of exercising agency by speaking out about their victimization, author-narrators may write to achieve upward socioeconomic mobility. The potential for such mobility is especially evident in the case of those author-narrators who leverage their books into careers, including activists like Kelek, Çileli, or James.[40] Yet as Rita Felski suggests, their gender is reified in the narratives of victimization to such an extent that the "grubby reality" of class rarely intrudes into public discourse on Muslim women's memoirs.

Financial exploitation is a routine element in the memoirs: author-narrators are often forced to work as virtual slaves in their homes or at jobs arranged by their families with their income funneled into accounts over which they have little or no control. The financial negotiations surrounding engagement and marriage also play a role, as does the familiar trope of selling a daughter to the highest bidder. Ayşe, for example, endured nearly two decades of financial exploitation, working up to eighteen hours a day and receiving only a small allowance from her mother-in-law while her wages supported an extended family and several of her husband's failed business ventures. Ewing also describes how one woman's escape was motivated primarily by conflict with her husband over money sent to his family in Turkey, and not because of physical abuse or the arranged nature of her marriage.[41] The fact that money is often a factor in author-narrators' decisions to flee is another instance of deviation from the familiar script of the Muslim woman victim, who remains poor but pure, fleeing for her freedom, not for upward socioeconomic mobility. The specific feminine trait idealized by this script is ultimately a kind of dependence—she trusts whatever she is fleeing toward to protect and support her, both physically and financially. But when Muslim women's memoirs include an account of life after the escape (and before publication), money is a constant concern.

Other parties also stand to benefit economically from the transformation of the author-narrator's experience into a marketable commodity: publishers and booksellers see financial profit, and increased attention to the issues these memoirs address can lead to more revenue for certain activist groups. The notion that oppressed Muslim women everywhere also stand to gain something from these books is a basic premise of the awareness-raising work the books are thought to do. Because these narratives are so ubiquitous, Muslim women trying to escape their families will be more confident about that choice, and receive more material assistance and support from German society—or so the argument goes.[42] Such narratives also arguably benefit conservative political goals by stoking moral panic: these stories complement xenophobic post-9/11 discourse and seem to prove the need for increased interventions, scrutiny of immigrants and minorities, and stricter regulation of immigration and integration.[43]

But some of these benefits are mostly hypothetical, and there are significant risks to this transformation as well. First and foremost is the very real possibility that women are being exploited as Muslim and their suffering redefined to suit the dominant discourse, sensationalized for maximum profit by greedy corporations, and trivialized by those in positions of power. In short, by sharing her story of victimhood, the author-narrator may be victimized all over again. On a different scale, there is the risk of these texts exacerbating the very same problems they are said to address by contributing to negative stereotypes about and racialization of Islam, fueling xenophobia and limiting possibilities for minority and Muslim women to participate in the public sphere. Ewing argues that narratives of this kind naturalize an extreme version of how Muslim women suffer, and her ethnographic research shows how they can limit possibilities for Muslim women who come into conflict with their families by operating as a model for and of the reality these women experience.[44]

Two common critical responses to the memoirs are tied to the risks and benefits described above. One is to view the genre as exploitative and insensitive, an example of a global industry satisfying the voyeuristic desires of audiences at the expense of vulnerable women. Given the differences between author-narrators and other producers and promoters, not to mention the often obscure processes of production, such a view is not without merit. However, it reinforces an impression of the author-narrators as both pitiful victims—first of Muslim violence and then of Western capitalism—and unrealistic stock figures, while eliding the potential these books have to bring critiques of the state and deviations from the script to the attention of readers. Despite the overdetermined nature of these books and the many valid critiques that can be made of their production and promotion, to discount the possibility that some women experienced the process of producing and promoting their memoirs as empowering (a process not usually described in the narratives themselves) would be to discount the possibility that their subjectivity predates the validation of their experiences by the interest of German and European audiences. Several author-narrators have said that the practice of putting their stories in print was in fact empowering for them, and the appetite audiences have demonstrated for such narratives has brought some women fame as well as personal and financial security.

Sabatina James, for example, has noted in interviews and on her personal website that the increased visibility she gained by writing a best-selling memoir means she is less likely to be attacked by her family.[45]

Another view reverses the roles of victim and exploiter. In this view, author-narrators are defrauding publishers and audiences by manufacturing or exaggerating their suffering and performing the Muslim woman victim to play on European anxieties about Islam. Such a view also devalues the narratives as more or less false; women are granted significant power and cultural awareness but are also revealed as dangerous, scheming, and untrustworthy. Several examples of this view are evident in 2003 Austrian news coverage of James after her former ghostwriter went to the press with allegations that her memoir was not true.[46] Concerns about the truth of Muslim women's memoirs and the integrity of their author-narrators are supported by a few instances in which narratives of this sort available in German translation have been proven false and pulled from the market by publishers.[47] This view also calcifies the victim status of the Muslim woman by suggesting that true victims are always silent.

The financial circumstances surrounding women's experiences are just one way that socioeconomic class is marked in and around their memoirs. Class plays an exceptionally complex role for participants in this industry, as class status is reflected by the nature of their engagement with the books. Like the figure of the oppressed Muslim woman, author-narrators tend to be marked as working class in their memoirs. They or their parents are often immigrants and many of the memoirs devote some pages to the difference (or hoped-for difference) in class status to be gained by leaving the country of origin for the destination. Emphasis is often placed on both their economic hardship and ignorance about basic Western practices: several books include scenes describing the heroine's first encounter with Western plumbing; James writes about her bafflement when given a knife and fork with which to eat on a flight from Pakistan to Austria.

Education has a major impact on perceptions of class (and the author-narrator's control over the production and promotion of her book), and the heroine's quest for or lack of formal education is a common theme. Her family usually fails to value education, especially the education of females. This trait is not only a marker of working-class status within a European framework but is also considered typical of Muslims and is a standard part of the familiar script. Education also has an impact on perceptions of authenticity: though better educated author-narrators such as James tend to play a greater role in production and promotion and more often go on to careers as activists and public speakers, the truth of their stories is also more often called into question, and they are more often and more harshly criticized for their prominence. Uneducated author-narrators, on the other hand, are thought of as more likely to be exploited by the industry, which reveals assumptions about their purity, not to mention their (in)ability (as "true" victims) to use available resources and navigate powerful institutions, despite evidence to the contrary.[48]

The higher socioeconomic status of the professionals involved in these memoirs, including contributing writers, publishers, reviewers, and activists, is evident not only in the social and economic security that puts them in a position to facilitate the author-narrator's participation in the public sphere but also in the degrees of distance they demonstrate from the stories themselves. As Rita Felski notes, class difference is "shaped by consumption practices and lifestyle patterns that do not bear any simple relation to the basic division between capital and labor."[49] In this case, the difference is shaped by ways of consuming these memoirs: how or whether the books are read as paid labor, altruism, or entertainment is reflected in different kinds of commentary and criticism. Class differences are especially evident in the undercurrent of criticism suggesting that oppressed Muslim women ought to find a more "honorable" way to improve their situation than by capitalizing on their suffering, a way that does not betray the "frugality, decency, and self-discipline" expected of the poor.[50]

Conclusion

Examining the production, promotion, and socioeconomics of Muslim women's memoirs, picking at the discursive knots that have formed around the figure of the Muslim woman victim, and identifying moments when author-narrators depart from the familiar script have tested the coherence of Muslim women's writing as a category. Once we look past the sensational marketing of these memoirs to the diversity of experiences they describe, the expectation that author-narrators present a single, coherent, and stable self to each of the numerous audiences they address in producing and promoting their memoirs emphasizes the extent to which they are understood as figures rather than individual, autonomous subjects. While it is widely accepted that audiences shift throughout the process of production and promotion (from co-author to editor to publicist to interviewer, for example), shifts in the self presented to the public at these stages can suggest inauthenticity, which has significant negative consequences for the status of an autobiographical narrative.

While categories of life writing such as testimonio and autoethnography cannot fully account for these memoirs, feminist theories of women's life writing offer a potentially helpful approach. These theories often define women's selfhood as fragmented and relational.[51] Leonore Hoffmann, for example, treated the autobiographical text as a construction of the self in the act of telling its story to a real or implied audience, an approach that takes the subjectivity of the author-narrator as a basic premise.[52] Treating the self that is constructed in and around the text as plural, shifting as audiences shift, allows greater consideration of the complex inequalities that structure the relationship between Muslim women's writing and the broader category of women's writing.

To what extent, then, is the category of Muslim women's writing related to the broader category of women's writing in German? Muslim women's writing is not simply a subset or qualification of women's writing; instead, it complicates and in some cases (like that of Inci Y. and coauthor Jochen Faust) challenges popular understandings of women's writing as explicitly bound by the gender of the writer and implicitly shaped by ideas and assumptions about her class, faith, sexuality, and ethnicity. At the same time, Muslim women's writing does not enjoy the same cultural status that other women's writing in German does. Its designation as trivial literature has as much (or more) to do with the social and discursive position of the author-narrator as with the literary merits of her work. Paradoxically, the author-narrator's status as a member and victim of a racialized minority group—the very group she is understood to have rejected, in an act that is practically necessary for the production of this narrative type—is both what granted her a voice, however small, in public debates about that group, and what prevents her voice from being attended to more carefully.

Even though Muslim women's texts address many of the same themes as other women's writing, the complexity of their perspective is obscured by sensational marketing; the memoirs' commercial success relies on the marginalization that women's writing works so hard to avoid. Such circumstances call for a more flexible critical approach to Muslim women's writing as well as women's writing at large—one that considers "the various social conditions that may affect the desire to speak or remain silent about the self," such as the tension between social and economic justice, the moral panic that allows specific individual experiences of violence to be seen as uniform, and especially the way that gender intersects with and shapes other articulations of difference.[53] Examining these categories and the relationship among them raises important questions about authorship, life writing, and the self, but especially about the possibility of intersectional analysis that comes from the provisional use of seemingly simple labels. It remains to be seen, however, whether the use of such categories as a method of critiquing the inequalities that produce them can actually reduce their power to shape both lives and literature.

Notes

[1] Yasemin Yildiz, "Turkish Girls, Allah's Daughters, and the Contemporary German Subject: Itinerary of a Figure," *German Life and Letters* 62, no. 4 (2009): 465.

[2] I use the term author-narrator to refer to the women listed as authors of these books in order to draw attention to two key points: the fact that they rarely (if

ever) write the memoirs by themselves, and the sense in which their primary discursive positioning as narrators-in-the-flesh, as the actual women whose experiences so fascinate audiences, is crucial for the genre.

[3] On amazon.de, for example, they have been cross-listed under "Biographien und Erinnerungen: Frauen" (biographies and memoirs: women [men's personal narratives are the unmarked majority]), "Biographien und Erinnerungen: Religion: Islam" (biographies and memoirs: religion: Islam) and "Biographien und Erinnerungen: Soziales: Flucht & Emigration" (biographies and memoirs: social issues: flight and emigration).

[4] Sabatina James (pseud.), *Sterben sollst du für dein Glück: Gefangen zwischen zwei Welten* (Munich: Knaur Taschenbuch Verlag, 2004).

[5] Ayşe (pseud.) and Renate Eder, *Mich hat keiner gefragt: Zur Ehe gezwungen— eine Türkin in Deutschland erzählt* (Munich: Blanvalet Verlag, 2005).

[6] Renate Maurer, "Hinter Mauern und Schleiern: Bücher der Anklage von Deutsch-Türkischen Autorinnen," Deutschlandradio Kultur, May 9, 2006, http://www.dradio.de/dkultur/sendungen/literatur/481659/.

[7] Renate Eder, in conversation with the author, Munich, Germany, 27 May 2009.

[8] James, *Sterben sollst du für dein Glück*, 10.

[9] Beverly Weber, "Freedom from Violence, Freedom to Make the World: Muslim Women's Memoirs, Gendered Violence, and Voices for Change in Germany," *Women in German Yearbook* 25 (2009): 199–222.

[10] Fatima El-Tayeb, *European Others: Queering Ethnicity in Postnational Europe* (Minneapolis: University of Minnesota Press, 2011).

[11] Lila Abu-Lughod, "The Active Social Life of 'Muslim Women's Rights': A Plea for Ethnography, Not Polemic, with Cases from Egypt and Palestine," *Journal of Middle East Women's Studies* 6, no. 1 (2010): 2.

[12] Chantelle Warner, *The Pragmatics of Literary Testimony* (New York: Routledge, 2013), 28.

[13] Abu-Lughod, "The Active Social Life," 2.

[14] Although author-activists such as Kelek have been roundly criticized for claiming the right to speak for Muslim women, their work is still treated as representative of all Muslim women's memoirs that address forced marriage or other "crimes of honor."

[15] Or, among more critical audiences, the belief that the author-narrators believe this.

[16] Gayatri Chakravorty Spivak, *Other Asias* (Malden, MA: Blackwell, 2008), 32.

[17] Serap Çileli, Introduction to Ayşe, *Mich hat keiner gefragt*, 7. Çileli is citing the Buchari and Muslim hadith collections as the origin of the quote she uses. Ahadith (the plural form) report the teachings or sayings of Muhammad, and are important supplements to the Qur'an for some Muslims. Buchari and Muslim are two of the most important Hadith collections. Emphasis original; original German: "Eine Jungfrau soll ohne ihre Einverständnis nicht verheiratet werden. Und genügend als (Zeichen der) Zustimmung soll **ihr Schweigen** sein (wegen ihrer natürlichen Schüchternheit)."

[18] Ayşe, *Mich hat keiner gefragt*, 126. Original German: "Der Islam spielte bei uns in der Familie eigentlich keine besonders große Rolle."

[19] Riem Spielhaus, "Religion und Identität: Vom deutschen Versuch, 'Ausländer' zu 'Muslimen' zu machen," *Internationale Politik* 3 (March 2006): 28–37.

[20] Matti Bunzl, "Between Anti-Semitism and Islamophobia: Some Thoughts on the New Europe," *American Ethnologist* 32, no. 4 (2005): 499–508.

[21] El-Tayeb, *European Others*.

[22] Jonathan Gray, *Show Sold Separately: Promos, Spoilers, and Other Media Paratexts* (New York: New York University Press, 2010), 17.

[23] Yildiz, "Turkish Girls," 467.

[24] Ibid.

[25] Hülya Kalkan, *Ich wollte nur frei sein: Meine Flucht vor der Zwangsehe* (Berlin: Ullstein Taschenbuch, 2006).

[26] Inci Y., *Erstickt an euren Lügen: Eine Türkin in Deutschland erzählt* (Munich: Piper Verlag, 2005).

[27] James's former coauthor leaked provocative topless photos of her to the Austrian tabloid press, unleashing a storm of publicity and harsh criticism about the perceived incongruity between the very existence of her sexuality and her purported Christian piety. German and international media alluded to Sürücü's sexuality in early coverage of her murder by her younger brother in 2005 (quickly termed an honor killing), but shied away from the topic once it became clear that she was not in a monogamous, committed relationship at the time of her death. Kekilli's past work in pornographic films was reported by *Bild-Zeitung* in 2004, shortly after she became famous for her role in the film *Gegen die Wand* (Head-On, 2004). The ensuing scandal led to a rift with her parents and some rather smug commentary in the German media.

[28] Weber, "Freedom from Violence," 200.

[29] James, *Sterben sollst du für dein Glück*, 10.

[30] Curiously, the figure of the Muslim woman in German literature has long been portrayed as speaking for herself, even when this speech was actually created by white Germans. Yeşilada cites Goethe's Suleika as a prime early example of such a paradox. Karin Yeşilada,"Die geschundene Suleika: Das Eigenbild der Türkin in der deutschsprachigen Literatur türkischer Autorinnen," in *Interkulturelle Konfigurationen: Zur deutschsprachigen Erzählliteratur von Autoren nichtdeutscher Herkunft*, ed. Mary Howard (Munich: Iudicium Verlag, 1997), 95–114.

[31] Maurer, "Hinter Mauern."

[32] Renate Eder, in conversation with the author, Munich, Germany, 27 May 2009.

[33] Part of the familiar script involves the Muslim woman victim's desire to make herself sexually available to non-Muslim men, and the author-narrators' wish to choose their own sexual partners is often misconstrued as such. Since these memoirs and the discourse surrounding them are so heteronormative, female coauthors are understood as less threatening.

[34] Maurer, "Hinter Mauern."

[35] The German Islam Conference was initiated in 2006 by then Minister of the Interior Wolfgang Schäuble, with the goal of improving dialogue between the German state and Muslims living in Germany.

[36] "Terre des Femmes," Terre des Femmes, e.V., accessed April 3, 2013, http://www.terre-des-femmes.de/.

[37] Weber, "Freedom from Violence."

[38] Inci Y., *Erzähl mir nix*, 36–37. Original German: "Die Träume vieler türkischer Frauen, die geglaubt hatten, aus Zwangsehen und geistiger Unterdrückung ausbrechen zu können, scheitern. . . . Um zu überleben, verkaufen sie dort am Ende das einzige Kapital, das ihnen ihre Eltern mit auf den Weg gegeben haben: ihre Weiblichkeit."

[39] Rita Felski, "Nothing to Declare: Identity, Shame and the Lower Middle Class," *PMLA* 115, no. 1 (2000): 43.

[40] Activists often have higher socioeconomic status prior to publishing their books, which likely plays a role in their careers as well as in the tone and amount of criticism they receive.

[41] Katherine Pratt Ewing, *Stolen Honor: Stigmatizing Muslim Men in Berlin* (Palo Alto, CA: Stanford University Press, 2008), 90.

[42] Çileli, in her introduction to Ayşe, *Mich hat keiner gefragt*, 11.

[43] See, for example, Ewing, *Stolen Honor*, 221; El-Tayeb, *European Others*; and Yasemin Yildiz, "Governing European Subjects: Tolerance and Guilt in the Discourse of 'Muslim Women,'" *Cultural Critique* 77 (Winter 2011): 70–101.

[44] Ewing, *Stolen Honor*, 67.

[45] Sabatina James, "Sabatina—Tagebuch," *sabatina.at*, 13 September 2003.

[46] Günter Traxler, "Der verschlungene Weg zu Jesus," *Der Standard*, 13 June 2003, http://derstandard.at/1329881. Leutgeb also exposed James's interest in sex and money, widely perceived as scandalous.

[47] For example, the case of American author Norma Kouhri's memoir *Forbidden Love*, which was shown to be false by an Australian book critic and removed from shelves by Random House (and from the German-language market by Rowohlt) in 2004.

[48] The heroine's experience of oppression and abuse is often thought to persist as long as it does in part because of her inability to access or navigate available social services. But studies suggest that Turkish women actually use these services more than women of German or Eastern European background. See Weber, "Freedom from Violence," 17.

[49] Felski, "Nothing to Declare," 34.

[50] Ibid. As Felski's interpretation suggests, it would be preferable to behave more like the iconic honor-killing victim Hatun Sürücü, who not only worked with state authorities to escape her family but also pursued training to become an electrician rather than trying to profit from her story (which did not stop the countless others who did profit from her story after she died).

[51] Marjanne E. Goozé, "The Definitions of the Self and Form in Feminist Autobiography Theory," *Women's Studies* 21, no. 4 (September 1992): 425.

[52] Leonore Hoffman, Introduction to *Women's Personal Narratives: Essays in Criticism and Pedagogy* (New York: Modern Language Association, 1985).

[53] Felski, "Nothing to Declare," 33.

6: Popfeminism, Ethnicity, and Race in Contemporary Germany: Hatice Akyün's Popfeminist Autobiographic Works *Einmal Hans mit scharfer Soße* (2005) and *Ali zum Dessert* (2008)

Mihaela Petrescu

IN RECENT YEARS several scholars have investigated the role of popfeminism, a term coined in 2007 by Sonja Eismann, which denotes Germany's own version of contemporary feminism.[1] While these scholars have scrutinized the relationship between popfeminism, pop literature, and neoliberalism, and they have pointed out the absence of concepts of race and ethnicity in numerous popfeminist texts, they have paid little attention to those popfeminist works that do analyze the intersections between sexuality, race, and ethnicity.[2] In this essay I address this gap by investigating the humor-inflected popfeminist autobiographical works *Einmal Hans mit scharfer Soße* (An Order of Hans with Hot Sauce, 2005) and its sequel, *Ali zum Dessert* (Ali for Dessert, 2008) by the Turkish-German journalist Hatice Akyün.[3] As is typical for popfeminist writing, Akyün uses pop tropes such as sampling, remixing, and resignification to present an independent, career-oriented woman who enjoys consumer empowerment and sexual agency while, significantly, she is also critical of the sexism and racism that operate in German society. The celebration of consumerism is a fundamental aspect of popfeminism that resignifies consumption as pleasure, which contrasts with its rejection in second-wave feminism. While Akyün shares with other popfeminist writers the use of an individualist approach manifested in the form of the autobiography, her books stand out because they emphasize sexual agency in the context of a modern, highly cross-cultural Turkish-German female identity.

Akyün is not the only female author to explore the identity of modern Turkish-German women, a topic also depicted in Iris Alanyali's *Die blaue Reise* (The Blue Journey, 2009), Dilek Güngör's *Unter uns* (Among Us, 2004) and *Ganz schön deutsch* (Very German Indeed, 2007), and Hilal Sezgin's *Typisch Türkin?* (Typical Turkish Woman?, 2006).[4] While all these books examine the complexity of contemporary, modern

Turkish-German female identity and defy stereotypes about Muslim families generally viewed as oppressive toward women, there are significant differences between them and Akyün's work. Neither Alanyali's nor Güngör's jovial books display the sexual openness and incisive scrutiny of racism and sexism present in Akyün's texts. Furthermore, whereas Sezgin's work criticizes the intersectionality of sexism and racism, her project differs from Akyün's generically and stylistically, as it is a collection of interviews of first- and second-generation Turkish-German women in which humor plays no role.[5]

Akyün's popfeminist autobiographies present exemplary interventions into the discursive representation of Turkish-German women in the twenty-first century. As Weber states, Akyün normalizes not only the professional Turkish-German woman, illustrated in the books by Akyün herself, but also the religious Turkish woman, represented mainly by Akyün's traditional mother.[6] Moreover, Akyün contributes to the normalization of the history of post-Second-World-War work migration to Germany: by including an episode about a first-generation female Turkish guest worker in her second book, Akyün sheds critical light on what has traditionally been considered the absence of women from the 1960s influx of Turkish laborers to the FRG.[7] Akyün thus renders what Leslie Adelson calls a "touching tale," that is to say a narrative that serves as a point of critical reorientation for German history because it "commingle(s) cultural developments and historical references generally not thought to belong together."[8]

Because Akyün portrays a strong and modern female identity, her texts constitute, as Yeşilada argues, a counterexample to the "Suleikalism" that marked the early biographical and autobiographical literature of female Turkish-German writers, which reflected the negative views held about their authors by Germans.[9] Furthermore, as Weber points out, Akyün's writing stands in stark contrast to the victim narratives of Necla Kelek and Seyran Ateş, which are more popular than Akyün's work because they reinforce negative German views about Muslim women as powerless victims of domestic violence.[10]

In contrast to the rejection of Islam on which the process of "becoming German" is stipulated in victim narratives, I argue that by employing sampling, remixing, and resignification—achieved via multiple forms of humor, including self-humor and humor that targets ethnic stereotypes—Akyün's texts emphasize the richness of both Turkish and German culture. In this manner, they also highlight the reciprocal influence and cultural learning that unfolds between Turks and Germans. I maintain that by celebrating emphatically this cross-cultural identity, Akyün suggests that she, and by extension other minority representatives who cherish such an identity, are better equipped to deal with an increasingly transcultural, globalized world.[11]

In addition to victim narratives, another literary genre in relationship to which Akyün's work has been considered is what Yeşilada terms "chick lit alla turca," a Turkish-German version of the international genre of US- and British-influenced chick lit. On the one hand, Akyün's texts do share with chick lit alla turca the depiction of a modern, urban, financially and sexually independent thirty-something woman of Turkish-German heritage.[12] On the other hand, however, there is a fundamental distinction between them: while chick lit alla turca is fiction, Akyün's texts constitute an autobiography bolstered by pop tropes and popfeminist views.[13]

Einmal Hans mit scharfer Soße (2005)

The defining pop traits of Akyün's first popfeminist autobiographical book are the humorous sampling and remixing of ethnic stereotypes. The popfeminist strategy of remixing allows Akyün to reevaluate key clichés about Turkish and German identity by bringing them into tension with one another. Thus she chisels away at the negative connotations often attached to a traditional female Turkish identity, such as an association with the domestic realm and the headscarf. At the same time, she samples elements that are usually associated with a Western female identity, including identity performance, consumerism, the beauty industry, and sexuality, which she incorporates into her popfeminist Turkish-German identity, thereby normalizing the latter.

Akyün addresses the widespread stereotype of Turkish women's definition via domesticity by means of her mother, who is mainly relegated to the space of the kitchen. She de-emphasizes the centrality of the domestic sphere for a traditional Turkish woman by noting humorously that in addition to being a homemaker her mother is also a rebellious person who always speaks her mind and gets her husband to do what she wants, and who ultimately holds the reins in their marriage. The link between a traditional Turkish female identity and the domestic sphere is furthermore enhanced by the detailed descriptions of typical Turkish foods her mother prepares, such as "meze," "turşu," "mücver," and the recipes for Turkish honey, Döner, and baklava, culinary examples that exoticize Turkish culture. However, this culinary self-exoticization also functions as a celebration of the diversity of Turkish gastronomy and contains a critical impetus, namely to rectify German misperceptions about Turkish food being mainly vegetarian and about the Döner as a representative Turkish dish. In contrast to her mother, Akyün does not define herself through domesticity: as she states with self-irony, she owns one pot, still in its original wrapping, while the fridge serves to store her face lotions, not her own gastronomic creations.

The culinary realm also plays a defining role in the title of Akyün's book, which humorously expresses her wish for a partner by sampling both German and Turkish culture. The former is invoked via the proper name Hans, used by Turkish people to refer to a generic German male, a name that Akyün uses metonymically for order and reliability. Turkish culture is reflected in the gastronomic detail "scharfe Soße" (hot sauce), a metaphor for the passion she wants her dream man to have. I disagree with Yeşilada, who argues that the culinary metaphor of the title emphasizes a conventional relationship between Turkish female identity and the domestic realm.[14] Rather, I claim that the act of ordering food expressed in the title reveals the agency of the female subject: she places a metaphoric order in which she clearly positions herself as the agent of consumption. With her playful and humorous phrasing Akyün underlines her agency, which stands in contrast to the object position a woman occupies in both traditional Muslim and Western discourses on female identity.

Another element that defines the perceived conservatism and victimization of Turkish women is the headscarf, which Akyün describes by sampling different opinions about it, including her own, her mother's, and that of her older sister, Gönül. While she herself does not don a headscarf because she does not feel good wearing it, Akyün explains that for her mother and for Gönül, sporting it is a sign of respecting Islamic tradition. Furthermore, for Gönül the headscarf is an exclusive fashion accessory: for her collection of over fifty headscarves by high-end fashion designers Versace and Valentino, Gönül paid significant sums (between 100 and 400 Euro per scarf). Akyün thus reveals that the headscarf is not only an expression of religiosity but also a fashion statement and the manifestation of global consumerism's incursion into Muslim tradition. While she acknowledges that some women are forced into wearing a headscarf, an act she adamantly criticizes as chauvinistic and hegemonic because it relieves men of the responsibility to control their fantasies, in presenting her family's diverse views about it Akyün complicates simplistic Western views of the headscarf by showing that there are many different reasons for wearing and renouncing it.

There is one instance in which Akyün does, however, wear the headscarf precisely according to the hegemonic understanding she criticizes, namely as protection from the male gaze during a two-week stay in Kabul, Afghanistan. Albeit particularly dramatic due to the war setting, this is but one of several examples of identity performance mediated via fashion, examples that reveal Akyün's transcultural and popfeminist identity. The earliest illustration of identity performance in Akyün's life happens when, as a child, she had to change the Wrangler jeans she wore during the four-day-long car trip from Duisburg to Akpınar Köyü, her parents' native village in Turkey, and instead wear a long skirt and a headscarf. At that time Akyün was too young to understand the performative implications of her actions, for which she was not the decision-making agent, since she was merely following her mother's request to change clothes. However, she is an agent of identity performance when she starts to take off her headscarf on the way to school, and more tellingly, when, as an adult woman visiting her parents in Duisburg, she stops at the outskirts of town to change her short skirt for a long one. As Akyün states, she does not feel obligated to do this, nor does she feel bothered by it. Rather, she views her identity performance as an acknowledgment that she lives with two cultures and that she can interact playfully with both.

The items that most highlight the performativity of Akyün's popfeminist identity are her high heels, which she resignifies as an expression of female power and pleasure. Akyün views her collection of designer high heels not only as a manifestation of elegance and sexiness but also as a mark of female fearlessness, courage, and determination:[15]

> High Heels erfordern Mut und Entschlossenheit, und sie sind eine ganz neue Art von Frauenbewegung, die auf zehn Zentimeter hohen Absätzen daherkommt. Vielleicht finde ich High Heels so sexy, weil sie eine unwiderstehliche Mischung aus Risiko, Tollkühnheit und Eleganz darstellen. (*H*, 101)

> [High heels demand courage and determination, and they are a very new form of "women's movement" coming along on heels ten centimeters high. Maybe I find high heels so sexy because they represent an irresistible mixture of risk, daredevilry, and elegance.]

Akyün celebrates high heels through the humorous double entendre of the phrase "Frauenbewegung." On the one hand, "Frauenbewegung" can be translated as a new way for women to move, while on the other hand, it functions as a reference to a new feminist movement, one that does not deny or limit the female pleasure of consumerism, as second-wave feminism did. What the two interpretations share is the celebration of the pleasure women get from wearing high heels as well as the self-assured and sexy attitude they help women project. With a great sense of irreverent humor, Akyün equates her high heels to a religious experience, "Schuhe sind meine Religion" (*H*, 99; shoes are my religion), "Mein Schuhregal ist mein Hausaltar" (*H*, 102; my shoe-rack is my home-altar), while she also makes fun of her expensive consumerist habit, which caused her to spend enough money on shoes to buy a medium-size car. Significantly, her high heels, this most symbolic expression of her popfeminist identity, bring about the comical resignification of a staple of Turkish domesticity, the vitrine. While in a traditional Turkish home such as her mother's the vitrine holds mocha cups, Akyün has repurposed hers, centrally located in the living room, as a display window for her most prized thirty pairs of high heels. Thus what is put on display is not the domesticity of a Turkish homemaker but the stylish fierceness and consumer power of an independent woman.

Another vector of Akyün's popfeminist identity is her critical nod toward the beauty industry, against which she juxtaposes home-made Turkish products and self-beautification processes such as threading, waxing, and bathing in milk and honey. While Yeşilada is right to point out that the bath scene reinforces the long-standing Oriental cliché of the Other bathing, she does not acknowledge the wider context in which it is embedded, namely Akyün's critical gesture toward the beauty industry.[16] By providing a simple, cost-efficient, and healthy bath recipe based only on natural ingredients, Akyün points out that, traditional as they might be in some ways, Turkish women are less duped by the costly and chemical-laden cosmetics industry. Simultaneously, she also raises awareness about the benefits of ethnic beautification processes such as threading and waxing, and when she uses the latter on her German friends, she imparts a hands-on cross-cultural experience. Overall, Akyün's popfeminist resignification of beautification practices contrasts with the rejection of such endeavors typical of second-wave feminism.

Akyün also rediscovers values promoted by second-wave feminism such as the refusal to shave, which was a political statement against male hegemony over women's bodies and an expression of liberated female sexuality. These feminist views resonate in Akyün's critique of the beauty industry's normative recommendation that women have hair-free legs, a critique that is defining for popfeminism.[17] Akyün's act of sometimes not shaving is a self-disciplining strategy that she occasionally employs to stop herself from having sex on first dates.[18] The fact that she has developed such a self-inhibiting practice and her candid and humorous admission that this strategy does not always work are clear indications of Akyün's sex-positive attitude. The latter is also evident from several amusing innuendoes,[19] as well as from Akyün's self-assured remarks that she has had intercourse without being married, and that her physical relationships with men were intense.

While early in the book Akyün states that it is challenging to live in two worlds that are difficult to bring together, it becomes clear as the text progresses that she places great importance on cross-cultural values, mutual cultural learning, and an interlaced German and Turkish identity. For instance, the humor and ironic ethnic stereotyping of the passages that describe her hopes for an ideal man bring to mind the works of Şinasi Dikmen and Osman Engin, famous for their satiric depictions of the reciprocal formulaic typecasting of Turks and Germans.[20] Thus Akyün desires a man who would smoothly unite German attributes such as respect, punctuality, and diligence with Turkish qualities such as passion and the ability to make elaborate compliments, flirt, and dance.[21] To highlight the essential role reciprocal cultural learning plays in her own life as well as in today's globalized world, Akyün points to a few personal examples, including the fact that her best friend, Julia—a German—learns various Turkish proverbs from her and uses them aptly in her interactions with Akyün, and that Akyün herself eventually adopts Julia's habit of making lists. Additionally, Akyün describes a larger-scale example of cross-cultural learning, namely the German appropriation of the Turkish habit of grilling in public spaces. Akyün reminds us that this process did not happen suddenly or without an uproar over the so-called "Türkenwiese" (Turks' meadow) in Berlin's Tiergarten park, which led to a face-off between CDU representatives and members of the Green party.[22]

Akyün views the interconnections, similarities, and differences between German and Turkish culture as a twofold enrichment of her existence:

Ich fühle mich in beiden Welten zu Hause, der deutschen und der türkischen, bin weder in der einen noch in der anderen nur Gast und schöpfe aus vollen Zügen aus zwei reichhaltigen Kulturen. (*H*, 183)

[I feel at home in both worlds, the German and the Turkish, I am not merely a guest in either, and I draw to the fullest extent from two enriching cultures.]

She emphasizes this double enrichment through unequivocal statements—"ich profitiere lieber von den Highlights beider Kulturen" (*H*, 35; I prefer to profit from the highlights of both cultures)—and references to her "Heimweh" (*H*, 56; homesickness) for both Germany and Turkey. Likewise, she underscores her cross-cultural and multivalent, popfeminist identity based on the several vantage points (ethnic, racial, religious, and social) from which she can define herself at all times:

Ich . . . bin zwar Türkin, aber auch Deutsche, Ausländerin, Muslime, Deutsch-Türkin, Journalistin oder ein Miststück, je nachdem, wer mich gerade betrachtet. Und ich empfinde es als Reichtum, diese Widersprüche in mir zu vereinen. (*H*, 185)

[I am . . . indeed a Turkish woman, but also a German one, a foreigner, a Muslim, a German-Turk, a journalist, or a bitch, depending on who happens to behold me. And I feel that uniting these contradictions in myself enriches me.]

A further key concept for Akyün's transcultural self-understanding is her metaphor of the tumbleweed:

Wenn ich meine Situation schon mit einem Bild beschreiben sollte, dann würde ich sagen, ich bin ein Tumblewheat [sic]. Tumblewheats sind die Strohgebilde, die man in Westernfilmen manchmal herumfliegen sieht. Sie werden vom Wüstenwind aus ihrer Verwurzelung gerissen und rollen und springen so lange, bis sie dank eines Regengusses irgendwo wieder Wurzeln schlagen. Dann erblühen sie für kurze Zeit, vertrocknen und fliegen weiter ziellos durch die Wüste. (*H*, 181)

[If I were to describe my situation with an image then I would say that I am a tumbleweed. Tumbleweeds are those straw-formations one can sometimes see flying around in Western films. They are uprooted by desert winds and roll around and jump until they lay roots somewhere thanks to a downpour. Then they bloom for a short time, dry out, and fly on aimlessly through the desert.]

Using the pop effect of recognition, Akyün evokes the image of the tumbleweed, known mainly from American Westerns, and resignifies it for her self-definition as a modern woman. On the one hand the image of the tumbleweed brings about visual associations of drifting aimlessly and thus suggests a rough, nomadic life. On the other hand, however, Akyün's resignification of the cinematic metaphor reveals the defining role the environment plays in the process of belonging. Here she offers a counterpoint to the widespread discourse of the 1980s and 1990s, according to which integration was failing in Germany because of the Turkish lack of interest in and desire for it.[23] The qualities Akyün cherishes, including the resilience and adaptability of a tumbleweed or mutual cultural enrichment, are relevant assets in today's globalized, transcultural world, and they contour Akyün as perfectly equipped to function in it.[24]

Finally, Akyün's book achieves what many popfeminist works do not: it sheds critical light on both sexism and racism.[25] Akyün reveals sexism in German society at large and within her own family. Although some of her examples might be deemed negligible, they do expose how deeply ingrained sexism is, for example via German idioms that help socialize children and reinforce gender barriers. In this sense she zooms in critically on the expression "kleiner Mann" (little man), which instills a sense of worth in young boys as it emphasizes their development into men, and its rather demeaning equivalent for girls, who are referred to as "Mäuschen" (little mouse), a word that achieves little in terms of identity building.[26] Akyün disapproves of the sexist double standard that condemns women who date younger men but does not apply to men who date younger women. Furthermore, she takes a critical stand against the sexism of the national discourse that blames middle-class, educated women and second-wave feminism for Germany's falling birth rate, while in reality, she argues, in Germany's neoliberal, male-dominated business world women often have to suppress their desire for a child in order to prove themselves.

Akyün describes a chauvinist and violent episode that unfolds in her family between herself and her youngest brother, who insults her and with whom she consequently starts a fight that includes biting, torn-out hair, bruises, and bloody noses. The determination to stand up for herself verbally and physically illustrated in this episode also manifests itself in Akyün's actions against essentialism, discrimination, and racism. After Akyün experiences what it is like to be essentialized as unique and exotic, she learns to use such occurrences to her own advantage for good part-time jobs and entrance into dance clubs, which reveals her popfeminist impetus to mix together various, often divergent, attitudes. Akyün's first encounter with what she calls "Diskriminierung" (*H*, 170; discrimination) happens in a physical-education class in grade school, where a peer refuses to hold her hands because presumably Turks stink. After school, Akyün settles things in a fight.[27] It is intriguing that what Akyün rather vaguely terms discrimination is an illustration of racism for a non-German critical reader. In this sense, it is important to recall the German reluctance over the past decades to employ the concept of race because of its historic misuse in anti-Semitic discourses of the Third Reich. Instead, in Germany the term has been replaced with the more evasive form "ethnicity," which, however, has become so commonplace that it "runs the risk of dethematizing racism."[28] Against this background, Akyün's example of what she considers discrimination is relevant, because it reveals that she has internalized the German reserve vis-à-vis the term race.

There are several other examples in which Akyün tackles racism, although under the cautious label discrimination. For instance, she consistently points out the ignorance behind the unreflected racism of various people: that of her editors, who change the spelling of her last name to forms more accessible to them; of Julia, who, years into their friendship, wants to know if Akyün was supposed to have her own forced marriage; and that of individuals who assume that she is not punctual and that hot weather does not bother her because of her southern origin. When her mother is faced with the "Diskriminierung" of a sales person who yells at her and tells her in incorrect, simplified German that she is not allowed to touch the merchandise, Akyün reacts firmly: she satirizes the employee by asking her to repeat the sentence in correct German, tells her that her behavior is "ausländerfeindlich" (*H*, 169; xenophobic), and asks her to apologize to her mother. While she cannot change the fact that she and her family are the objects of racism, Akyün acts decisively and publicly against being its victim. This is particularly well indicated by her verbal reaction to the racism displayed by those people who comment with amazement on the fact that she speaks impeccable German. Her reply, a simple sentence full of wit and sarcasm, "Danke, Sie aber auch!" (*H*, 171; Thank you, you do too!), signals that Akyün does not let herself be regarded as special because of her command of German. Furthermore, with self-assuredness and irony, the answer forces the speaker to reflect on his or her own problematic statement.

One event in particular shocks Akyün because of its severity: the xenophobic attacks from May 1993 that took place in Solingen, when four Germans set fire to a Turkish home, an act that claimed the life of five Turks. Paradoxically, although she is shaken and saddened by the attack, Akyün remarks that she is ashamed to act publicly on her feelings, a shame she considers fundamentally German. This incapacity to act publicly brings to mind the German guilt complex, which Katherine Pratt Ewing defines as a "post-Holocaust fear of appearing racist."[29] Peter Schneider and Necla Kelek assert that this German guilt complex has led to the tolerance of radical Turkish customs such as honor killings, which have almost ceased to exist in Turkey, yet continue to be practiced by conservative Muslims in Germany.[30] However, it is not fear of being deemed racist that prevents Akyün from acting publicly shortly after the racialized violence at Solingen, but the realization that she has appropriated an unsettling German mode of thinking and behaving that reinforces her Germanness in a negative way.

Despite its merits as a popfeminist text that uncovers racism, Akyün's book has its own blind spots in that it employs racism in an inaccurate synopsis of Germany's treatment of Turkish guest workers and in its views about Eastern Europe during the Cold War. Akyün claims that for her parents, integration into German society failed because they always intended to return to Turkey and therefore excluded themselves from Germany's vision of a multicultural society. However, to position Germany's treatment of first-generation Turkish guest workers under the optimistic auspices of a multicultural society is historically inaccurate. As Mark Terkessidis demonstrates, Germany did not understand and define itself as a multicultural society between 1961, the year when Turkish guest workers started arriving in the FRG, and the caesura year 1989.[31] Furthermore, even the reforms that ensued after Germany's reunification in 1990, such as the liberalization of the naturalization procedures in the early 1990s, and the 1999 citizenship reform that rejects dual citizenship, do not sustain the smooth and peaceful German view of multiculturalism that Akyün puts forth, but rather one that is highly controversial.[32] Likewise, stating that Germany was keen on demonstrating that it had overcome racism is an oversimplification, since it offers no historical points of reference and glosses over the racism Akyün herself has adamantly critiqued in other sections of her book.

Also surprising is Akyün's othering of Eastern Europe in the passages in which she describes her family's car journeys from Germany to Turkey. Former Yugoslavia is viewed in a mixture of negative clichés as the "Vorhölle" (*H*, 51; pre-hell) because of its barren landscape, unfriendly inhabitants, and rudimentary toilets. Employing similarly demeaning and inferiorizing images, she depicts Bulgaria as the "richtige Hölle" (*H*, 52–53; real hell) because of its corrupt border guards and poor villages.³³ While one cannot deny the negative portrayal of these two Eastern European countries, one should also acknowledge the potential of these passages to function as "touching tales" as they disclose the links between Turkish guest workers in Germany and Eastern Europe during the Cold War.³⁴ Negative as they are, these passages are relevant because they evoke the oppressive living conditions in the Eastern Bloc, where regular Western items such as Coca-Cola and chocolate were a luxury and often used as bribes, and where, despite official claims by their respective Communist governments, people often lacked basic amenities.³⁵

Ali zum Dessert (2008)

Akyün's second book continues her popfeminist autobiography and its critical approach to sexism, racism, and consumerism (in this case, the industry for pregnant women and new mothers), while it also reveals significant critical details about the first generation of female Turkish guest workers, thus giving contour to yet another "touching tale." Akyün is very critical of her own status as "expert" on migration and integration issues, because it was bestowed on her in large part by the media. She observes ironically that her severe lack of knowledge would prevent her from accepting a hypothetical invitation from Wolfgang Schäuble, Germany's minister of the interior at the time, to join a conference on the topic of migration. Her self-criticism further disparages the expert status the media has bestowed on feminist activists Necla Kelek and Seyran Ateş, both participants in the *Deutsche Islam-Konferenz* (German Islam Conference) initiated by Schäuble in 2006. Unlike Kelek and Ateş, who claim the right to "represent" the issues of immigrant women, for which they have been repeatedly criticized, Akyün refuses this representational role.³⁶

While the sequel engages critically with aspects of ethnic identity, it also reads like chick lit, because of its thematic focus on a woman who balances her career, single life, and search for love, a focus that is much more emphatic than in the first book. Furthermore, affinities with chick lit underscore the narrative suspense of Akyün's budding relationship with Ali, an intelligent, handsome, and charming Turkish-German journalist working for a Berlin television station, and of Akyün's pregnancy. In addition, the defining chick lit elements of interlaced humor and romance are apparent from the diverse narrative strategies Akyün employs, such as a romantic cliffhanger conclusion (chapter 3), the insertion of a soap-opera-like passage and of Ali's love letters and emails to her (chapter 4), and romantic twists and turns (particularly chapters 4, 5, and 6).

As in the first book, in *Ali zum Dessert* Akyün constructs a popfeminist female identity by employing the humor-based pop tropes of sampling and resignification. The humor, however, is at times more sarcastic and derisive, occasionally even dark in comparison to Akyün's first text. Self-deprecating comical observations abound, a stylistic trait that emphasizes the second book's affiliation with chick lit, if one bears in mind Suzanne Ferris and Mallory Young's observation that chick lit often uses self-mocking humor.[37] For example, Akyün makes fun of the fact that she stooped low enough to date her muscular but not very bright fitness trainer, and that in contrast to her youth, when she used to turn people's heads in admiration, it is now Ali who has this impact. The instances in which Akyün mocks Julia's small breast size and the pregnancy weight gained by US actress Katie Holmes, whom she likens to a walrus, and the statements in which she compares her own newborn daughter to a baby gorilla display a rather dark humor, which one also encounters in chick lit novels such as Karen Duve's *Dies ist kein Liebeslied* (This Is Not a Love Song, 2000).[38] Akyün's satiric assertions about her own child and about Holmes undermine basic assumptions about what constitutes an acceptable comportment vis-à-vis motherhood, and in this sense her writing participates alongside other recent German literature by women in providing redefinitions of the maternal for the twenty-first century.[39]

By exposing racism and sexism Akyün's second work continues the author's critical approach to German society. But she also self-reflexively reveals her own racist sexism, which is brought into focus through her first serious relationship with a Turkish-German man. Akyün exposes instances of unreflected racism, including that of a doctor who misinterprets Ali's tears of joy at seeing his newborn daughter as an expression of patriarchal Turkish masculinity offended that the child is not a boy; the xenophobia of a landlord who refuses to rent to foreigners;[40] and the covert racism of a bureaucrat who compliments Akyün and Ali on their perfect command of German. With relentless self-irony and self-criticism Akyün also divulges that in the process of getting to know Ali she discovers clichés in her own thinking, namely her own racism about Ali's language skills, and her racist gender stereotyping of Ali as unreliable, jealous, patriarchal, and violent—prejudices that initially cause her to refuse his attentions. By trenchantly exposing her own unflattering opinions, Akyün underscores negative components of her Germanness, since through her socialization in Germany she is inadvertently the carrier of racism and sexism. Thus, while it follows thematic conventions of chick lit, Akyün's book also pushes boundaries toward redefining popfeminist writing by acknowledging the complex intersectionality of sexism and racism.

Another misperception Akyün refutes concerns first-generation female Turkish guest workers, and in this context she is among the very few to reject the assumptions that Germany had no or only few such laborers. In contrast to her own mother, who focused on caring for her family and was not employed in Germany, Akyün reveals that Ali's mother was an assemblywoman at Siemens. Although she was illiterate and initially barely spoke German, over time Ali's mother made numerous innovative suggestions in the workplace, for which she received several prizes. Brief as it may be, this episode provides one more "touching tale" for German history and clarifies not only that first-generation female Turkish guest workers did come to the FRG but also that some even achieved public recognition for their accomplishments.[41]

While Akyün is critical of both German and Turkish values—in some areas the former are preferred over the latter and vice versa—overall, the text promotes a mélange of traditions and attitudes associated with both countries. Akyün criticizes, for instance, the German consumer industry for pregnant women, which prescribes that mothers-to-be engage in Lamaze, yoga, and water gymnastics classes, as well as in various activities with their babies post-birth. The attitude that Akyün critiques the most incisively is Germany's aversion to children, which she considers to be the actual reason for the country's demographic problems. While in *Einmal Hans* Akyün points out that Germany's neoliberalism infringes on women's plans for motherhood, here she explores alternative causes of the country's demography debates:

> Nicht die geringen Geburtenraten sind das Problem, nicht generelle Zweifel oder finanzielle Sorgen, ob man sich für ein Kind entscheidet oder nicht, sondern die Kinderfeindlichkeit, mit der existierende Kinder und ihre Bezugspersonen überall konfrontiert werden. . . . Ich kann nicht verstehen, warum Kinder hierzulande in Geschäften, öffentlichen Verkehrsmitteln, Cafés und Restaurants als störend empfunden werden. Deutschland braucht nicht nur Elterngeld und Erziehungsurlaub, nicht nur Kitas und Ganztagsschulen, sondern vor allem eine Atmosphäre, in der Kinder willkommen sind. (*A*, 181–82)

> [The problem is not the low birthrate, not the general sense of doubt or financial concerns regarding whether one decides in favor of a child or not, but rather the animosity toward children that existing children and their caregivers face everywhere. . . . I cannot understand why children are deemed disturbing in stores, public transportation, cafés, and restaurants in this country. Germany needs not only parenting benefits and childcare leave, not only daycare centers and a longer school day, but primarily also an atmosphere in which children are welcome.]

The passage above resonates with the critical discussion of the demography debate presented in the popfeminist text *Wir Alphamädchen* (We Alpha Females), whose authors explore the lack of appropriate childcare facilities and trained personnel, and the conservative, antifeminist climate that erroneously links Germany's falling birthrate to women's emancipation.[42] In addition, Akyün speaks out against the overt hostility mothers and children face in a variety of public places, which she contrasts with the positive attitude toward children in Turkey.

This is not to say that Akyün is less outspoken about other Turkish customs. For instance, she is critical of Turkish traditions that cause her extended family to beleaguer her at the hospital and present her baby with gold jewelry, and according to which she is not allowed to leave the house with the newborn for forty days. While she seeks to balance different Turkish and German motherhood practices, when it comes to her relationship with Ali, Akyün emphasizes repeatedly that she favors German over Turkish parameters. In this sense her narrative is sex-positive, reflecting the feminist understanding that women may choose to have sexual relationships without being married. At the same time, she engages in a courting ritual that she resignifies in a popfeminist manner, indicating that she would like to propose marriage to Ali herself, when the time is right for her. Into this German-Turkish collage she also interweaves a high appreciation of the Turkish dedication to personally taking care of one's parents in their old age.

While she acknowledges these divergent Turkish and German traditions, here too Akyün promotes a transcultural identity bolstered by cross-cultural learning experiences. For example, she narrates humorous episodes in which her German friends follow the Turkish tradition of eating pieces of red ribbon in hopes of finding the right man. Akyün is also determined to celebrate both Christmas and *Zuckerfest* and to allow her daughter the freedom to eat pork. She demonstrates a strong appreciation of bilingualism and cross-cultural learning as facilitators for an enhanced understanding of the world. On the one hand, the transcultural hope that concludes her book, namely that Germans will one day learn to celebrate the *Zuckerfest* just as she, Ali, and her daughter celebrate Christmas, denotes a certain utopianism. On the other hand, it also indicates that she and Ali have a heightened cross-cultural understanding and sociocultural pragmatism, which give them an edge in today's globalized world.

Conclusion

Akyün's two books form a popfeminist autobiography that bears affinities with chick lit and chick lit alla turca. As I have demonstrated, Akyün's sex-positive texts reveal a popfeminist subject who is an avid consumer and an insightful chronicler of the era of globalization as well as a vociferous critic of racism and sexism—a critique other popfeminist writers do not articulate. Akyün's humorous autobiographical books provide an alternative history that challenges the victim narratives that constitute the dominant discourse on Muslim women in Germany. Furthermore, by drawing on central pop tropes such as sampling, remixing, and resignification, which she interweaves with humor about ethnic stereotypes, Akyün positions herself firmly in both German and Turkish culture. Akyün's popfeminist autobiography resists essentializing long-standing concerns of women's writing such as female identity, sexuality, and motherhood as merely female issues. By arguing in favor of a cross-cultural identity, which she considers necessary for successful interactions in our globalized world, Akyün creates a model of transcultural women's writing for the new millennium.

Notes

[1] Sonja Eismann, ed., *Hot Topic: Popfeminismus heute* (Mainz: Ventil Verlag, 2007). Consider also "Contemporary Women's Writing and the Return of Feminism in Germany," ed. Hester Baer, special issue, *Studies in Twentieth and Twenty-First Century Literature* 35, no. 1 (Winter 2011); Hester Baer, "German Feminism in the Age of Neoliberalism: Jana Hensel and Elisabeth Raether's *Neue deutsche Mädchen*," *German Studies Review* 35, no. 2 (2012): 355–74; Mirja Stöcker, ed., *Das F-Wort: Feminismus ist sexy* (Königstein: Helmer, 2007); Meredith Haaf, Susanne Klingner, and Barbara Streidl, *Wir Alphamädchen: Warum Feminismus das Leben schöner macht* (Hamburg: Hoffmann & Campe, 2008); and Jana Hensel and Elisabeth Raether, *Neue deutsche Mädchen* (Reinbek bei Hamburg: Rowohlt, 2008).

[2] This absence is particularly surprising since race and ethnicity are fundamental both in third-wave feminism in the United States, which has significantly influenced German popfeminism, and in discussions of intersectionality in German academic feminism, with which popfeminism has a tense relationship. For more on the latter see Baer, "German Feminism," 356. An important exception to this absence is the work of scholars Beverly Weber and Karen Yeşilada, who have analyzed the intersections of sexuality, race, and ethnicity in their scholarship. Texts by Weber include "Freedom from Violence, Freedom to Make the World: Muslim Women's Memoirs, Gendered Violence, and Voices for Change in Germany," *Women in German Yearbook* 25 (2009): 199–222; *Violence and Gender in the "New" Europe: Islam in German Culture* (New York: Palgrave Macmillan, 2013); "Work, Sex, and Socialism: Reading beyond Cultural Hybridity in Emine Sevgi Özdamar's *Die Brücke vom Goldenen Horn*," *German Life and Letters* 63, no. 1 (January 2010): 37–53. Works by Yeşilada include "Die geschundene Suleika: Das Eigenbild der Türkin in der deutschsprachigen Literatur türkischer Autorinnen," in *Interkulturelle Konfigurationen: Zur deutschsprachigen Erzählliteratur von Autoren nicht-deutscher Herkunft*, ed. Mary Howard (Munich: Iudicum, 1997), 95–114; "'Getürkt' oder nur 'anders'? Das Türkenbild in der türkisch-deutschen Satire," in *The Image of the Turk in Europe from the Declaration of the Republic in 1923 to the 1990s*, ed. Nedret Kuran Borçoğlu (Istanbul: Isis, 2000), 205–20; "'Nette Türkinnen von nebenan'—Die neue deutsch-türkische Harmlosigkeit als literarischer Trend," in *Von der nationalen zur internationalen*

Literatur: Transkulturelle deutschsprachige Literatur und Kultur im Zeitalter globaler Migration, ed. Helmut Schmitz (Amsterdam: Rodopi, 2009), 117–42.

[3] Hatice Akyün, *Einmal Hans mit scharfer Soße: Leben in zwei Welten*, 2nd ed. (Munich: Wilhelm Goldman Verlag, 2007), and *Ali zum Dessert: Leben in einer neuen Welt* (Munich: Wilhelm Goldman Verlag, 2008). Further references to these works are given in the text using the abbreviations *H* and *A* respectively. All translations are my own. Akyün's third book titled *Ich küss dich, Kismet: Eine Deutsche am Bosporus* [I Kiss You, Kismet: A German Woman at the Bosporus] (Cologne: Kiepenheuer & Witsch, 2013) was published in fall 2013, too late to be included in this essay.

[4] See Iris Alanyali, *Die blaue Reise* (Reinbek bei Hamburg: Rowohlt, 2006); Dilek Güngör, *Unter uns* (Berlin: Ebersbach, 2004); Güngör, *Ganz schön deutsch* (Munich: Piper Verlag, 2007); and Hilal Sezgin, *Typisch Türkin?* (Freiburg: Herder, 2006).

[5] Sezgin's *Typisch Türkin?* recalls Feridun Zaimoglu's *Koppstoff*. Feridun Zaimoglu, *Kanak Sprak/Koppstoff: Die gesammelten Mißtöne vom Rande der Gesellschaft* (Cologne: Kiepenheuer & Witsch, 2011). For more on Zaimoglu see Maria Stehle, *Ghetto Voices in Contemporary German Culture: Textscapes, Filmscapes, Soundscapes* (Rochester: Camden House, 2012), 20–63. For more on Sezgin see Weber, *Violence and Gender*, 161–65.

[6] Weber, *Violence and Gender*, 155. Weber analyzes only Akyün's first book but some of her observations, for example, about professional Turkish-German women, also apply to the sequel.

[7] For more on the perceived absence of women among Turkish guest workers see Mark Terkessidis, *Migranten* (Hamburg: Rotbuch Verlag, 2000), 21; and Christine Huth-Hildebrandt, *Das Bild von der Migrantin: Auf den Spuren eines Konstrukts* (Frankfurt am Main: Brandes & Apsel, 2002).

[8] For more on the concept of "touching tales" see Leslie Adelson, *The Turkish Turn in Contemporary German Literature: Toward a New Critical Grammar of Migration* (New York: Palgrave Macmillan, 2005), 20.

[9] Yeşilada, "'Nette Türkinnen,'" 118. Although Yeşilada makes this observation only in connection to Akyün's first book, it also holds true for the second. For more on "Suleikalism" see Yeşilada's "Die geschundene Suleika."

[10] Weber, *Violence and Gender*, 137–72, particularly 168. Other victim narratives include Serap Çileli, *Wir sind eure Töchter nicht eure Ehre* (Munich: Blanvalet, 2006); Hülya Kalkan, *Ich wollte nur frei sein: Meine Flucht vor der Zwangsehe* (Berlin: Ullstein Taschenbuchverlag, 2006); Ayşe [pseud.], *Mich hat keiner gefragt: Zur Ehe gezwungen—eine Türkin in Deutschland erzählt* (Munich: Blanvalet, 2007); Inci Y. [pseud.], *Erstickt an euren Lügen: Eine Türkin erzählt* (Munich: Piper Verlag, 2005). For more on these texts, see Lindsay Lawton's chapter in this volume.

[11] A similar idea has been suggested by Mushaben, who argues that East Germans have adjusted more thoroughly to the late-capitalist consumer society than West Germans and that they will surge ahead in the neoliberal economic order. Mushaben predicts this economic edge for minorities as well, although parenthetically. Joyce Marie Mushaben, "*Be Careful What You Pray For*: Employment Profiles among East and West Germans," *German Studies Review* 33, no. 3 (2010): 574.

[12] *Einmal Hans* has been made into a film directed by Buket Alakuş and released in 2014. This transformation from book to screen follows the trajectory of several American and British chick lit novels and thus emphasizes the book's proximity to chick lit. For more on this trajectory, see Suzanne Ferriss and Mallory Young, *Chick Lit: The New Woman's Fiction* (New York: Routledge, 2006).

[13] In "Nette Türkinnen" Yeşilada foregoes analyzing this combination by repeatedly categorizing Akyün's first book as a novel (129, 132, 133), without providing a critical explanation. Intriguingly, Weber, too, delivers a confusing genre characterization: in *Violence and Gender* she wavers between viewing Akyün's work as a pop autobiography (140), an example of Turkish German women's pop lit (151), and an example of Yeşilada's chick lit alla turca (151), and she incorrectly refers to Akyün as a novelist (143). The confusion arises from the fact that Weber neither explains the relationship between her various labels nor analyzes the pop elements that could clarify how she employs the term pop autobiography.

[14] Yeşilada, "'Nette Türkinnen,'" 132.

[15] Akyün's popfeminist view on high heels is similar to that presented in the famed American television series *Sex and the City*, to which she makes direct reference in *Einmal Hans mit scharfer Soße* (99, 101).

[16] Yeşilada, "'Nette Türkinnen,'" 132.

[17] For more on this criticism see Li Gerhalter, "Wie Angora: Körperbehaarung ist out—und krause Politik," in *Hot Topic: Popfeminismus heute*, ed Sonja Eismann, 90–99; and the section on "Die Schönheitslüge" in Haaf, Klingner, and Streidl, *Wir Alphamädchen*, 53.

[18] Akyün's refusal to shave differs substantially from the elaborate shaving practices described in Charlotte Roche's novel *Feuchtgebiete* (2008; published in English as *Wetlands*, 2009). For more on Roche, see Carrie Smith-Prei, "'Knaller Sex für alle': Popfeminist Body Politics in Lady Bitch Ray, Charlotte Roche, and Sarah Kuttner," in Baer,"Contemporary Women's Writing and the Return of Feminism in Germany," 27–30. See also the article by Smith-Prei and Maria Stehle in this volume.

[19] See for example Akyün, *Einmal Hans*, 8, 82–83, 93–94.

[20] For more on the works of Dikmen and Engin see Yeşilada, "'Getürkt' oder nur 'anders'?," 205–20.

[21] Yeşilada suggests that Akyün's search for a German partner with Turkish attributes is a subversive reaction to the Turkish reethnicization of the 1990s that occurred through import brides and grooms and was sparked by German xenophobic attacks. Yeşilada, "'Nette Türkinnnen,'" 135.

[22] For more on the "Türkenwiese" see Klaus Hartung, "Let the Berliners Barbecue in Peace!" in *Germany in Transit: Nation and Migration, 1955–2005*, ed. Deniz Göktürk, David Gramling, and Anton Kaes (Berkeley: University of California Press, 2007), 445–46.

[23] For an analysis of the presumed Turkish lack of interest in integration see Terkessidis, *Migranten*, 30–37.

[24] The understanding that Turkish Germans maneuver within the global order with ease is also present in Sezgin, *Typisch Türkin?*, 136–37.

[25] Interestingly, while Yeşilada points to Akyün's critique of sexism, Weber acknowledges only Akyün's criticism of racism, and thus both analyses remain incomplete.

[26] Haaf's project is another popfeminist work that exposes the sexism embedded in the German language. See Haaf, Klingner, and Streidl, *Wir Alphamädchen*, 137–48.

[27] In her discussion of violence in Akyün's book, Weber disregards the two important examples of Akyün literally fighting against the ethnic discrimination she encounters in school and against her brother's sexism. By not considering these examples Weber ignores Akyün's insistence on asserting herself against the sexism and racism of German and Turkish society. See Weber, *Violence and Gender*, 152–55.

[28] See Helma Lutz, Maria Teresa Vivar, and Linda Supik, *Fokus Intersektionalität: Bewegungen und Verortungen eines vielschichtigen Konzepts* (Wiesbaden: VS Verlag, 2010), 19.

[29] Katherine Pratt Ewing, *Stolen Honor: Stigmatizing Muslim Men in Berlin* (Stanford, CA: Stanford University Press, 2008), 162.

[30] Peter Schneider, "The New Berlin Wall," *New York Times*, 4 December 2005. Necla Kelek, *Die fremde Braut: Ein Bericht aus dem Inneren des türkischen Lebens in Deutschland* (Cologne: Kiepenheuer & Witsch, 2005), 270–71. See also Yasemin Yildiz, "Governing European Subjects: Tolerance and Guilt in the Discourse of 'Muslim Women,'" *Cultural Critique* 77 (Winter 2011): 70–101.

[31] Terkessidis, *Migranten*, 16–29, 30–37.

[32] See Karen Schönwälder and Triadafilos Triadafilopoulos, "A Bridge or Barrier to Incorporation? Germany's 1999 Citizenship Reform in Critical Perspective," *German Politics and Society* 30, no. 1 (Spring 2012): 57–58.

[33] A similarly negative view of Bulgaria is presented in Alanyali's account, whereas there Yugoslavia is described in more positive terms. See Alanyali, *Die blaue Reise*, 200.

[34] See Adelson, *The Turkish Turn*, 20–22.

[35] For more on life in communist Bulgaria see R. J. Crampton, *A Concise History of Bulgaria*, 2nd edition (Cambridge: Cambridge University Press, 2006), 193–211. For more on Yugoslavia during the Cold War see Patrick Hyder Patterson, *Bought and Sold: Living and Losing the Good Life in Socialist Yugoslavia* (Ithaca, NY: Cornell University Press, 2011), 294–319.

[36] For further criticism of Kelek and Ateş see Weber, *Gender and Violence*, 137–51, and Weber, "Freedom from Violence," 207–10. For a critical approach to Kelek see also Yildiz, "Turkish Girls, Allah's Daughters, and the Contemporary German Subject: Itinerary of a Figure," *German Life and Letters* 62, no. 4 (October 2009): 477–81. See also Tom Cheesman, *Novels of Turkish German Settlement: Cosmopolite Fictions* (Rochester, NY: Camden House, 2007), especially 112–17.

[37] Ferriss and Young, *Chick Lit*, 4.

[38] For more on Duve's black humor see Brenda Bethman, "Generation Chick: Reading *Bridget Jones's Diary*, *Jessica, 30.*, and *Dies ist kein Liebeslied* as

Postfeminist Novels," in Baer, "Contemporary Women's Writing and the Return of Feminism in Germany," 146.

[39] For more on motherhood in contemporary German literature see Alexandra Merley Hill, "Motherhood as Performance: (Re)Negotiations of Motherhood in Contemporary German Literature," in Baer, "Contemporary Women's Writing and the Return of Feminism in Germany," 74–94.

[40] This theme also appears in Sinasi Dikman, "Wohnungssuche," in *Hurra, ich lebe in Deutschland* (Munich: Piper Verlag, 1995), 68–74.

[41] For a critical reconsideration of the role of female Turkish guest workers in the FRG see Weber, "Work, Sex, and Socialism," 37–53.

[42] See Haaf, Klingner, and Streidl, *Wir Alphamädchen*, 153–78.

7: The Awkward Politics of Popfeminist Literary Events: Helene Hegemann, Charlotte Roche, and Lady Bitch Ray

Carrie Smith-Prei and Maria Stehle

Since the mid-2000s there has been a marked uptick across the Western world of discussions surrounding the validity and effectiveness of feminism today.[1] Terms such as "postfeminism" or "lifestyle feminism" are increasingly used to characterize a popular interest in making feminism palatable through depoliticization, even as political actions are publicly evaluated as successes or failures on the basis of criteria more appropriate for their second-wave forebears. These discussions either brand feminist cultural production as successful activism against a sexist, mainstream, and consumerist culture, or condemn it as mere media sensation that points to the failure or ineffectuality of feminism today. This production of unclear political meaning speaks to the current situation of contemporary feminisms in both popular and academic discourse.

The label of women's writing used in this volume is particularly illustrative of the pitfalls of such desire for clear evaluation, for it suggests that a neat categorization along easily delineated gender lines corresponds productively with literary work geared toward consumption by a specific, self-identified female audience. The term "Popfeminismus" (popfeminism), which emerged in Germany alongside these other terms to reference a feminism entangled in popular culture, offers one way of undoing the categorical delineation. Popfeminism uses feminism to draw from, disturb, and rewrite popular culture, but also uses popular culture to draw from, disturb, and rewrite feminism. The circular result contains an inherent awkwardness that we suggest is politically legible.[2]

In this essay, we explore how that awkwardness is a useful concept for the production, consumption, and analysis of a branch of contemporary "women's writing" that understands itself or is received as both feminist and popular, because it offers a way out of the failure/success binary. In so doing, it problematizes the existence of the category of women's writing altogether, even while it confirms that in feminist literature, beginning a discussion with a notion of women's writing is potentially necessary. Awkwardness embraces the ambivalence of effectiveness in feminist creative work today that refuses clear meaning-making by nevertheless showing how its own position is intentionally (if ambivalently) political.

We use a popfeminist methodology to propose awkwardness as a theoretical tool for political interpretation. The term popfeminism here has a threefold function: first, as a way to situate ourselves within a political discourse that is popularized; second, as a term that describes the literary events we are analyzing, which have been consumed en masse, produced in tandem with popular response, and/or clearly integrate the popular into their conception; and third, as a perspective that we as researchers take, that is, one that captures our own personal investment in approaching creative work that emerges out of or engages with popular culture. Awkwardness, in turn, has formed what we are calling a *Suchbegriff*, a search term that allows us to mine for the political in popfeminist creative work. As a search term, it is always on the move within or in between texts, sometimes within the content, sometimes in the narrative or poetic collision of media or material, sometimes at the level of reception or theorization, sometimes inherent to the author's or reader's body, and always retreating from view. Awkwardness draws attention to normative representations of sexuality, gender, and race, and to the power of prescriptive regimes of representation, while also representing the collapse of standard discursive frameworks that might easily describe these representations. As such, we suggest that theorizing the awkward can get at the complicated meanings and unstable positions of the political in popfeminist literary work.

Throughout the following, we engage in a broader discussion of both popfeminism as a methodology and awkwardness as a political tool, into which we embed an examination of three non-discrete ways in which awkwardness is produced in feminist literary texts and events. We discuss Helene Hegemann's *Axolotl Roadkill* (2010) and the unwieldy material form of the text itself; the challenges made to the reader's preconceptions or emotions in Charlotte Roche's *Feuchtgebiete* (2008; published in English as *Wetlands*, 2009) and *Schoßgebete* (2011; published in English as *Wrecked*, 2013); and Lady Bitch Ray's *Bitchsm* (2012) and the text's author-driven interaction with external factors.

By examining the production of awkwardness in texts of three publicly contested writers, we develop a basis for larger political considerations. These authors are all located at the intersection of commercial success, ideological agendas, and digital proliferation in and for the twenty-first century, and they are equally subject to the fickle ebb and flow of popular interest. Furthermore, we describe these textual moments as literary events because Hegemann, Roche, and Ray are not merely literary authors but also creative entrepreneurs. In all three cases, the literary is but one aspect of their popfeminist political intervention. The literary text itself, therefore, has an unstable and awkward position within the creative, political work of our objects of study as (self-)deconstructive, fleeting, and irreverent.

Popfeminist Methods

Awkwardness in popfeminist literary events evokes feminist traditions of creative work, but it also points to their failures—including the failure to create the desired effects—in today's contexts. As Sonja Eismann outlines in her introduction to *Hot Topic*, popfeminism provides a feminist approach to pop culture, but it also critiques and redefines both feminism and pop culture: "Popkultur [sollte] duch feministische Strategien perforiert und erschüttert werden" (pop culture [should] be perforated and rocked by feminist strategies).[3] Eismann's attempt to reclaim feminism for a new generation is both a reaction against the popular understanding of feminism as second-wave feminism, which in German popular opinion was often rather narrowly understood as represented by Alice Schwarzer,[4] and a reinsertion of the radical voice missing from post- and lifestyle feminism.[5] In Eismann's summation, feminism is not an abstract concept but instead a politics penetrating all realms of life as "gelebte Alltagskultur" (lived everyday culture).[6] But while popfeminism is a playful politics of personal and individual experience taken to a theoretical level, it is constantly in danger of becoming an object of consumption, for it uses pop culture on a global scale to look for local spaces of change and resistance. For this reason, popfeminism is subject to the manner in which both feminist politics and pop culture are reliant upon globalized economic mechanisms, even as these are radically rewritten, manipulated, or clashing in popfeminist works.

Using a popfeminist methodology means exploiting the awkwardness of the material as we search for a politically productive feminist perspective that does not rely on clear definitions and representations of meaning. Lauren Berlant offers us a way of defining this ambivalent position as political. In *Cruel Optimism* she writes of the optimism produced by the neoliberal promise of the so-called good life as follows:

> [Optimism] is cruel when the object/scene that ignites a sense of possibility actually makes it impossible to attain the expansive transformation for which a person or a people risks striving; and doubly, it is cruel insofar as the very pleasures of being inside a relation have become sustaining regardless of the content of the relation, such that a person or a world finds itself bound to a situation of profound threat that is, at the same time, profoundly confirming.[7]

Cruel optimism, therefore, is the continued belief that success is on the horizon if only this object is attained or that scene experienced, the object or scene being precisely that which stands in the way of attaining the promised success. The object/scene of cruel optimism can be love, the desire for the good life, or the wish for the political. If we consider the two parts of the neologism, popfeminism works very clearly within the cruel-optimistic framework. Feminism creates a relation, or in Berlant's words "an attachment," to such objects/scenes as liberation from gender-based oppression, freedom (of expression), choice of sexuality, or economic equality, all of which cruelly promise clarity of meaning (goals, intent) and productivity (success, failure).[8] Conversely, pop culture creates an attachment based on economically driven consumerism, which cruelly promises global belonging and status through mass participation. The attachment in each case lasts only because the promises have not (yet) been fulfilled.

Popfeminist texts and literary events are found (or consciously place themselves) in the middle of such relations that uphold cruel optimism; however, they also engage with and exploit the assumptions that underlie these relations. To begin with, feminist causes remain at the center of their narratives, but emotional attachments are mainly formed via critical negativity to those causes. Furthermore, the texts and events (and their authors) act as objects of popular consumption, but negative emotions and critical negativity vis-à-vis these objects emerge as the primary points of the performance. Therefore we claim that popfeminism makes visible cruel optimism, because it openly uses feminist and neoliberal attachments while positioning itself negatively against them. As such, popfeminism refuses to accept conventional understandings of success or failure as key to the feminist project, nor is it evaluative in its consumption or coding of neoliberal pop. Awkwardness emerges in the circularity, and it is here that we read the complicated and messy positions of the political.

Standard theoretical approaches to popfeminist creative work, including literary events, cannot properly capture, explain, or engage with these circularities. Each approach ends with the unfulfilled promise of clear meaning or evaluation. Our perspective in the following discussion of awkwardness and literary events accounts for this problem by mimicking the popfeminist position, which is squarely in the middle of a complicated engagement with the cruel optimisms of feminist politics. This means that in our readings and analysis we harness the shifting perspectives (among objects and media, writers, and publics) and embrace the cruelty in the pop coding of feminism and the feminist coding of pop.

First Literary Event: The Aesthetic Production of Awkwardness—*Axolotl Roadkill*

Axolotl Roadkill by Helene Hegemann demonstrates what the collapse of standard theoretical frameworks looks like in literary-aesthetic practice.

When the novel hit German bookstores in late January 2010, it was praised by journalists in regional and national newspapers, in magazines, and in a variety of literary blogs as the great coming-of-age novel on a par with *The Catcher in the Rye*, applicable to an entire disillusioned generation of "millennials,"[9] not the least because its author, who had already written a short story and a play and directed a film, was then only seventeen years of age. The hype was exacerbated and complicated on February 5 of that same year, when Hegemann was revealed to have plagiarized content from a selection of pop-cultural and digital sources. Despite the final tally of a "mere" one plagiarized page out of the novel's more than two hundred pages, confirmed by an extensive source list provided by the author and publishing house in a second printing run, the scandal raged on well into the spring, fueled by the author's and the novel's participation in and disturbance of the literary establishment, including a clear questioning of the publishing industry and masculine critical tradition.[10]

The implications of the firestorm of debate for the literary establishment come jarringly together with the novel's aesthetic quality. The novel follows Mifti, a girl of sixteen—self-described as a victim of affluent neglect—who lives with her two elder half-siblings in well-to-do squalor in an apartment in Berlin, their leftist artist-father residing with his girlfriend in a separate apartment nearby. The novel is without plot, narrative arc, or clear direction, and instead can be described as a loose collection of vignettes made up of Mifti's drug use, the Berlin club and party scene, demeaning and often violent sexual encounters, emotional confusion and pain, familial dysfunctionality, and snide attacks lobbed at the thirty-something cultural, artistic, and intellectual scene that makes up Berlin Mitte, Friedrichshain, and Prenzlauer Berg. Aesthetically, the novel is awkward; both narrative voice and poetic form occupy a threshold in between text forms and media varieties, a threshold that also describes the position of the adolescent. This same quality becomes charged in a feminist-political sense when the implication is taken into account that the narrator, and by extension the author, is an emotionally distressed and sexually empowered no-longer-child and not-yet-adult. The narrative-poetic awkwardness emanating from the novel consistently disturbs any clear-cut reading of abuse, misguidance, or naiveté on the part of the author, thereby questioning the motives of the literary establishment in the scandal.

The novel is written in angular, bristly, and provocatively unwieldy language, the building blocks of which reference, cite, and intersect with a variety of textual styles and media. The terms intertextuality and intermediality both offer potential interpretative frameworks for understanding this aesthetic construction; however, neither suffices on its own: while intertextuality is interested in the communication of symbolic meaning as text references collide,[11] intermediality takes into account the materiality of that collision.[12] In *Axolotl Roadkill* the symbolic and material interactions are at odds. The novel's language is created from a mixture of symbolic text and material media forms, ranging from invented compound words, emails, text messages, letters, dialogues, and found prose, which in turn might include television taglines (such as Pro7's "We love to entertain you"), song titles and lyrics (including riot grrrl band L7's "You've made my shitlist" or lyrics by Leonard Cohen), as well as media sound bites (from Franz Beckenbauer, for example).[13] Aside from suggesting that reading is a form of pop-cultural consumption, such text and media sources have no internal relationship to the novel. The disconnect between the symbolic and material level of the novel's language resonates also in its construction of adolescent narrative subjectivity: Mifti's descriptions veer off course, her prose is interrupted, and her communication with other figures is often stilted and broken. In her discussion of intertextuality, Julia Kristeva identifies a threshold that is crossed when texts and subjectivities interact within a narrative. This threshold, Kristeva notes (in keeping with Hannah Arendt), is an "in-between zone" that creates a "social melting pot, a political openness and most of all a mental plasticity."[14] The threshold is essential to understanding the disconnections and their effects in *Axolotl Roadkill*. The novel produces seams and cracks over which the reader trips. The "inter" here is not a unifying concept but instead a divisive one.[15]

This threshold, or "inter," also describes the adolescent, who is standing at the developmental precipice that is adulthood, and mobilizes this position accordingly, for the narrator of *Axolotl Roadkill* is very aware of her self-positioning at this threshold as culturally constructed. For example, she describes adulthood as buying sofa covers, understanding Foucault, and "mich zu Tode schämen für alles, was ich hier . . . in diesen Computer reinhacke" (being ashamed to death of everything I . . . bang into this computer here).[16] If adolescence is a state of "being or becoming," as well as a time of heightened sexuality, rebellion, volatility, and freedom from norms, then here that state also includes cultural production—including textual self-creation—even as this is playfully and self-referentially disregarded.[17] Adolescence, as the so-called awkward age, thus has a direct impact on the text's narrative poetics; in its language, the text, like its narrator, is awkward, struggling for its unique voice: "Mir wurde eine Sprache einverleibt, die nicht meine eigene ist" (I was given a language that is not my own).[18]

The political implications of this awkwardness become clear when we turn to the cultural meaning of adolescence. Carsten Gansel reminds us that because the physical and emotional signs of adolescence occur as a process contained within culture, it is important to interpret the relationship between adolescence and culture.[19] Mifti seems cognizant of this fact. Her self-introduction to the readers proceeds as follows:

1. Ich habe meine von Analsex, Tränen und Leichenschändung geprägte Patchworkgeschichte verloren.
2. Ich habe eine offene Entzündung im Rachen.
3. Meine Familie ist ein Haufen von in irgendeiner frühkindlichen Allmachtsphase steckengebliebenen Personen mit Selbstdarstellungssucht. Im äußersten Fall wird von deren Seite aus mal ein popkultureller Text über die Frage verfasst, weshalb die Avantgarde TROTZDEM bauchtanzt, aber das war's auch schon.[20]

[1. I have lost my patchwork history that was written by anal sex, tears, and corpse defilement.
2. I have an open sore in my throat.
3. My family is a heap of random people with an addiction to self-performance stuck in omnipotent fantasies of early childhood. In the extreme case, they might write a pop-cultural text on the question as to why the avant-garde NEVERTHELESS belly dances, but that's about it.]

These disjointed statements display the narrative voice's self-positioning at a threshold that is located between childhood and adulthood, is rebelliously textual, and is wrought with cultural expectations surrounding childhood. The narrator says early in the text: "Ich weiß komischerweise genau, was ich will: nicht erwachsen werden" (17; Oddly, I know exactly what I want: not to grow up). This positioning of the no-longer-child and not-yet-adult at a desired-for eternal threshold references the neotenic salamander, the axolotl, in the novel's title. That the "Roadkill" of the title appears toward the end of the book with reference to Mifti's writing style ("'You write like a roadkill,'" 190; English in original), further cements female adolescent development within the textual aesthetics.

The childish yet self-aware voice collides in the novel with sexual precociousness, which ranges from anal-sex to same-sex desire. This removal of supposed innocence is where the awkwardness takes on political implications. In the introduction to *Curiouser*, editors Steven Bruhm and Natasha Hurley write of the dominant cultural narrative that children are innocent of sexual desire: "People panic when that sexuality takes on a life outside the sanctioned scripts of child's play." That panic is felt acutely with the queer child, who conforms to neither asexuality nor the "blissful promises of adult heteronormativity."[21] Kathryn Bond Stockton, in *The Queer Child*, makes a claim that all children are queer children, for they are foreign and strange to adults, and their assumed "innocence is queerer than we ever thought it could be."[22] When we examine where the child has grown sideways, as Stockton calls it, away from the narratives of innocence and asexuality but not up toward adulthood, then we see the political implications of our "cultural ideals" (13). Mifti's refusal to grow up is not classically childish, à la Peter Pan, as our cultural ideals would have it. She has grown sideways; Mifti is not innocent, is decidedly sexual, and is also enormously and depressively exhausted. The text thus presents readers with their own cruelly optimistic stance toward societal expectations for girls, a stance that also counters lifestyle feminism's positive coding of empowerment. Further, it uncovers the cruel optimism in the literary establishment's titillated desire to participate in the plagiarism scandal: the condemnation from older authors and the outrage of literary critics spoke as much to the desire to consume the event as it did to their potentially outmoded understanding of publishing in the digital age. That much of this condemnation and outrage was couched in sexualized, gendered, and age-driven terms in the national newspapers returns that consumption circuitously back to the author/narrator herself.[23] The awkwardness associated with adolescence becomes a political aesthetic in both the text and its reception.

Awkward Political Emotions

As seen in this reading, although the production of awkwardness can occur within the text, it also resonates outward to the reader. The reader's experience of the raw and uncomfortable aesthetics of *Axolotl Roadkill* equals in emotional tenor the distress and depression experienced by the narrator. This means that awkwardness has an emotional dimension. Further, emotions indicate that politics are at work. In the multiauthored introduction to the edited volume *Political Emotions*, Janet Staiger claims that "perhaps we truly encounter the political only when we *feel*,"[24] which implies that politics, perhaps defined here in a rather narrow sense as relating to social relationships, authority, and power, are always affective. Further, as Ann Cvetkovich states in that same introduction, the close connection between gender and emotion has long been a concern for feminists,[25] and the often-stated affective turn is not new to feminist thought since, as a main slogan of second-wave feminism, the private or emotional sphere was thought of as political. What the affective turn stands for in Cvetkovich's view, however, is the call to "perform ideology critique in new ways" or to "do the work of critique differently," which could mean that one formulates "new ways of thinking the relations between the emotional, the cultural, and the political for those who are tired of reading cultural objects in order to decide if they (or the emotions they produce) are good or bad for politics" (6).

Similarly, popfeminist creative work, including literary events, can and should not be evaluated on the basis of whether they "work" or "don't work" according to a certain political perspective, since the work or event itself might aim to question this particular kind of cruel optimism; rather, the question should be *how* they work. This means that awkwardness is not just a question of descriptive form, affect, or viscerality. The provocative potential of popfeminist literary events is located in their production of awkwardness as a process. Popfeminist awkwardness emerges from a position between commercialism and a critical stance against it; between political appropriation and the attempt to undermine such an appropriation. Awkwardness is a self-deconstructive, self-reflexive tool, as well as a tool for attacking social norms and categories.

In this context we follow the lead of Sianne Ngai, who investigates the "politically ambiguous work" of an "aesthetics of negative emotions."[26] The uncomfortable emotional dimension of awkwardness produces the political ambiguities in popfeminist activism. Such negative affect, as J. Halberstam writes in *The Queer Art of Failure*, "provides the opportunity . . . to poke holes in the toxic positivity of contemporary life."[27] Awkwardness is a negative affect that helps us to see how popfeminism pokes holes in what could be read as a form of toxic positivity—or the cruel optimisms—of an individualized, hedonistic, and privileged lifestyle feminism and an apolitical postfeminism.

Second Literary Event: The Awkwardness of the Audience—*Feuchtgebiete* and *Schoßgebete*

Discussions about whether Charlotte Roche's novels *Feuchtgebiete* and *Schoßgebete*[28] can be considered feminist texts abound; the fact that Roche's literary events in many ways *are* this question often leads to a rather circular discussion. To approach Roche's texts as awkward literary events allows us to discuss not if but how they engage in feminist politics and to read the texts as a new form of feminist critique. In their awkwardness they "poke holes" into "toxic positivity" and position themselves clearly against feminism's cruel optimisms. Like *Axolotl Roadkill*, both of Roche's novels are first-person narratives told from the perspective of emotionally disturbed women who try to come to terms with their familial past, their sexuality, and various physical ailments, but unlike Hegemann's novel, they do so within conventional aesthetic and formal structures. Thus, in contrast to Hegemann's aesthetic awkwardness, any clear discursive framing of Roche's literary texts collapses when uncomfortable encounters at the level of plot collide with expectations, both those produced by the texts and those brought to the text by the reading public, in the process of reception. In their popfeminist political interventions, they expand the category of the literary to include the broader context of media reception and circulation.

The texts create plot-based tensions by combining disturbing psychological experiences with embarrassing or disgusting physical conditions, like an anal fissure in the case of *Feuchtgebiete* or intestinal worms in the case of *Schoßgebete*. These emotional and physical disturbances are narratively intertwined with explicit (and in some cases raunchy or pornographic) descriptions of sexual encounters and sexual fantasies. While these tensions in and of themselves might produce uncomfortable feelings in the reader, the fact that both texts directly address, and thus create expectations around, traditional feminist questions surrounding physical norms, motherhood, sexual liberation, and sexual self-realization politicizes this awkwardness. Added to this is the receptive awkwardness: *Feuchtgebiete*, which became a bestseller within a month of publication, was understood as a phenomenon—a true event—leaving the reception process to produce a broad variety of conflicting emotional responses ranging from disgust to celebration; *Schoßgebete*, on the other hand, was received solely in standard literary-critical terms. In both cases, the reception finds itself rubbing up against the texts' intended politics: *Feuchtgebiete* engages the audience's emotions by inciting, for example, feelings of disgust, arousal, or amusement, but it fails the reader on all these emotional accounts by explaining away the experience and thereby questioning the legitimacy of the emotional responses it triggers; while received literarily, *Schoßgebete* is in parts a self-deconstructive failure of a self-help book, and thus builds an inherently unstable relationship to its subject and audience.

Feuchtgebiete tells the story of eighteen-year-old Helen Memel as she lies in her hospital bed, where she is recovering from surgery necessitated by an anal fissure. The story is told entirely from Helen's perspective as she obsesses over her body, remembers sexual adventures, and plots ways to subvert hygienic conventions or bring her divorced parents back together. In the media, the novel was discussed mainly for its subversive approach to female hygiene and Helen's experimentation with bodily fluids and smells. Praised by some as a new feminist manifesto and critiqued by others as pornographic trash, the text triggered strong reactions across Germany. Roche's readings of *Feuchtgebiete* were extremely popular, especially among young, educated women; almost every major newspaper published reports about the novel or Roche's readings, or printed interviews with Roche; she was one of the most popular talk-show guests on almost every show on German television that year.[29] In the process of this production of awkward moments in media reception, a rather strange emotional relationship forms among text, author, and readers' bodies. Sentences like the very first of the novel, "Solange ich denken kann, habe ich Hämorrhoiden" (as long as I can remember, I have had hemorrhoids), phrases like "zurück zum Arschrasieren" (back to ass shaving), or hygienic strategies such as the use of vaginal fluid as perfume[30] trigger confused reactions in readers. These range from amusement to sexual tension to embarrassment, because of their blunt, matter-of-fact, or dirty flirtatious tone; such reactions may lead readers to understand the text alternatingly as amusingly politically subversive, obsessive, or even disgustingly psychologically disturbed.

Such a reception puts readers and audience members, together with the author and her character, into the confused but nonetheless political position of the self-challenging, questioning feminist. At times it appears as if Helen's actions and thoughts are subversive and political—she explores her sexuality, expresses her desires and needs, and rebels against conventional notions of female body image or appropriate female behavior—but then she reverts to the position of a hurt, insecure, and psychologically disturbed young woman. Further, *Feuchtgebiete* plays with the neoliberal notion of individual self-realization absorbed by mainstream and lifestyle feminisms, by showing a young woman who exaggeratedly tries to attain self-realization and, for the most part, fails. In that way Roche reveals the optimistic cruelty of such notions and their often pseudo-feminist positions, while at the same time embracing them. For example, when Helen describes her relationship to motherhood by explaining her sexual games with avocado pits, which she calls her "Biodildo" (organic dildo), and then ends this reflection just as her mother enters her hospital room, the text creates a tension by connecting the validation of individual sexual self-exploration to questions of motherhood:

> Dank meiner gut trainierten Scheidenmuskeln kann ich [den Avocadokern] nachher wieder rausschießen lassen.... Näher komme ich an eine Geburt nicht ran.... Ich will wirklich seit ich denken kann, ein Kind haben. Es gibt aber bei uns in der Familie ein immer wiederkehrendes Muster. Meine Urgroßmutter, meine Oma, Mama und ich. Alle Erstgeborene. Alle Mädchen. Alle nervenschwach, gestört und unglücklich. Den Kreislauf habe ich durchbrochen.... habe mich sterilisieren lassen.... Als ich die Augen aufmache, sehe ich Mama über mich gebeugt.[31]

> [Thanks to my well-trained vaginal muscles I can shoot the avocado pit back out.... I can't come closer to a birth.... I've really always wanted a child as long as I can remember. But in my family there's a pattern that keeps repeating. My great-grandmother, my grandmother, Mama, and I. All first born. All girls. All weak-nerved, disturbed, and unhappy. I've broken the cycle.... been sterilized.... When I open my eyes, I see Mama leaning over me.]

In this paragraph Roche combines the tensions inherent to neoliberal forms of feminism—the tension between the sexual power of her masturbation experiments and her self-identification as weak and disturbed, the desire for motherhood and her decision against procreation—with a strange concept of motherhood that is located somewhere between popular readings of Freud and Second Wave feminists' rebellion against their mothers. In such examples of sexual experimentation, but also in psychological explanations, Roche's text functions as a complex commentary: it reaffirms goals of both Second Wave and lifestyle feminisms, but exaggerates and deconstructs these. Roche's strategy is indicative of popfeminist literary events, for she locates these goals squarely within and against the cruel optimism of feminist self-realizations. Although Helen is a rather unreliable voice, the text neither questions nor validates her perspective. *Feuchtgebiete* does not offer a clear position from which to evaluate the text and its voice; on the contrary, the novel and its narrator create an insecure position for readers.

Schoßgebete, Roche's second novel, is told from the perspective of Elizabeth Kiel, a sex-obsessed, psychologically disturbed, and insecure mother. She thinks about sex with her husband Georg, her therapy, her skills as a mother, the intestinal worms with which her family is infected, and her family history, which is marked by the traumatic death of her three brothers in a car crash. More clearly than *Feuchtgebiete*, this text is based on autobiographical experiences,[32] and as a whole, it is not as playful, exaggerated, or excessive as Roche's first novel. Instead, *Schoßgebete* creates the painful realization in the reader that there is a little bit of Elizabeth Kiel in most women. This realization is distressing since the (coping) strategies Elizabeth develops exist only to be deconstructed within the text. While *Schoßgebete* is not as pop, not as funny, and rather differently awkward than *Feuchtgebiete*, a popfeminist perspective on the affective responses that the book produces helps to develop a reading of the text outside the feminist vs. antifeminist binary, which critics again employed.[33]

On a narrative level, *Schoßgebete*, like *Feuchtgebiete*, produces awkwardness by combining explicit and detailed sex scenes, such as the one between Elizabeth and her husband that opens the text, with Elizabeth's often-insecure attempts to be a good mother. For example, after having sex with her husband, she washes herself and decides: "In dieser Stunde koche ich was gesundes" (23; I will cook something healthy during this hour). It further produces awkwardness in its narrative positioning as an advice book, or in Hester Baer's words "a how-to manual,"[34] on how to have good sex with your husband, how to cook healthy food, and how to raise your daughter. As was the case with *Feuchtgebiete*, as a reader one can connect emotionally to Elizabeth's desire for sexual and familial perfection, and is positioned, along with Elizabeth, as searching for such solutions. But the text also fails its readers on this level, since any "solution" that Elizabeth suggests—for successful parenting, satisfying marital sex, effective therapy—fails. Elizabeth, for example, strategizes at great length about how to respond to her daughter's fears, only to compensate for her own inability to deal with her emotional trauma; she prepares for a visit to the brothel to please her husband, and, although she enjoys it, her attempts to satisfy his sexual needs do not seem to address her desire to cheat. The text reveals the abundance of advice on how to do the "right" thing and how to be "successful," be it from feminists, leftists, health or beauty columns, or women's and parenting magazines, as anything but helpful and instead cruelly optimistic. Any given advice, such as that received from Elizabeth's therapist, Frau Drescher, is deconstructed and rendered silly or dysfunctional, only to leave the reader searching for more advice. While there is something liberating about subverting the notion of the self-help book, it is also profoundly unsettling, particularly when that subversion takes place as a replication.

The political intervention of the text lies in the fact that it does not present a position for readers outside this kind of circularity. The only position left for readers leaves them implicated, complicit, or just as confused as the narrator. This is particularly poignant with regard to Elizabeth's relationship to her own body: "Ich will mich im Spiegel angucken können und denken: Mann, sehe ich sexy aus . . . Das will ich. Kein Schönheitswahn, kein Hungern mehr. Ich bin eine kleine sexy, gesunde, richtig gut gebaute Frau. Fuck, ja!" (256; I want to be able to look at myself in the mirror and think: Man, I look sexy . . . That is what I want. No beauty craze, no more starvation. I am a small, sexy, healthy, really well built woman. Fuck, yeah!). Rather than living this empowered relationship to her own body in the narrative, Elizabeth constantly obsesses over her physical appearance. These sentiments are not presented as mutually exclusive, and the text reveals how contradictory and unstable corporeal perceptions are. In such passages the cruel optimism of body politics surfaces and locates *Schoßgebete* squarely within a popfeminist political discourse.

The awkwardness in Roche's literary events originates in the position of the self-directed, self-challenging feminist and emerges in the process of reception as well as in Roche's (multi-)media circulations. She exploits the cruel optimism of feminism mainly by questioning the legitimacy of any emotional responses that her texts might produce; she exploits the cruel optimism of pop by making entirely uncomfortable the object/scene that promises participation in the consumer event (the books themselves but also her readings and media appearances). Popfeminist readers are invited to identify with the painful, physical, and sexual emotions the texts describe; they must ask why they are feeling aroused, disgusted, or amused as they confront the cruelty of the claim that bodies are our own (*Feuchtgebiete*) and that sex can be whatever we as women want (something that manifests itself in both texts, albeit differently). This freedom of sexual and physical expression, or simply the idea that one is in control of one's own body and one's physical and emotional well-being, appears as desirable and impossible—thus awkwardly political.

The Awkward Body Politics of Sex

Awkwardness works against cruel optimisms by embracing them only to playfully deconstruct them. Such awkwardness, as has become apparent in the above discussion, is often produced via the sexual body. The complex position of the body in popfeminism in general and in our case studies in particular, its location between text, material authenticity, and projection screens, is crucial for a political understanding of popfeminist literary texts and their reception. The body is present here as perception, representation, and manipulation: there is no "real" body outside the mediated body, and the mediated body is always also physical. In these texts, bodies become hyper-visible as sites for emotion, be it pain, pleasure, lust, or depression; at the same time, bodies are the main objects for playful deconstruction. Such textual representations of bodies create political emotions in the popfeminist literary events we discuss here.[35]

The political female body in popfeminism is caught in the push and pull of feminism and pop, taking traditionally feminist body concerns—abortion rights, contraception, eating disorders, pornography—to a media-oriented level that includes also traditionally antifeminist approaches such as glossy images of highly stylized, normative, sexy, and even pornographic female bodies. While an understanding of the body as "Rohstoff" (raw matter)—a place of individual formation and play and for individual self-stylization, as some contemporary feminisms would argue[36]—could produce a rather apolitical understanding, awkwardness complicates this notion of the body. Popfeminism recognizes but also manipulates the traditional feminist belief that the body is "sinnstiftend" (makes meaning), and that it is representative of a masculine dominated system.[37] In their popfeminist manifesto *Wir Alphamädchen* (We Alpha-Girls, 2008), which has often been criticized as depoliticized, Haaf, Klinger, and Streidel define body styling as the woman's decision. No longer is it only a response to male-dominated beauty culture: instead, it becomes an expression of individual liberties, which includes also the negative, injured, or otherwise imperfect body (53). In Hegemann's and Roche's texts, such body styling is revealed as a sometimes painful and most definitely negative process that is culturally coded, whether this cultural coding is related to the randy sexual body of the adolescent (as is the case in *Axolotl Roadkill* and to some extent *Feuchtgebiete*[38]) or that of the mother (*Schoßgebete*). Such approaches confirm the continuing entanglement of the personal and the political and break down essentialist ideas of femininity, natural beauty, and sex—including those solidified in earlier forms of feminism. They also question what feminist body politics might mean in the contemporary setting: there is no strategy of writing (about) the body that places the body outside cultural norms.

Popfeminist literary events politicize the body by presenting and embracing sex as awkward. In their depictions of sexualized bodies, they reference both the messy second-wave feminist discourse about pornography and the rather superficial embracing of pleasure and sex in lifestyle feminisms. Further, emphasizing the body as sexual, or to go one step further, depicting the female body as always and only sexual, popfeminist texts mirror the politics of pop culture. They also reduce much of their feminist political intervention to the sexualized body and the emotional politics that surround it. We locate the politics of popfeminism in this tension between pop-representation of sexualized bodies and references to feminist discourses about pornography and pleasure. The text *Bitchsm*, our third literary example, exemplifies this tension. The text further points to a lacuna in German popfeminist discourse: the politics of race.

Third Literary Event: Author-Driven Awkwardness—*Bitchsm*

After struggling to finish the manuscript and searching for a publisher, "Lady Bitch Ray" (aka Dr. phil. Reyhan Şahin) published *Bitchsm* in 2012 with a small publisher, Panini Verlags GmbH, in collaboration with her own publishing company, Vagina Style-VS-Verlag. *Bitchsm* is a playful mixture of a how-to-book and a political manifesto. Not only is it sex-positive in its approach to the female body, but it also suggests that successful female emancipation starts (and ends) with sexual liberation. The subtitle "Emanzipation—Integration—Masturbation"[39] further implies that the text addresses the relationship between sexual liberation and racial discrimination, confirmed by sections of the text that respond directly to media debates in Germany about headscarves in public schools, honor killings, and the failed integration of "foreigners" in general.[40] The book is part women's magazine, part pin-up/soft-porn magazine, part feminist manifesto in a traditional sense, and part essayistic political intervention into the discourses about integration and sexism in Germany. However, we read this text as a literary event, because of the context in which it was published, its multimedia reception, its formal use of intertextual and intermedial elements in an experimental collage, and its very clear development of a narrative-performative voice in the character of Lady Bitch Ray.

Indeed, it is the text's narrative-performative perspective that unifies these potentially disparate elements, for this perspective is consistently hedonistic and centered around female pleasure and lust. As a literary event, *Bitchsm* is a response to and builds upon the media frenzy that developed in 2008 around the provocations of porn-rapper and sex-activist Lady Bitch Ray, whose voice drives the "narrative." She first appeared in public when she launched a lawsuit against her former employer,

Radio Bremen, for firing her on the basis of her online appearances as Lady Bitch Ray in May 2006. She approached the German tabloid paper *Die Bildzeitung* with her story, and because of the scandal-appeal of a highly educated Turkish-German porn-rapper, the paper gladly published her story, with many others following suit. In the following months Ray became a short-lived media phenomenon. She appeared on talk shows and in interviews, published more rap videos online, started her own label, and triggered furious as well as enthusiastic responses in chat forums and in the comments to her videos and other media appearances.

Bitchsm builds on the media phenomenon of the Turkish-German porn-rapper and the media frenzy caused by her aggressive sexuality and her claim to be a new feminist voice. The text begins with a "philosophical definition" and ethics (concerning primarily female solidarity), then it offers "Ficktipps" (fuck tips) and beauty advice. The second half of the book directly addresses questions around cultural politics, racism, sexism in hip hop, family politics, and Turkish identity in Germany. Each chapter is illustrated with a range of photos that are "soft-porn style," as is much of the writing. The photos show the author wearing self-designed lingerie as she demonstrates various sexual practices and exercises to improve self-esteem and sexual pleasure, elements that she also explores in the text. In large part *Bitchsm* is a sex-positive manual for female body styling, and although at times it slips from sex-positivity to sexploitation, this body styling, in contrast to that in *Feuchtgebiete*, does not originate in negation or negativity vis-à-vis the female body, nor does the gross, sick, or painful body appear in the text. Instead, Lady Bitch Ray describes the sexual, sexualized, and sexy female body as a site for and source of power, as is clear from the cover notes: "Für emanzipierte Bitches, deren Muschi nicht genug kriegen kann und andauernd juckt—steht auf, wenn ihr Fotzen seid! Bitchsm 2012, yeah!!" (For emancipated bitches whose pussies can't get enough and always have the itch—stand up if you are a cunt! Bitchsm 2012, yeah!!). At the same time, it turns this emancipation back on itself: the front and back cover show a black and white Rorschach-like smear, the caption reading "Original-Votzenabdruck von Lady Bitch Ray" (original impression of Lady Bitch Ray's cunt); suddenly, the sexual body of the author-narrator is a little too close for comfort.

This closeness is mimicked in the book's approach to its audience. The introduction, for example, veritably screams the following directly at its readership:

> Liebe Hunde und Hündinnen, genießt dieses mutterfickende Werk! Bitchsm for Bitches, Bitchsm for Live [sic], Biaaaaaach!!! Ihr könnt es nicht mehr ignorieren. Endlich kann ich Bitchsm veröffentlichen und kein Schwanz redet mir dazwischen. Geschrieben von Mushido—der buschigen Muschi von Lady Bitch Ray. (17)

[Dear dogs and bitches, enjoy this motherfucking work! Bitchsm for bitches, bitchsm for live [sic], biaaaaaach!!! You can't ignore it any more. Finally I can publish bitchsm and no dick can interrupt me. Written by Mushido—Lady Bitch Ray's bushy pussy.]

Lady Bitch Ray's provocative and playful use of antifemale aggressive language recoded as empowerment also becomes self-referential through her amalgamation of the name of controversial German rapper Bushido with "muschi" or pussy. To this she adds the "Fußnutte" (her playful neologism made of footnote and *Nutte*, whore):

Ich hatte Frau Alice Schwarzer gefragt, ob sie das Vorwort für dieses Bitchsm-Werk schreiben will, sie hat mir leider nicht geantwortet, dann hat's meine Fut verfasst. Ist doch viel fotziger geworden! (17)

[I asked Ms. Alice Schwarzer if she wanted to write the foreword to this Bitchsm work, unfortunately she did not answer, then my twat wrote it. It became much twattier.]

Bitchsm transforms negative semantics around female sexuality that often have a citational quality, to become culturally intertextual in nature. Moreover, the text's performative position with regard to its audience, and its assertiveness vis-à-vis racial politics, clash with gender politics. This intersectionality and intertextuality create a messy politics that consistently slips from interpretation. In an attempt to counter racialized stereotypes of victimized Turkish women in Germany, stereotypes that German mainstream feminism—from Alice Schwarzer to lifestyle feminism—endorses and fosters, *Bitchsm* employs the violent language of pornography and the sexist imagery of pop culture to create its pleasure-obsessed, hedonistic, and aggressive voice. Thus the text highlights the tensions that intersectional approaches to racial and sexual discrimination can present. *Bitchsm* tries to escape the traps of either racist or sexist essentialism by playfully circling the line between both. Lady Bitch Ray therefore poses the question of political agency and of who is in control of awkwardness in yet a different way. The character of Lady Bitch Ray is purposely out of control, which puts her in control of the mess she is creating.

Bitchsm is a product of Lady Bitch Ray's own self-located position among media forms; as a YouTube star, MySpace artist, talk-show aficionado, and tabloid sideshow, her rap-artist persona develops within the circulation among television, online, and print media. As an author she taps into and uses (and is thus dependent upon) the intermediality of that circulation, while also exposing the sometimes dire consequences for women of just such modes of circulation. The awkwardness that results can be explained by popfeminism: the pop culture that embraces the sexualized female body for consumption is utilized in the feminist critique. The danger of this approach is that critique itself becomes pop—thus the ambivalence of the political position. In the example of Lady Bitch Ray, that pop culturally coded object is her own sexual body, which she reclaims for feminism in her text. The importance of this circulation among media is also true for Roche and Hegemann. Our understanding of Roche's literary events as awkward, and thus as readable for their popfeminist political potential, depends on her own role as a television moderator and regular appearance in mainstream media outlets before and after publication of her novels. Finally, the politics of Hegemann's aesthetics take on popfeminist qualities in conjunction with her media branding first as a sexually precocious child prodigy and then as a literary bad girl, both aspects to be found awkwardly embedded in the text itself.

Circling Back: Concluding Thoughts from Awkward Positions

In the literary events described here, the use of pop culture in tandem with feminism to criticize mainstream sexist and consumerist society is caught in positions of circular political practice. Out of these positions emerge facets of the awkward—be they internally produced in the text form itself, produced in concert between text and reception, or driven by the author—two of which, the emotional and the sexual, were examined in greater depth here. Awkwardness is a search term that allows us to poke holes in the standard popular and academic approaches to feminist creative work, revealing much about how feminist discourse today participates uncritically in the cruel optimism upholding pop culture. Our search has also tried to poke holes in the approach to understanding women's writing as a useful category for literature broadly speaking and for politically engaged literature more specifically. The politics in the texts we discuss here are fleeting and often political only within a certain, messy discourse; authors take on various roles, create characters, and present themselves as in motion or as (adolescently) evolving. Moreover, in the act of reading these texts, the female reader—often that reader implicated under the label women's writing—is confronted with her own awkward politics, for in consuming the books she participates in hugely popular literary events driven in many cases by an often leeringly horny (male) critical public.

We suggest, therefore, that popfeminist researchers employ this searching, deconstructive, and questioning feminist eye in their analyses of contemporary feminist cultures, what we call our popfeminist methodology, and we stress that identifications can take multiple and shifting forms in a web of normative constructions of gender, sexuality, ethnicity, and national belonging. This is mirrored on a formal level, since none of the events we discuss here are strictly, or only, "literary." Literary texts are but one facet of the political interventions these artists make. Popfeminist interventions into the feminist literary market "mess" with literature: they cite and sample digital texts to create a literary text, they propel the literary into digital proliferations, or they compress digital performances and their reception into a book. Aside from what we discuss on the level of content, that is, the creation of awkward emotions and bodies, on a formal level, Hegemann, Roche, and Ray define an awkward *Handlungsraum* (space for intervention) for popfeminist texts that calls for a redefinition of what literature, feminist literature, and, by extension, feminist political writing might be in the twenty-first century.

Notes

[1] For an interesting recent discussion of the debates surrounding "new feminism" in the media see Anna-Katherina Messmer, "Neuer Feminismus?" *taz: die Tageszeitung*, July 12, 2013, 12.

[2] This article represents one part of a larger research project, "Technologies of Popfeminist Activism," funded by a grant from the Social Sciences and Humanities Research Council (Canada), examining art activism, digital cultures, and awkwardness in a broad range of popfeminist creative production.

[3] Sonja Eismann, *Hot Topic* (Mainz: Ventil Verlag, 2007), 10. All translations from the German are our own, unless otherwise noted. Three of the four literary texts examined have been published in English translation; our translations of them here are our own.

[4] For a more detailed description of the evolution of German feminism, see Myra Marx Ferree, *Varieties of Feminism: German Gender Politics in Global Perspective* (Palo Alto, CA: Stanford University Press, 2012).

[5] Eismann, *Hot Topic*, 10. Of course she is not alone in this. Jana Hensel and Elisabeth Raether clearly and vehemently position themselves against Schwarzer in their book *Neue deutsche Mädchen* (Reinbek bei Hamburg: Rowohlt, 2008).

[6] Eismann, *Hot Topic*, 12.

[7] Lauren G. Berlant, *Cruel Optimism* (Durham, NC: Duke University Press, 2011), 2.

[8] Ibid., 1.

[9] See Mara Delius, "Mir zerfallen die Worte im Mund wie schlechte Pillen," *FAZ*, January 22, 2010, http://www.faz.net/aktuell/feuilleton/buecher/rezensionen/belletristik/helene-hegemann-axolotl-roadkill-mir-zerfallen-die-worte-im-mund-wie-schlechte-pillen-1913572.html.

[10] For example, it was nominated for the prestigious Leipziger book prize, prompting a host of established authors to sign a declaration decrying intellectual theft. See "'Leipziger Erklärung': Literaturstars mobilisieren gegen Hegemann,"

Spiegel Online, March 15, 2010, http://www.spiegel.de/kultur/literatur/ leipziger-erklaerung-literaturstars-mobilisieren-gegen-hegemann-a-683716.html.

[11] See Julia Kristeva, "'Nous Deux' or a (Hi)story of Intertextuality," *Romanic Review* 93, no. 1–2 (2003): 7–13. For a good summary see also William Irwin, "Against Intertextuality," *Philosophy and Literature* 28, no. 2 (October 2004): 227–42.

[12] On theories of intermediality, see, for example, Joachim Paech, "Paradoxien der Auflösung und Intermedialität," in *HyperKult: Geschichte, Theorie und Kontext digitaler Medien*, ed. Martin Warnke, Wolfgang Coy, and Georg Christoph Tholen (Basel: Stroemfeld, 1997), 331–68, accessed July 15, 2013, http://www.medientheorie.com/doc/paech_paradoxien.pdf.

[13] Helene Hegemann, *Axolotl Roadkill* (Berlin: Ullstein, 2011), 7, 13, 44, 172.

[14] Kristeva, "(Hi)story," 9.

[15] For another interesting reading of Hegemann's work, see Emily Jeremiah, "The Case of Helene Hegemann: Queerness, Failure, and the German Girl," *Seminar: A Journal of Germanic Studies* 49, no. 4 (2013): 400–413.

[16] Hegemann, *Axolotl Roadkill*, 17. See Rachael McLennan's summary in McLennan, *Adolescence, America, and Postwar Fiction* (New York: Palgrave Macmillan, 2009).

[17] Stephen Burt, *The Form of Youth* (New York: Columbia University Press, 2007), 3–4.

[18] Hegemann, *Axolotl Roadkill*, 49. See Burt, *The Form of Youth*, for a discussion of poetics and individuality.

[19] Carsten Gansel, "Adoleszenz, Ritual und Inszenierung in der Popliteratur," in "Popliteratur," ed. Heinz-Ludwig Arnold and Jörgen Schäfer, special issue, *Text + Kritik* (2003): 234–57.

[20] Hegemann, *Axolotl Roadkill*, 12.

[21] Steven Bruhm and Natasha Hurley, "Curiouser: On the Queerness of Children," in *Curiouser: On the Queerness of Children*, ed. Steven Bruhm and Natasha Hurley (Minneapolis: University of Minnesota Press, 2004), ix–xxxviii; here, ix.

[22] Kathryn Bond Stockton, *The Queer Child: On Growing Sideways in the Twentieth Century* (Durham, NC: Duke University Press, 2009), 5.

[23] This produced such headlines as Sebastian Hammelehle's "Axololita Overkill" or Iris Radisch's "Die alten Männer und das junge Mädchen" (The Old Men and the Young Girl). Sebastian Hammelehle, "Hegemanns Quellenliste: Axololita Overkill," February 18, 2010, http://www.spiegel.de/kultur/literatur/0,1518,678708,00.html. Iris Radisch, "Die alten Männer und das junge Mädchen," Zeit.de, February 19, 2010, http://www.zeit.de/2010/08/Helene-Hegemann-Medien.

[24] Janet Staiger, Ann Cvetkovich, and Ann Reynolds, "Introduction: Political Emotions and Public Feelings," in *Political Emotions*, ed. Janet Staiger, Ann Cvetkovich, and Ann Reynolds (New York: Routledge, 2010), 4; emphasis in original. See also Berlant, *Cruel Optimism*.

[25] Staiger, Cvetkovich, and Reynolds, "Introduction," 5.

[26] Sianne Ngai, *Ugly Feelings* (Cambridge, MA: Harvard University Press, 2007), 1.

[27] J. Halberstam, *The Queer Art of Failure* (Durham, NC: Duke University Press, 2010), 2–3.

[28] Charlotte Roche, *Feuchtgebiete* (Berlin: Ullstein, 2009) and *Schoßgebete* (Munich: Piper, 2011). *Feuchtgebiete* was first performed as a play at the Neues Theater Halle under the direction of Christina Friedrich in 2008; subsequently the text was performed as a play at the Theaterforum Kreuzberg in Berlin, at the Brandenburger Theater, and at the Theater Liga in Hamburg. A film version premiered in August 2013. German director Sönke Wortmann's film adaptation of *Schoßgebete* was released in 2014.

[29] As we argue elsewhere, these television appearances produced a specific kind of awkwardness, for the often-male talk-show hosts engaged in discussions of the book that, because of Roche's clever media strategy, turned the pornographic gaze from Roche's text and author personality to the talk-show hosts themselves, challenging them to confront their own preconceptions about female sexuality. This meant that awkward passages in the text that are based on detailed and exaggerated descriptions of the female body, its smells, and its fluids were transferred to the male body. See Carrie Smith-Prei and Maria Stehle, "*Awkwardness* als Provokation: Gedankenspiele zu Popfeminismus, Körperpolitik und der Vermarktung literarischer Frauen," in *Fiktionen und Realitäten*, ed. Marion Schulz and Brigitte Jirku (Frankfurt am Main: Peter Lang, 2013), 215–30. See also, for example, Roche's visit to the Harald Schmidt Show.

[30] Roche, *Feuchtgebiete*, 8, 10, 19.

[31] Ibid., 40–41.

[32] See Hester Baer, "Sex, Death, and Motherhood in the Eurozone: Contemporary Women's Writing in German," *World Literature Today* (May/June 2012), 61.

[33] See Schwarzer's response to the text, or Alice O'Keeffe, "Wrecked by Charlotte Roche—Review" *Guardian*, May 8, 2013, http://www.guardian.co.uk/books/2013/may/08/wrecked-charlotte-roche-review. On Schwarzer's response, see Christian Buß, "Schwarzer attackiert Roche: Häschen im Bett, Oma im Kopf," *Spiegel Online*, August 15, 2011, http://www.spiegel.de/kultur/literatur/schwarzer-attackiert-roche-haeschen-im-bett-oma-im-kopf-a-780345.html.

[34] Baer, "Sex, Death, and Motherhood," 61.

[35] Carrie Smith-Prei, "'Knaller Sex für alle': Popfeminist Body Politics in Lady Bitch Ray, Charlotte Roche, and Sarah Kuttner," in "Contemporary Women's Writing and the Return of Feminism in Germany," ed. Hester Baer, special issue, *Studies in Twentieth and Twenty-First Century Literature* 35, no. 1 (Winter 2011): 18.

[36] Mirja Stöcker, *Das F-Wort: Feminismus ist Sexy* (Königstein: Helmer, 2007), 37. See also Meredith Haaf, Susanne Klingner, and Barbara Streidl, *Wir Alphamädchen: Warum Feminismus das Leben schöner macht* (Hamburg: Hoffmann & Campe, 2008), 66.

[37] Eismann, *Hot Topic*, 109.

[38] For a reading of both Mifti and Helen in terms of youthful rebellion, see Hannelore Schlaffer, "Die Göre—Karriere einer literarischen Figur," *Merkur: Deutsche Zeitschrift für europäisches Denken* 742, no. 3 (2011): 274–79.

[39] Lady Bitch Ray, *Bitchsm* (Stuttgart: Vagina Style Verlag/Panini Books, 2012). Lady Bitch Ray's homepage and blog, accessed July 14, 2013, http://www.lady-bitch-ray.com/tx-bl/tag/bitchism/.

[40] For a more detailed academic discussion of the headscarf debates, see, for example, Beverly Weber, "Cloth on Her Head, Constitution in Hand," *German Politics and Society* 22, no. 3 (Fall 2004): 33–64.

8: The Indictment of Neoliberalism and Communism in the Novels of Katharina Hacker, Nikola Richter, Judith Schalansky, and Julia Schoch

Helga Druxes

L<small>EFTIST CULTURAL CRITIC</small> Jeffrey Nealon argues that "we've experienced an intensification of postmodern capitalism over the past decades, an increasing saturation of the economic sphere into formerly independent segments of everyday cultural life."[1] The new global economy elevates competitiveness to its guiding principle, mandating a national quest to maintain "Konkurrenzfähigkeit des Standorts Deutschland" (competitiveness of Germany as a business hub).[2] At the same time, since the rise of neoliberalism in the 1990s, intensified technologies of the self, widely promoted by popular culture and the advertising industry, insinuate that individuals should take a functionalist approach toward themselves as sites of experience, or conceive of themselves and their physical bodies as reified projects for self-marketing and improvement in a normative marketplace.[3] This imprinting is so pervasive that it is difficult to resist; it presents itself in the guise of self-actualization, or even as entertainment.[4]

The writers under consideration in this chapter present a strong critique of neoliberalism by addressing these pervasive effects. Katharina Hacker, Nikola Richter, Julia Schoch, and Judith Schalansky want readers to question which common goods are foundational for a liveable society, what the proper ratio of work versus leisure is, and how to recover or attain for the first time a sense of shared intimacy. Moreover, their works critique the evacuation of the public good as a shared civic responsibility from the public sphere, chronicling the neoliberal shift onto individuals as entrepreneurs, "equipped," in economist Mirowski's judgment, "with promiscuous notions of identity and selfhood, surrounded by simulacra of other such selves . . . a world where competition is the primary virtue, and solidarity is a sign of weakness."[5]

While women's bodies were already commodified and relegated to the status of consumers in the Western capitalist marketplace, women in the neoliberal era are disproportionately affected by this renewed punitive intrusion into their psyches, urging them to submit to the dictates of perpetual self-interventions in the guise of a new freedom to realize the self. Moreover, as Hester Baer has pointed out, compared to women in other EU countries, German women are underrepresented in leadership positions in the workplace, and those who work are more likely to do so part-time.[6] Baer touches upon the critical interpretations of neoliberalism as an ideology of submerged misogyny. Neoliberalism pretends that sexism no longer exists in the dynamic new marketplace. The constructivism of neoliberalism applies to all elements of society except the marketplace itself, which is seen as monolithic and bracingly free of moral accountability.

Within the contradictions of state socialism's economic planning, women were alternately urged to seek advanced qualifications for the workplace, or incentivized to bear three or more children at a young age; they were either encouraged to take pride in their performance as workers, or shunted back into traditional female spheres. In Eastern Bloc communism, the state was a kind of behemoth whose dictates, no matter how irrational, could not be questioned.[7] Counterintuitively, neoliberalism and state socialism converge in the notion that a person is caught up in a cycle of self-optimization for the sake of an entity that offers no coherent justifications for its demands.

While the increasing saturation of everyday life by economic imperatives can be observed wherever neoliberal economies hold sway, these processes are keenly resisted by writers Judith Schalansky and Julia Schoch, who were born in the GDR and grew up there in the late seventies and early eighties under state-controlled socialism. Too young to engage in much overt public dissidence at the time of the GDR's demise, they nonetheless harbored subversive ideas about the school system and the family collective, which were the loci of the social control they experienced most vividly up to that point. But after the collapse of communism as a social system—the implosion of the Honecker regime and the fragmentation of the Eastern Bloc—came the moral bankruptcy of neoliberal capitalism, which falsely implied that women now faced a level playing field of entrepreneurial opportunity and freedom to choose. Paternalism is at the bottom of both the cult of the state and the cult of the market. The emblems of power in Schalansky's and Schoch's novels are male, which points to the continued subjugation and marginalization of women.

While Schoch and Schalansky face the neoliberal marketplace with systematic skepticism, their central characters are sidelined, or opt out radically by becoming hapless gamblers or committing suicide. Schoch and, to a lesser extent, Schalansky embrace states of suspended animation in their works, with dreaming and make-believe emerging as respites from the failures of both state socialism and neoliberal capitalism: "Für einen Moment kann man beruhigt sein, die Welt, sie wartet noch" (For a brief moment, one can be calm. The world is still waiting).[8]

By contrast, women writers raised in a capitalist market economy bring to bear a different set of political concerns, focusing their critique on emotional stunting, anhedonia, and superficial interpersonal relations, as well as the rootlessness of globalized workers who are not given any incentive to insert themselves into the existing local frame. Born in the Federal Republic, writers Katharina Hacker and Nikola Richter target amorphous social phenomena, such as the global nature of work and its ramifications for the alienation of sons and daughters from their families, friends, and partners. This psychic numbing and disavowal come in the wake of an unprecedented wave of state privatization and urban gentrification occurring since the mid-eighties in Germany and since the Thatcher era in the United Kingdom.

Sociologist Christoph Butterwegge terms this ongoing process an epoch of "Staatsvergessenheit" (the state forgetting its obligations).[9] German left-of-center intellectuals point out that democracy and minority rights cannot be quantified and monetized—these, defined neither by untrammeled greed nor cost-cutting, are normative communal values that constitute the legitimation of the state (102). Butterwegge goes on to state: "Im viel beschworenen 'Zeitalter der Globalisierung' gilt das Soziale erst recht als Luxus, den sich selbst eine wohlhabende Industrienation wie die deutsche nicht mehr leisten kann" (194; In the much-evoked "era of globalization" social programs seem ever more a luxury, which even an affluent nation like Germany can no longer afford). As the long-term studies (begun in 2002) of the Heitmeyer team of Bielefeld sociologists document, this perception leads to widespread middle-class resentment against socially weak groups. Even the well-off experience anxiety about future social resource availability and a sense of disorientation, and these feelings create a climate of "de-solidarization and anomie."[10] The well-educated white-collar class of the former West either finds itself caught up in a global race for professional opportunities, jettisoning its social lives and moral qualms, or, like Hacker's Isabelle in *Die Habenichtse* (2006; published in English as *The Have-Nots*, 2008), drift into undeserved positions that turn them into appendages of others.

Katharina Hacker and Nikola Richter

Hacker presents us with obtuse protagonists who are stunted by neoliberal intensification: the German yuppies Isabelle and Jakob in *Die Habenichtse* are materialistic globetrotters, blurrily out of touch with their own emotions. They are willfully incurious about Germany's Nazi past, even as they are surrounded by its lingering aftereffects. Nor are they concerned about the plight of their underclass neighbors. Hacker removes this affluent, well-educated young German couple from Berlin to London, where Jakob is hired by an old Jewish private banker, whose firm specializes in the restitution of real estate looted by the Nazis and the GDR regime. Isabelle, an illustrator and graphic designer, simply tags along as Jakob's wife to live in an urban neighborhood she finds appealing for its Bohemian mixing. Hacker quickly reveals that this well-educated but amateurish drifter does not observe carefully, failing to sense the simmering class tensions in the area. Isabelle's daily promenades, taken at a leisurely pace and characterized by self-absorption, and which take her from her beautiful house out to the park and the tube station to travel into the center of the city, irritate her underclass next-door neighbor, Jim. He squats next door in one of his client's apartments and, as we learn from his inner monologues, is an abused male prostitute and drug runner. He turns his class rage against his new neighbors by stalking Isabelle and eventually holding her hostage. The neighbors on the other side of Isabelle's house are a working-class family terrorized by the father, an alcoholic wife-beater and abuser of his two children, a teenage son and a mentally handicapped younger daughter named Sara. Even though Isabelle overhears ample daily evidence of violent altercations, she does not intervene, or contact any state institutions, thus becoming complicit in Sara's murder.

Hacker deliberately chooses, then undermines, the home as a symbol of respite from a brutally competitive social system. The family home might be seen as a repository of memories, but the sons and daughters of the German postwar bourgeoisie refuse to acknowledge their parents by largely cutting themselves off from them.[11] Isabelle thinks of her parents' house as "die graue Schuhschachtel" (the grey shoe box),[12] a disposable container. Similarly, Jakob inherits an old dresser from his grandparents with a drawer full of mementos, which are discovered by the movers when the drawer becomes dislodged in his new London home. Overly focused on legal questions about others' rights of succession to repossess family homes in the former East, Jakob neglects to ask questions about the history of his own foreign home and its neighborhood. He is preoccupied with fitting in and not seeming "posh," because a coworker indicates that this might be a bad thing, but by the same token he feels: "provinziell . . . oder wie ein Kind, das in die Welt reist" (*HN*, 87; provincial . . . or like a child traveling out into the world). Neither Jakob nor Isabelle has ever thought critically about each other's class background and unearned privileges, just as they are profoundly incurious about older people, and even about their best friends. Asked in confidence why she is marrying Jakob instead of just living with him, Isabelle cannot say. "Es ist so passend, antwortet Isabelle zögernd" (*HN*, 55; It is so appropriate to do this, Isabelle answers hesitantly). External events have favored Isabelle, who is pretty, with even features and a slim, prepubescent body. Lacking the desire to dig deeper, she vaguely intuits: "Immer war ihr etwas entglitten, wenn auch auf zufriedenstellende Weise" (*HN*, 32; something always slid out of her grasp, even if it happened in a satisfying manner). Jakob at least knows that he received his promotion to the London job because his peer Robert, who was slightly better qualified at the office, died in the attack on the Twin Towers. Faced with survivor's guilt, Jakob refuses to engage it, preferring to maintain his cynical attitude that death is merely a change in ownership contracts (which handily echoes a neoliberal mantra about human capital as reified without end). As portrayed by Hacker, these stupefied, alienated protagonists disavow both memory and civic engagement on behalf of weaker groups, whether they be European Jews of their own intimate circle, their neighbors, or the many individuals displaced and dispossessed in the ongoing global wars.

Hacker alludes to Orwell's distopian *1984* when she describes the post-9/11 scene as a state of continuous warfare in which "nothing had changed" for affluent first-world white-collar workers. Jakob lists a litany of recent gruesome wars and terrorist events,

> Namen und Dinge, die für sie hier nicht mehr bedeuteten als die Verwicklungen und Dramen einer Fernsehserie, über die alle sprachen, wie sie über *Big Brother* gesprochen hatten. Und jetzt sprachen sie alle über den Krieg im Irak. Wie viele Tote hatte es im letzten Irak-Krieg gegeben? (*HN*, 93)

> [names and events that did not mean any more for these people over here than the convoluted plots and dramas of a TV series everyone was talking about, just as they used to talk about *Big Brother* in the past. And now all of them were talking about the Iraq war. How many dead had there been in the last Iraq war?]

Orwell's action is set in London in the 1980s, where his central characters, Julia and Winston, still struggle to rebel against an inhumane system, because they are able to retrieve dulled emotions like compassion and love and manage to restore critical thought through dialogue. In the London of 2003, Hacker's characters are either docile or intermittently violent, but they all draw the same memory blanks when it comes to their own responsibility for, or complicity with, disaster and death-dealing. Hacker's protagonists refuse to remember, observe empathetically, or show consistent support to other beings—symbolized in its most minor variant in the limping of a cat that Isabelle saw the little girl next door hit with a big branch. Although Isabelle then brings the cat into her own space to feed it, she viciously pushes it off the windowsill when the animal returns, ascribing the cat's visible limp to old age. Similarly, Isabelle and Jakob at various times hear the girl next door being beaten but do not intervene or even discuss the problem with each other. Being so self-absorbed and willfully naive makes Isabelle easy prey for the violent squatter Jim, who periodically lashes out by killing cats and maiming women. Jim imprisons Isabelle with Sara, the handicapped girl, whom he severely beats up before leaving the area. He rages at Isabelle for being so impassive: "Nichts sieht man in deinem Gesicht, grade mal ein bißchen Angst. . . . Das Mädchen stinkt, merkst du das nicht?" (Your face shows nothing, barely a little fear. . . . The girl stinks, don't you notice that?). Jim also orders Isabelle to "open her eyes" to the injured Sara, after which he cuts off all Isabelle's hair at the scalp so that "your husband will at least see that something has happened to you" (*HN*, 300; English in the original). The class tensions between a poorly qualified underclass—whose only capital is their bodies—and a new internationally mobile financial manager class erupt in physical violence in Hacker's text, but this violence succeeds mainly in doing more damage to other members of the underclass. It is doubtful whether Isabelle and Jakob will handle their privileged status differently at the close of the novel, as Jakob insists that "es ist aber nichts passiert" (but nothing happened), and instructs the numb Isabelle: "Wir müssen hineingehen . . . wir können hier nicht stehenbleiben" (*HN*, 307–8; we have to go inside . . . we cannot stay out here). Jakob's conformism spurs him on to reerect a façade of normalcy rather than attempting to better understand what happened. These two affluent and entitled characters take no responsibility for their own actions, and do not engage or empathize with individuals from diverse class backgrounds. As the title of the novel suggests, they truly have nothing.

Hacker's negative assessment of the corporate worker is supported by the depiction of eager but hapless novices on the job market, the eponymous characters in *Die Lebenspraktikanten* (The Life Interns, 2006) of Nikola Richter's lightly fictionalized account. These young men and women become stuck in a loop of unpaid internships, which lead only to further pseudo-opportunities for advancement. Economists Herbert Schui and Stephanie Blankenburg argue that since the mid-1990s, everywhere in Europe conceptions of work are rapidly changing as a consequence of privatization and fewer government subsidies. In a depoliticizing rhetorical move, discussions have become focused on the efforts of the individual job seeker:

> Die Teilhabe am Markt ist Sache der Eigeninitiative: Jeder, der will, kann Arbeit finden, wenn er oder sie sich nur genügend anstrengt. Die Grundwerte der neoliberalen Weltsicht—Ehrlichkeit, Sparsamkeit, Privatheit und negative Freiheit—haben reformerische Wertvorstellungen, wie Solidarität, Partizipation und Emanzipation, ohne jeden Zweifel erfolgreich verdrängt. An die Stelle von organisierter Interessenvertretung und öffentlicher Debatte ist die schweigende Gemeinschaft der "Steuerzahler/innen," der "Aktieninhaber/innen" und der "Leistungsträger" getreten, öffentliche Beamte und Staatsangestellte sind zu "Managern" geworden.[13]

[Market participation is now a matter of taking the initiative on one's own: anyone who wants to can find work; he or she just has to invest enough effort. The basic values of the neoliberal world view—honesty, frugality, privacy, and negative freedom—have without a doubt successfully replaced reformist concepts, such as solidarity, participation, and emancipation. What has replaced the organized representation of interests and public debate is the silent community of "taxpayers," "stockholders," and "service providers"; public officials and state employees have turned into "managers."]

Richter chronicles the everyday lives of young people in the precariat, always looking for another temp job and living in a state of permanent readiness: one of her characters says "daß wir heute unsere Leben wochenweise organisieren müssen. Wenn eine Sache klappt, können wir uns nicht darüber freuen und kurz durchatmen, sondern müssen schon die nächste planen" (that today we have to organize our lives on a week-by-week schedule. If something works out, we cannot enjoy it and take a breather—we already have to be planning the next thing).[14] Parents are not shown as understanding, but insist on a neoliberal mantra of "Das Leben ist kein Zuckerschlecken" (*L*, 12; Life is not a bowl of cherries). Anglicisms like "career center," "branding," and "knowledge management" veil the permanent state of economic insecurity in which these young workers are caught up. A job advisor counsels Anika that she should simply go on applying, that her job letter looks great, but that she cannot offer any specific pointers. Her friend Linn, by contrast, has learned to fashion herself anew for every new job opening, regularly juggling seven different applications—"sie kann sich für sehr unterschiedliche Profile zurechtstutzen oder auch erweitern" (*L*, 21; she can prune her resume to match very different profiles, or expand it). Several of the stories show how the job seekers become obsessed by frugality, as if this self-management would lead to an actual job. Time efficiency is the maxim of the employers, who often interview in the company cafeteria, so that they can multitask and save money at the same time. Chris, one of the highly mobile interns for a humanitarian aid organization, works and travels so much that he suffers from burnout syndrome, unable to enjoy his time off between assignments. Since the late 1990s, burnout has been on the rise in Germany, in part because doctors learned to diagnose this illness.[15] Economist Ursula Engelen-Kefer criticizes German state tactics of temporarily removing young people from the unemployment rolls by enrolling them in publicly financed "ABM" (Arbeitsbeschaffungsmaßnahme, or work opportunity measure) slots, which do not lead to further employment, but only to another short-term program. Moreover, she mentions that only one-fifth of German businesses still train their own aspirants, which indicates the extent to which training has been outsourced and divorced from actual job openings.[16]

Those who manage to get taken on, like the character Giulia, quickly find that they are expected to work much longer hours than their contract stipulates:

> Ihre 40-Stunden Woche wird oft zu einer 60-Stunden Woche. Als ob die Arbeit wie ein Magnet mehr und mehr Arbeit anziehen würde, als ob das Arbeithaben dazu qualifizieren würde, noch mehr Arbeit zu haben. (*L*, 166)

> [Her 40-hour work week often turns into a 60-hour week. As if work was like a magnet, attracting more and more work, as if having work would qualify one only to be given more work to do.]

A side-effect of work time bleeding into private time, according to Richter, is that her characters' social lives atrophy. Nils "kommuniziert den ganzen Tag und [will] dann abends nicht noch mehr kommunizieren" (*L*, 84; communicates all day long and does not want to do more of it at night); similarly, Giulia "will nicht offen für alles sein. Während ihrer Freizeit versucht sie im Allgemeinen alle Kontakte zu vermeiden, die nichts mit ihrer Arbeit zu tun haben" (*L*, 173; does not want to be open to anything. In general, during her leisure time, she tries to avoid any contacts that are not work-related). This model of urban sociologist Richard Sennett's "'flexible human' cannot afford the time for a family, either because of money issues or because of the geographical mobility that the managers of transnational corporations demand."[17] Richter exposes the new ideology of the depoliticized novice worker, who only tries to adapt to current market conditions. As Giulia puts it in a tense conversation with her formerly leftist mother, a '68er: "Ich erschaffe mir nicht irgendwelche rebellischen, staatsfernen Nischen . . ., sondern versuche durch die Eingliederung in das Bestehende herauszufinden, welcher Platz für mich bereitgehalten wird und wo ich hineinpasse" (*L*, 136; I am not carving out some rebellious anti-government niche . . ., but rather trying to find out by integrating into existing structures which spot is available to me and where I fit in). Such docile compliance leads to political and ethical values being subsumed under the rubric of private engagement, such as volunteering. Access to such activities (presumptively open to all) is based on class privilege, as a recent German poverty study shows.[18] Three-quarters of workers in the precariat have no time to demonstrate for their rights or do lobbying. In the new turbo-capitalist Germany, as elsewhere in the Eurozone and the globalized labor sphere, "democracy is not measured according to values, but construed as a market model."[19] As Wilhelm Heitmeyer describes it, Germany has entered a phase of "Demokratieentleerung" (hollowing out of democracy).[20] Its substitute becomes a myopic working on the self as a "bundle of skills," as economist Mirowski avers: "As for laborers in the service sector, the 'feminization' of the workforce through part-time casualized work with erosion of seniority and benefits has been recast as a 'blending of service, shopping and religion.'"[21]

In Richter's account, the more level-headed protagonists Nils, Viktor, and Linn, who had become exposed to critical thinking as philosophy students, choose local networks and partners over foreign job opportunities, risking unemployment. Nils surprisingly rediscovers his ethnic roots in the Balkans and markets a type of funnel cake inspired by family recipes, becoming a small business entrepreneur: "Er fühlt sich in seiner Theorie der kleinen Zellen bestätigt: je kleiner die zu organsierenden Einheiten sind, desto mehr Einsatz kann der Einzelne zeigen, desto mehr wird der Einzelne gefragt, desto übersichtlicher ist es" (*L*, 188–89; He feels that his theory of small units is correct: the smaller the units are that need to be organized, the more engagement an individual can demonstrate, the more each individual is tasked to participate, the more it becomes manageable). His baking project grows into a catering company that provides food and entertainment for private parties. Yet such a turn toward locally produced merchandise and event management is not really a way out of the neoliberal marketplace, since it, too, shores up a service economy where people can buy social events and experiences rather than create their own.

Hacker and Richter are aware of the emotional numbing and alienation that seem to be the price of continuous adaptation to shifting labor-market demands. Hacker describes an erosion of the social collective, where individuals do not take action to protest social violence and protect others, and are even unsure how to respond when such violence happens to them. Richter analyzes the psychic toll of constant mobility and the economic imperative of regarding oneself as a competitive commodity. Their protagonists go to international locations in search of work, but they do not become passionate about the new setting, as they either have little free time to experience it, or, as in Hacker's novel, chiefly approach it through yuppie social rituals such as going out for drinks after work. Figures from older generations remain opaque in *Die Habenichtse*, as is the case with Mr. Bentham, Jakob's employer and mentor, largely because Jakob is unimaginative and does not question or make deductions based on visual evidence that presents itself to him. Isabelle's parents are isolated, bourgeois homeowners who never leave the provinces and who do not even meet their daughter's new husband or her coworkers. In Richter's *Lebenspraktikanten*, parents are unwilling or unable to grasp the challenges facing their sons and daughters in their endless quest for stable paying jobs. Richter insists on the legitimacy of her generation's personal emotional needs: close friendships, meaningful recognition in the workplace, and gestures toward political agency for the new precariat class.

However, even temporary workers' rights to insurance, for example, are not demanded publicly and are merely tested out behind closed doors in a meeting with the boss.

Judith Schalansky and Julia Schoch

Schalansky's portrayals of the character deformation brought on by neoliberal ethics are powerful and may represent the most incisive feminist critique of globalization in contemporary German women's writing. In *Der Hals der Giraffe* (The Giraffe's Neck, 2012) her metaphor of the gradual development of the giraffe's deformed neck in the evolutionary process suggests that the human animal is likewise susceptible to environmental cues. Schalansky presents the corrosive personal and social effects of such a deformation through the character of Inge Lohmark. By peering inside Lohmark's isolated and warped mind, readers are forced to ask what would constitute a liveable society.

Schalansky grew up on the Eastern periphery of the GDR, in Greifswald, a city in rural Pomerania. Both she and Julia Schoch use the topos of the journey to distant lands to sharpen their critique of conditions at home. In Schalansky's fictional universe, remote islands play a key role (*Atlas der abgelegenen Inseln* [Atlas of Remote Islands, 2011]), as does the figure of the female sailor, who functions as a cipher for the female experiential quest (*Blau steht dir nicht: Matrosenroman* [Blue Is Not Your Color: Sailor Novel, 2008]). But the author's attention is at the same time never far from the local and its homely constraints, as in *Der Hals der Giraffe*, where Schalansky chronicles the entropy of a stunted female life lived out in the provinces.

Inge Lohmark is a victim of retrenchment: her job will soon disappear because of the dwindling demographic in this rural outpost of an increasingly globalized economy. Neoliberalism is provocatively posited as if it were an impersonal force, sweeping across the already denuded East and causing it to atrophy even further. The financialization of everyday life and people's intimate relationships mesh with the earlier instrumentalization of people by the Communist Party to produce grotesquely inhumane social behavior. Schalansky suggests that such noxious traits were acquired within particular political-economic constellations, which implies that they could also be undone if environmental conditions were to change. Negativity and the narrator's clinical tone are meant to provoke the reader to imagine a counter-narrative where characters would take moral responsibility for their own actions and rebuild the social collective through a process of democratic negotiation and contestation. In any case, all of Schalansky's young female characters dismiss the parent generation as corrupt, in some cases embracing the grandparent generation as more promising mentors. In *Blau steht dir nicht*, the grandfather represents a craggy individualism that thrives on eccentricity and is willing to foster a nonconformist imagination in his granddaughter.

Schalansky gave *Der Hals der Giraffe* the subtitle *Bildungsroman*, beckoning her readers into the vitriolic mind of a biology teacher and the deepest, dullest recesses of a coercive country school, where what transpires is a stubborn refusal to educate or be educated in a broader sense. Soon this isolated place and its unsympathetic antiheroine begin to call into question the entire project of a collective formation enacted too brutally. As Schalansky implies, we might consider the current state of affairs, namely neoliberalism applied too aggressively, to be both a troubling analogue to forced collectivization carried out in various Eastern Bloc dictatorships, and a variant of biologistic Darwinism.

In regard to the GDR's Stalinist heritage, *Der Hals der Giraffe* suggests that a worker's productivity was emphasized to the detriment of humane values. As Inge Lohmark[22] remembers:

> Das Land als Labor. Experimente, für die Pflanzen kastriert wurden, um zu verhindern, daß sie sich selbst befruchteten. Eine Armee von Bauern, die mit Pinzette und Pinsel bewaffnet aufs Feld zog, um Staubbeutel zu entfernen und Pflanzen künstlich zu bestäuben.[23]

> [The countryside [or: the country] as a laboratory. Experiments where plants were castrated to prevent them from pollinating on their own. An army of peasants, going to war equipped with pincers and brush to remove pollen sacs and pollinate plants artificially.]

Strategically deploying homonyms such as countryside/country, field/theater of war and a political allusion to the GDR state as a self-proclaimed "nation of workers and farmers," Schalansky satirizes the nation-building project of communist East Germany that was modeled upon the Soviet Union: "Von der Sowjetunion lernen heißt siegen lernen. Das prägte einen fürs Leben" (*HG*, 138; To learn from the Soviet Union means to learn how to be victorious. That imprinted you for life).

Today's global capitalist ventures have already seeped into the remote farm country that provides the setting for *Der Hals der Giraffe*, with Wolfgang, Inge's crude husband, switching over from farming dairy cattle to raising ostriches in an effort to adapt to the demand for exotic produce and stave off bankruptcy. But the area itself is rapidly depopulating, as its residents leave for the West in search of jobs and better living conditions, thereby ruining the remaining infrastructure. Inge's principal, Kattner, a West German originally sent east by the federal government to teach social studies in the newly unified country, tries to downplay the dire personal and political impact of their own school closing, by putting it into context:

So neu und so dramatisch einmalig sind sterbende Landschaften überhaupt nicht. Anderswo werden auch Schulen geschlossen. Auch im Westen. Im Ruhrgebiet. Halb Niedersachsen steht leer. Das ist eine ganz allgemeine Entwicklung. . . . Dem Osten geht es sogar noch gut. Hier wurde ja wenigstens noch Geld reingesteckt. Die ganzen neuen Straßenlampen, die Autobahn. (*HG*, 44)

[Dying areas are nothing new or especially tragic. They are closing schools in other places, too. In the West, too. In the Ruhr valley. Half of Lower Saxony has emptied out. You see it everywhere. . . . The East is actually faring quite well. Here at least they did still invest some money. All those new streetlights, the highway.]

The financialization of all work time becomes apparent here: the teachers are to understand their dilemma as the inexorable development of a dynamic economy rather than a targeted political decision against which they could protest. In other words, they should console themselves for the loss of their livelihood with the prettified appearance of the region's streets. In fact, they are the casualties of a political decision, namely, to invest in a highway instead of in teachers.

This newly imposed functionalism combines all too neatly with the teachers' earlier socialization under the Honecker regime. They fail to establish solidarity with each other or to take proper charge of their students' social education. In a pivotal episode Inge is called to account for doing nothing to stop the hazing of a young girl in her charge. The principal threatens to terminate her contract and characterizes her as "verknöchert" (ossified). Like the one-sided development of the giraffe's long neck, Inge overdeveloped her desire for aggression and dominance in adaptation to an oppressive social system: "Man malte sich was aus. Und dann war es doch jeden Tag nur dasselbe. Den Umständen entsprechen. Den Umständen entsprechend" (*HG*, 212; You imagined a future. But then it was just the same routine everyday. You had to adapt to the conditions. According to the conditions).

Yet the comparison of Inge with a giraffe turns out to be superficial, and another shrewd misdirection. Like a joint badly set, Inge develops in another direction: the animal that comes to best represent her is the ostrich, with its stunted wings. Young ostriches attempt to run in a herd but end up running in ever-tightening circles and impeding each other's movement. The novel closes on the striking and sad vision of the ostriches dancing in an enclosed pasture, with Inge mesmerized by them, standing at the fence, while a swarm of crows swoops down from the sky, croaking. These serve as a reminder of flight, and in Northern European literature they are often used as a bad omen. Visually close to ravens, they might also allude to Inge's own bad mothering by evoking the specter of the "Rabenmutter" (uncaring mother; literally, raven mother). Like the ostrich and the giraffe, humans, too, originated in Africa, the novel tells us:

> Zwei Wüstenvögel, die alles beäugten und gedankenlos in die Weite starrten. Steppentiere. Das passte. Das hier war ja nichts anderes als Steppe. . . . Aber diese Strauße waren hier geboren, ihre Heimat hatten sie nie gesehen. Sie war ja auch noch nie in Afrika gewesen. (*HG*, 220)

> [Two desert birds, eyeballing everything and staring thoughtlessly into the distance. Creatures of the steppe. That was fitting. Here there was nothing but steppe. . . . But these ostriches had been born here; they had never seen their home. She had never been to Africa, either.]

The displaced birds mirror the existential homelessness of their human counterpart. The repetition of the word steppe not only echoes the African desert but also gestures toward the large steppe further East, in Siberia, which has a more overt political association with the Soviet gulag as a form of punitive political exile.

Some of the novel's secondary characters reach out to other continents, as if to flee its setting on the eastern periphery of Germany. Inge's absent daughter Claudia has gone off to distant "Amiland" (a pejorative designation for the United States) and does little to keep in touch. What at first appears as callousness reveals itself as the daughter's healthy instinct for self-preservation. In the present day, Inge tacitly condones the hazing of Ellen, a girl in her class. This weakness turns out to be a reenactment of an earlier—and until this moment in the narrative repressed—refusal to be a mother to her daughter. Claudia was also hazed in school in the GDR, and her mother was her teacher. Claudia appeals to Inge for help in front of the whole class (her abusers) by prostrating herself and crying out. But Inge refuses to comfort her, rigidly sticking to her script as the distant and authoritarian "Frau Lohmark." Claudia eventually leaves for the American West, where she and her mother later tour the Arizona desert and Indian villages. While Claudia excitedly explains about the prehistory of the desert—once a fertile ocean with undersea mountain ridges—Inge refuses to listen, or to imagine in her mind's eye a radically different environment teeming with life; she categorically notices nothing but "tote Landschaft" (dead landscape). Used to being in control, she is unwilling to reverse roles and let her daughter teach her, even just once. Inge rejects her American experience as "Alles zu groß, zu weit. Täler und Wüsten, Tagesreisen, Wochenreisen groß. Viel zu unübersichtlich" (*HG*, 156; Everything too big, too open. Valleys and deserts, as big as a day's journey, a week's journey. Much too confusing). The word "unübersichtlich" (literally: impossible to oversee) in connection to the rigidity of this particular character smacks of the Foucaldian Panopticon, with its pervasive surveillance emanating from the all-seeing guard in the watchtower, which the prisoners eventually come to internalize. Inge is extremely uncomfortable in a setting that cannot be exhaustively surveilled. The social system that left its stamp on Inge Lohmark is an unmerciful one. She manifests the ruthlessness of a cornered animal, and the psychic numbing of a captive human.

In the new foreword to the small-format reissue of her fictional, hand-illustrated travelogue entitled *Taschenatlas der abgelegenen Inseln* (Pocket Atlas of Remote Islands, 2011), Schalansky casts herself in the role of the cartographer, since she actually did study mapmaking and illustration before turning to writing as her métier.[24] She remarks: "Alle Projektionen stellen die Welt verzerrt dar" (All projections represent the world in a distorted way).[25] This is true of her school satire *Der Hals der Giraffe*. The two projects are linked in terms of their focus on human depravity in isolated places. In history, argues the author in *Taschenatlas*, explorers who colonized an isolated island and enslaved its inhabitants more often effected "die Schreckensherrschaft eines Einzelnen als [die] Verwirklichung der Utopie einer egalitären Gemeinschaft" (24: the reign of terror of a single individual rather than realizing the utopia of an egalitarian community). Inge Lohmark is one such autocrat, even though the coercive collective that shaped her is long gone.

In Schalansky's imaginary, the sailor becomes an oppositional figure of rebellious freedom; he is part of a collective that is on the move and explores new areas without getting pinned down. In *Blau steht dir nicht: Matrosenroman*, Jenny, a young girl resembling the author, becomes fascinated by the open sea and sailors. She often vacations at her grandparents' house on Usedom, an island near Sweden, but still on the northernmost periphery of the GDR. Tantalizingly close to the open sea and free travel, residents and tourists alike are surveilled by border patrols, lifeguards, and each other. Those who swim out too far are cautioned by megaphone to turn back immediately. The child does not understand the full political import of these events, but she feels the oppressive atmosphere of stasis: "Es bewegte sich einfach nichts" (Nothing moved at all).[26] Jenny fondly remembers walks to the beach with her sympathetic grandfather, a retired math teacher and lovable eccentric, who tries to enliven their daily routine with games and little adventures, such as trying to guess the weather and the temperature of the water, or collecting amber on the beach at dawn. This educator is a counter-model to the depraved teacher in *Der Hals der Giraffe*. But even he categorically opposes Jenny's professed desire to become a "Matrösin" (female sailor), saying that women bring bad luck on board ship. Any unusual deviation from gender norms is forbidden, rendered more illogical by the government's emphasis on women in "needed" traditionally male occupations such as engineer and crane operator. The child experiences this taboo as unfair, and she never gives up admiring sailors as an emblem of independence. Her grandmother tells her not to wear the blue suit her mother bought her, because it looks unbecoming. Given Jenny's brown eyes and hair, the grandmother proclaims: "Blau steht dir nicht" (Blue is not your color). The nine-year-old is admonished to be decorative, and presumably more feminine, by wearing bright colors like red and green.

Nonetheless, she does find a way out by becoming a naturalist, if not a sailor. While sailing the open sea is forbidden by the government, even though it beckons from close by, collecting debris churned up by the ocean is permitted—if grudgingly. Even as Jenny and her grandfather busy themselves at dawn on the beach, the local VOPO (police constable) challenges them. This climate of suspicion makes people taciturn, and there is an inherent sadness in a whole population of old men so hemmed in, still desiring to steer their own ship, but never being allowed to do so. However, some of the older men still speak Platt (Low German) to each other, to express a local identity that predates and trumps communism. Most wear dark blue hats with a back visor that look like captain's hats. Jenny comments: "So viele Kapitäne, und weit und breit kein Schiff" (*B*, 10; So many captains, and no boat to be found far and wide). After the fall of the Berlin Wall, Jenny and her mother travel immediately to West Berlin because of this pent-up desire to transgress.

The particular delight of this book is how Schalansky links Jenny's desire for the androgynous sailor suit with that of others who wore it across the centuries: those who were to become innovators, such as the Russian filmmaker Sergei Eisenstein, and those, such as Crown Prince Nikolai of Russia, who failed to live out their anticipated trajectory, creating a scandal through a tragic life and violent death. They alternate in the book with the long-forgotten surrealist French artist and lesbian photographer Claude Cahun (whom we can now admire as the gender-bending precursor of contemporary feminist artists such as Cindy Sherman) and the postwar writer Wolfgang Koeppen, a native of Greifswald. The adult Jenny herself will travel to New York City to take pictures, but she becomes fascinated by a sailor she sees in the street. She ends up at night in Chelsea in a gay club, where she is told "Sorry, no girls" (*B*, 85). Even in this land of supposed freedom her behavior is restricted because of gender. It is ironic that even though Jenny herself may be gay, she is excluded by gay men from their group, based only on her female body. Jenny is actually mimicking Claude Cahun's masculine swagger in her self-portrait as a sailor, a reproduction of her photograph we saw five pages earlier in her text: "Ich suche eine Lücke an der Bar, schiebe mich auf den Hocker, breite Knie und Schultern aus und betrachte die sich aalenden Körper.

Auftrieb durch Verdrängung. Wo ein Körper ist, kann kein zweiter sein. Wo ich bin, kann kein anderer sein. Das ist logisch, tut aber weh" (*B*, 84; I look for an opening at the bar, push myself onto the stool, spread out my knees and my shoulders and watch the luxuriating bodies. Buoyancy through pushing away. Where there is one body, there is no room for another. Where I am, there can be no other. That is logical, but it pains me). This crucial law of physical bodies is overcome in writing, because the narrator is free to imagine her affinity to others who felt ostracized before she came along.

In a 2009 interview about her island project, Schalansky argues that islands can be dystopian spaces, but that seekers deserve our empathy, because they are facing up to their own condition: "During my childhood in Greifswald everything beyond our tiny territory was unattainable. Between GDR and FRG ran the accidental divide of the atlas spine. The other side of the world was on the facing page. Our idea of freedom is conditioned by living landlocked. If the boat only arrives three times a year, there is no true freedom. . . . the GDR was an island."[27] As an avid reader of maps, the young Schalansky became aware of the arbitrariness of the GDR's isolation and longed to experience what lay beyond. In her fiction she subjects her female characters to conditions of being marooned in the hinterlands of the former East Germany to tease out their resilience against Orwellian conformism, yet in resisting conformism they also damage a younger generation.

Both *Blau steht dir nicht* and *Taschenatlas* are projects of reclamation. On her path to adulthood, Schalansky resented the ideological self-dramatization of the GDR as an island of communism in a sea of hostile capitalists, just as she chafed under the heteronormativity of imposed career goals and the sexist projections of male peers. Attracted to the prospect of remote island living as a voluntary intellectual choice, she repurposed this idea to signify a space for self-recovery, an autonomous vantage point from which the normative systems such as communism, sexism, and neoliberalism can be understood as parallel to one another and may consequently be critiqued. Her youthful reinvention as a "Matrösin," a designation that does not exist as such in German, allows her protagonist to express a cosmopolitan desire for world citizenship that originates in a genuine, and necessarily non-objectifying, interest in others and their life-worlds. Schalansky's readers are invited to embark on this journey by carrying her handy vade-mecum in their pockets, readily available as they go about their own daily routines.

Julia Schoch's female characters share with Schalansky's the desire for far-flung travel combined with forays into devolved regions in Eastern Europe. Like Schalansky's ossified teacher, Schoch's female observers often sport nonfunctional limbs or a disfiguring skin disease. They feel relegated to the role of powerless bystander in neoliberal mediatized spectacles of crisis: for example, Claire in *Verabredungen mit Mattok* (Assignations with Mattok, 2004),[28] or the eastern backcountry wife and mother in *Mit der Geschwindigkeit des Sommers* (With the Speed of Summer, 2009).[29] But while Schoch's characters are more timid than Schalansky's, their efforts to break out of confining strictures culminate in rash, destructive gestures: they gamble away their life savings, they swiftly drown an enemy, or they commit suicide. These actions may be read as violent attempts to clear the way for a rebirth into a radically different life. Their shock value prompts a searching dialogue between the narrator and an individual who was once close to her, but who is now lost or absent, and whose place the reader must take.

Schoch was fifteen years old when the Berlin Wall fell. The fact that her father was a high-ranking army operative and communist true believer set the stage for intergenerational conflict. In her novel *Mit der Geschwindigkeit des Sommers*, Schoch portrays the keen disappointment with the outcome of the *Wende* in the former East via her female narrator's subdued sister, who ends up committing suicide on her first trip abroad when she realizes the full extent of her alienation. In her 2012 *Selbstporträt mit Bonaparte* (Self-Portrait with Bonaparte), Schoch revives the figure of the attractive male gambler from *Verabredungen mit Mattok*, relocating the gambler's origin from an Eastern Bloc country to the West. The female narrator, an academic freelancer whose assignments are precarious and make for an insecure lifestyle, finds herself drawn to his casual, superior attitude toward money, work, and relationships and attempts to mimic it. In an effort to assume risk, she ends up gambling away her life savings in one fell swoop to free herself from the careful way in which she has conducted her own life. Like his historical namesake, "Bonaparte" is a ruthless global player who also embodies the distracted ubiquity of neoliberalism. He travels seemingly effortlessly between the academy and the casino, between California, Las Vegas, Berlin, and a sleepy resort on the Baltic coast. Through her mimicry, the female protagonist also unmasks rapacious masculinity as a new model of neoliberal risk-taking. Schoch's gambler embodies the neoliberal ideal of "someone who revels in the opportunity to remake themselves ... who grasps rashly and imperiously for self-gratification."[30] The dominant but blurrily contoured kinetic male is merely a clever device deployed by the female narrator to lure readers into a philosophical dialogue that masquerades as a love story, as Schoch's title *Selbstporträt mit Bonaparte* (Self-portrait with/by means of Bonaparte) may suggest.

In an era when introspection has been supplanted by the spectacle of agile entrepreneurial selves (even if these might be in free fall), Schoch's female protagonists are tasked with interrogating themselves. Bonaparte's lover asks critically, "Aber was heißt: *mein* Leben? Und was heißt: *ich*?" (But what does *my* life mean? And what is this thing called *I*?).[31] These characters engage in self-questioning in order to confront the normative constraints of the social system they operate under and to release their own dimmed potential. Schoch's female protagonists, like Schalansky's, rebel in various ways against the aridity of the neoliberal environment in which they operate. The only way to attain a critical vantage point within the diegetic realm is to open up meditative spaces. These set their characters apart in a time-out-of-time, or a remote area away from urban sprawl. By adopting and performing the male stances of the scientist as cartographer and naturalist, or the gambler and painter, Schoch and Schalanksy expose the rigidity and the arbitrary arrangement of oppressive social systems. "Ich wollte dort [an der Ostsee] einen Aufsatz über die Arbeiten eines Malers schreiben, der sich mit der Versteppung von Landstrichen befasste" (I wanted to travel to the Baltic coast to write an essay about the works of a painter who depicted the desertification of regions) claims the female narrator of *Selbstporträt mit Bonaparte*.[32] Desertification is a catastrophic consequence of human mismanagement of natural resources. It is also a pointed reference to the economic flight of East Germans away from the East, an immediate consequence of the *Treuhand*'s economic restructuring of Eastern businesses by selling them out, often below value, to West German bidders who had no interest in boosting their viability.

Schoch focuses on the loss of pride in one's work in the shift from communism to neoliberalism. Anxious not to lose their work, however mundane and unskilled, neoliberal workers over-perform with officiousness. They become robotic and sporadically violent to vent their frustration. Claire's numb right hand is a symbol for the relegation of female workers back to the private sphere after unification. Unlike the new neoliberal model workers, Claire actively seeks to undo her marginalization and is constantly involved in reorienting herself in her new environment. She realizes its implacable sameness, as she turns the cracked binoculars away from the empty ocean in front of her toward herself and studies the material of her clothes. This apparent reification of her body is an optical distortion but also represents the Kafkaesque depersonalization that neoliberalism demands of those under its sway.

Conclusion

Hacker portrays how neoliberal Darwinism leads to urban class warfare, with underclass males reacting violently against their own relegation to permanent marginality and invisibility. In ascribing such violent impulses primarily to this group, she perpetuates white middle-class stereotypes about the working class as criminal and sexist. The female protagonist is still tasked with the emotional rehabilitation of males and children, and she is punished for her lack of interest, echoing traditional gender norms. Her affluent neoliberal agents are childlike somnambulists, who need to be shocked into an awareness of the facile solipsism of their worldview.

Schalansky, by contrast, chooses a provincial setting on the margins of the former East Germany to show the corrosive effects of global competition even in such a seemingly placid backwater, and her perpetrator is atypically a female protagonist in the education system. She wishes to point out the destructive effect a person in a position of authority may have on her charges, blaming both Inge herself and the coercive Stalinist dogma that shaped her. In the end, Inge is disciplined by a male authority and forced out of the workplace. She invokes a harsh determinism as the best life lesson for a new generation that has to compete in the neoliberal marketplace. Inge's inhumanity is an outcome of her reification by both GDR-era communism and the neoliberalism of the Federal Republic.

Richter and Schoch, on the other hand, choose individuals whose sense of agency is not so overtly defined as characteristic of a particular caste. Their diffuse treatment of disaffection and anomie attenuates their political critique, as they target phenomena rather than systemic root causes. In Schoch's case this may be due to her philosophical skepticism about all forms of grand economic and social schemes, be they communist or capitalist. Richter's protagonists, however, seem too mired in intergenerational misunderstandings and caught up in the rat race to create a political agenda that would oppose neoliberalism. Their attempts to become small-scale entrepreneurs by opening a stand, then a chain of stands in the marketplace resemble a "green" version of neoliberal ideology and bootstrap capitalism. Entirely missing are the systemic critique and coalition building with other disenfranchised groups on the left spectrum that used to characterize post-1968 feminism.

Both Richter and Schalansky (in *Atlas*) bend the genre conventions of narrative in the vignettes they string together. Schalansky lauds the transgressive curiosity of the seeker who reinvents herself by imagining other islands rather than nations, and radically other ways of being in her body. She especially exposes as shams the notions of stable gender and master narrative. Of the four authors, Schalansky's normative critique is the most mordant, because she explicitly articulates the convergence of the Stalinist model of communism with neoliberalism, unveiling the cult of paternalistic authority that undergirds each system. Furthermore, neither Schalansky nor Richter depicts sisterhood in the female protagonists' struggle to overcome paternalism, a fact that attests to the waning influence of feminism in women's literature today. In Schalansky's case, maverick allies are discovered in the past, with the understanding that a historiographic excavation is needed in the absence of a strong belief in the future. The ideology of communism with its relentless deferral of utopia to a distant future resulted in a disenchantment with grand revolutionary visions. The critical topography of islands is a useful model for understanding causality, providing a clearly defined environment where actions have visible impacts. The island biotope is a model for an impact study of neoliberalism, which itself masquerades as spontaneous order and demands flexible adaptation of human capital to volatile circumstances.

Readers explore this strange microcosm, only to be led back to their own distracted and fragmentary present to ask: who profits, and at what cost? While some organized youth resistance has been catalyzed by the harshness and cynicism with which globalized competition is waged according to the neoliberal screed, the movement has not yet become reflected programmatically in German women's literature. Nonetheless, negative states of being need to be seen as integral to the process of metamorphosis, as they can constitute key conditions for the emergence of new opportunities for connection and new political formations. East German women writers such as Schoch and Schalansky at least present readers with introspective female protagonists, and they condense their critique of neoliberal effects into salient metaphors that readers have to unpack. Less moralistic in tone than Hacker and Richter, they nonetheless hone in on neoliberalism's costs, especially for women. First in line to be affected by systemic inequality and insecurity in the economic sector, the women in all the novels considered here turn into bellwethers for a perniciously creeping dismantling of the self in the name of ecstatic reconfiguration and entrepreneurial opportunity.

Notes

[1] Jeffrey T. Nealon, *Post-postmodernism: or, The Cultural Logic of Just-in-Time Capitalism* (Palo Alto, CA: Stanford University Press, 2012), back cover.

[2] Christoph Butterwegge, Bettina Lösch, and Ralf Ptak, *Kritik des Neoliberalismus* (2006; repr., Wiesbaden: VS Verlag für Sozialwissenschaften, 2007), 199. All translations in this chapter are my own.

[3] June Deery, *Consuming Reality: The Commercialization of Factual Entertainment* (New York: Palgrave Macmillan, 2012).

[4] See Nealon, *Post-postmodernism*, 148. Nealon argues (based on Foucault's notion of biopower) that financialization has penetrated into all spheres of everyday life.

[5] Philip Mirowski, *Never Let a Serious Crisis Go to Waste* (New York: Verso, 2013), 92.

[6] Hester Baer, "German Feminism in the Age of Neoliberalism: Jana Hensel and Elisabeth Raether's *Neue deutsche Mädchen*," *German Studies Review* vol. 35, no. 2 (May 2012): 359–60.

[7] Mirowski, *Never Let a Serious Crisis Go to Waste*, 55.

[8] Julia Schoch, *Selbstporträt mit Bonaparte* (Munich: Piper, 2012), 9.

[9] Butterwege, Lösch, and Ptak, *Kritik des Neoliberalismus*, 103.

[10] Wilhelm Heitmeyer, *Deutsche Zustände Folge 5* (Frankfurt: Suhrkamp, 2007), 38. For a discussion of the parallel British scenario under Tony Blair's leadership see Heitmeyer, *Deutsche Zustände Folge 10* (Frankfurt: Suhrkamp, 2012), 43.

[11] For a detailed analysis of the symbolics of house and home, see Monika Shafi, "'New concept—new life': Bodies and Buildings in Katharina Hacker's *Die Habenichtse*," *Seminar* 47, no. 4 (2011): 434–46.

[12] Katharina Hacker, *Die Habenichtse* (Frankfurt: Suhrkamp, 2006), 78. Published in English as *The Have-Nots*, trans. Helen Atkins (New York: Europa Editions, 2008). Translations here are my own. Further references to this work are given in the text using the abbreviation *HN*.

[13] Herbert Schui and Stephanie Blankenburg, *Neoliberalismus: Theorie, Gegner, Praxis* (Hamburg: VSA Verlag, 2002), 176.

[14] Nikola Richter, *Die Lebenspraktikanten* (Frankfurt: Fischer, 2006), 14. Further references to this work are given in the text using the abbreviation *L*.

[15] An insurance report from 2011 shows the number of days missed at work has risen ninefold since 2004, with roughly one hundred thousand insured workers out sick in 2010. "Zahl der Burnout-Erkrankungen steigt," *Die Zeit*, April 19, 2011, http://www.zeit.de/karriere/2011-04/burn-out-erkrankungen.

[16] Ursula Engelen-Kefer, "Die Propagandamaschine läuft," July 3, 2013, http://www.taz.de/Debatte-Jugendarbeitslosigkeit/!119200/.

[17] Butterwegge, Lösch, and Ptak, *Kritik des Neoliberalismus*, 202.

[18] Nadja Klinger and Jens König, *Einfach abgehängt: Ein wahrer Bericht über die neue Armut in Deutschland* (Berlin: Rowohlt, 2006), 104–6.

[19] See Butterwegge's summary of economist Gary Becker's theses, *Kritik des Neoliberalismus*, 224.

[20] In Butterwegge, Lösch, and Ptak, *Kritik des Neoliberalismus*, 245.

[21] Mirowski, *Never Let a Serious Crisis Go to Waste*, 111.

[22] The name Lohmark can be read as a variant of Lamarck, Darwin's precursor, whose system turned out to be flawed.

[23] Judith Schalansky, *Der Hals der Giraffe: Bildungsroman* (Berlin: Suhrkamp, 2011), 139. Further references to this work are given in the text using the abbreviation *HG*.

[24] Judith Schalansky, *Taschenatlas der abgelegenen Inseln: Fünfzig Inseln, auf denen ich niemals war und niemals sein werde* (Frankfurt: Fischer, 2011).

[25] Schalansky, "Das Paradies ist eine Insel: Die Hölle auch," *Taschenatlas*, 15.

[26] Schalansky, *Blau steht dir nicht: Matrosenroman* (Frankfurt: Suhrkamp, 2011), 10. Further references to this work are given in the text using the abbreviation *B*.

[27] Roger Willemsen, "Warum machen Sie das? Judith Schalansky über ihren Atlas der abgelegenen Inseln," *Zeit Magazin*, October 8, 2009, http://www.zeit.de/2009/42/Willemsen-42/komplettansicht.

[28] Julia Schoch, *Verabredungen mit Mattok* (Munich: Piper, 2004).

[29] Julia Schoch, *Mit der Geschwindigkeit des Sommers* (Munich: Piper, 2009).

[30] Mirowski, *Never Let a Serious Crisis Go to Waste*, 119.

[31] Schoch, *Selbstporträt mit Bonaparte*, 11.

[32] Ibid., 20.

9: Sounds of Silence: Rape and Representation in Juli Zeh's Bosnian Travelogue

Jill Suzanne Smith

Same River, Different Sides

ON A SWELTERING SUMMER DAY in 2001, the writer Juli Zeh stood on the banks of the river Drina in Bosnia-Herzegovina, not far from the town of Srebrenica, where, in the summer of 1995, Serbian forces killed 8,000 Bosnian Muslims in plain view of United Nations peacekeeping forces. The Drina does not flow through Srebrenica, but it does flow through Višegrad, one of the first sites of the brutal expulsion of Muslims from northeastern Bosnia. As Zeh struggled to clear her mind of images of bloody corpses floating in the Drina near Višegrad, she turned her thoughts to another German-language writer who journeyed to former Yugoslavia: Peter Handke. Zeh writes:

> Da drüben auf der anderen Seite stand Peter Handke vor fünfdreiviertel Jahren, entdeckte eine schwimmende Kindersandale und wollte nicht herüberkommen. Was haben sie ihn dafür gescholten.[1]

> [Five and three-quarter years ago, Peter Handke stood over there on the other side, discovered a child's floating sandal, and didn't want to come over to this side. How they scolded him for that.]

This brief episode comes from Zeh's Bosnian travelogue *Die Stille ist ein Geräusch* (Even Silence Is a Sound, 2002), a literary rendition of the travel diary the author kept while on a five-week trip through Bosnia in 2001. With only her dog Othello as her constant companion, Zeh journeyed through various Bosnian towns and cities, taking in the landscape still marred by war and littered with landmines, and interacting with locals, with Western journalists, and with members of international peacekeeping forces. The text has a complex narrative structure; Zeh interweaves the first-person account of her trip through Bosnia with geopolitical references to the conflict in Yugoslavia and with cultural references, both implicit and explicit, to literary works by Hans Magnus Enzensberger and Joseph Conrad, contemporary films, and even the beloved Asterix comics.[2] The passage on Handke itself is multilayered, pointing first to a particular moment in Handke's own account of his 1995 journey to Serbia, *Eine winterliche Reise zu den Flüssen Donau, Save, Morawa und Drina oder Gerechtigkeit für Serbien* (A Winter Journey to the Rivers Danube, Save, Morawa, and Drina, or Justice for Serbia, 1996; published in English as *A Journey to the Rivers: Justice for Serbia*, 1997), and then to the controversy that immediately followed its publication in the *Süddeutsche Zeitung*.[3] The specific passage to which Zeh's text refers is one in which Handke indeed stands on the snow-covered banks of the Drina, on the Serbian side. As a child's sandal bobs to the surface next to his feet (or at least that is what he imagines), he realizes that he is not far from Srebrenica. He does not, however, venture to the Bosnian side of the Drina.[4] As Zeh intimates by mentioning the scolding of Handke, the author's perceived reluctance to visit Bosnia was understood by his critics as evidence for his political support of Serbia and, therewith, his denial of the realities of genocidal war.[5] Handke's central argument, however, was that the realities of war in Yugoslavia—in particular the war's causes—had been obscured by sensationalist media reports intent on shocking readers with stories of atrocities perpetrated by the Serbs.

It is apt that Zeh thinks of Handke as she gazes at the waters of the Drina, for the travel narratives of both writers deliver stinging critiques of the news media. At the outset of her text, Zeh claims that she is traveling to Bosnia because media reports have made her doubt the country's very existence. Through witty asides like "ausser *Spiegel* und *Stern* keine Pornomagazine" (besides *Spiegel* and *Stern* there are no porn magazines) and her unflattering portrait of a rotund British journalist who is working on an exposé on violence against women, Zeh criticizes the affect of "Betroffenheit" (the state of being emotionally "moved" or "touched") and the air of moral superiority exuded by Western journalists vis-à-vis the former Yugoslavia (*SG*, 11, 142). For his part, Handke accuses the media of presenting to readers oversimplified, exaggerated images of the warring factions—the Serbs, for instance, are described as "psychopaths"—and of allowing the Western European powers to obfuscate their own responsibility for the political disintegration of Yugoslavia and the onset of hostilities. He pleads for an alternative narrative and asks: "Wer wird diese Geschichte einmal anders schreiben, und sei es auch bloß in den Nuancen—die freilich viel dazutun könnten, die Völker aus ihrer gegenseitigen Bilderstarre zu erlösen?" (Who will someday write this history differently, and even if only the nuances—which could do much to liberate the peoples from their mutual inflexible images?).[6] Although Handke himself did not attempt to write such a nuanced geopolitical history of the

Yugoslav conflict, his travelogue proposes that literature plays an indispensable role in bringing readers closer to Yugoslav culture—or at least in disabusing them of false images of that culture. It does so by posing numerous critical questions that poke holes in the so-called facts reported and the overblown rhetoric used by the mainstream media, yet it is also poetic in its depiction of the Serbian landscape and people, and its polemic tone is frequently countered by questions that the narrator (the "I" that is presumed by critics and scholars to be Handke) directs back at himself. The questions themselves, the narrator claims, are essential to the achievement of justice, by which he means a more just representation of a very complex situation: "Es drängt mich nur nach Gerechtigkeit. Oder vielleicht überhaupt bloß nach Bedenklichkeit, Zu-bedenken-Geben" (I feel compelled only to justice. Or perhaps even only to questioning, to raising doubts).[7] In contrast to the news media, which often frame their questions in ways that predetermine the answers, Zeh's text, like Handke's, poses a myriad of questions that have no clear answers, or perhaps no answers whatsoever. And Zeh's work, like Handke's, is an experiment with a literary genre that defies easy categorization, an attempt to juxtapose "*eine* literarisch-subjektive Sichtweise" (*a* literary-subjective point of view) with that of "*der* objektiven oder pseudoobjektiven journalistischen Berichterstattung" (*the* objective or pseudo-objective journalistic form of reporting).[8] Zeh's use of the indefinite article for her own narrative marks it as open to critical reading and interpretation, while her use of the definite article for journalism mocks the media's self-proclaimed authority and undermines its claims of truth and objectivity.

It is also fitting, however, that in Zeh's travelogue she and Handke stand on opposite banks of the Drina, for Zeh's text differs from Handke's in several important ways. The first point of diversion between the two texts is their rather obvious temporal and spatial difference: whereas Handke chose to travel to Serbia in the mid-1990s in order to complicate the idea of Serbia as the land of the perpetrators, Zeh traveled to Bosnia-Herzegovina more than five years after the war's end in order to complicate the idea of Bosnia as the ravaged land of the victims. Even in 2001, the map at the German travel agency Zeh visits before her trip depicts Bosnia as "ein weißer Fleck" ("a white spot," meaning here "a blank spot"), as if it were not merely inhospitable to tourists, but uninhabited and uninhabitable, as if the war had wiped it off the map (*SG*, 9). Unlike Handke, whose contentious attacks on the media and, later, on the war crimes tribunal in the Hague were perceived as a defense of Serbia, Zeh refuses to choose political sides; in her travels she meets, questions, and listens to Croats, Bosnians, Serbs, and members of the international community.

Most important for this essay, Zeh's work deals with the gendered dimension of the Yugoslav wars—a central aspect of the conflict that

Handke ignores, namely the rape of thousands of Yugoslav women, the majority of whom were Bosnian Muslims. Zeh's text reminds readers that gender is inseparable from a discussion of the Balkan wars of the 1990s, in which the mass rape of women was systematically used as a form of warfare.[9] The absence of gendered violence in Handke's travelogue stands in stark contrast to its presence in Zeh's text, in the very scenes in which the two writers stand on the banks of the Drina. It is the image of the floating sandal and the childhood innocence it evokes that makes Handke think of the human tragedy that took place at Srebrenica and wonder how such an act of violence could have happened under the watchful eye of the UN. While it may be evocative of both life and innocence lost, the sandal is a fleeting image that characterizes Handke's own fleeting engagement with the specific acts of violence perpetrated by the Serbs in Srebrenica. Zeh, writing with postwar Srebrenica in mind, does not shy away from wondering how the town's current Serb residents could bear to live there: "Wie kann man von einem Küchentisch essen, der Unterlage einer Vergewaltigung war? In Betten schlafen, deren zerschossene, blutige Matratzen erst mal entfernt werden mussten?" (*SG*, 233; How can one eat from a kitchen table that served as the platform for a rape? Sleep in beds whose bullet-riddled, bloody mattresses first had to be removed?). This blatant mention of rape as a war crime is just one example of rape's pervasive presence in Zeh's travelogue: it surfaces as a memory in the hostile interaction between a Croatian and a Bosnian man, both of whom have befriended Zeh during her travels; it surfaces as a legitimate fear when Zeh is harassed by a Turkish hotel guest in Sarajevo and leered at by Serbian men; and it serves, as I will show, as a problem of literary and cultural representation, when Zeh contemplates the effects that wartime violence has on literature.[10] Handke does not give readers this side of the story, choosing instead to remain on the other side of the river.

By focusing on how Zeh's travelogue grapples with rape and its representation, in this essay I analyze a key aspect of Zeh's text that has, quite surprisingly, not yet received any attention in existing scholarly literature on her work.[11] This puzzling omission of any discussion of the gendered dimension of Zeh's text on Bosnia might be explained by the fact that Zeh herself resists the label of feminist author and rarely foregrounds gender in her writing, but this explanation, I would argue, is inadequate and does not do justice to the complex ways in which gender emerges in Zeh's writing. Although Patricia Herminghouse accurately describes Zeh as a "postfeminist" writer "for whom the struggle against 'the patriarchy' is no longer at the center of her political interest," she concludes all too hastily that Zeh "does not call attention to her gender in addressing social and political issues, neither in her prose fiction nor in the essays."[12] This argument simply cannot be made in reference to *Die Stille ist ein Geräusch*, a work that not only deals with wartime rape but also calls repeated attention to the author's gender by depicting her pervasive unease as a woman traveling alone. By highlighting the gendered dimensions of Zeh's travelogue, my essay brings her work into dialogue not only with well-known German-language writers such as Handke but also with feminist debates on rape from the 1990s. In so doing, it shows how contemporary German women's writing can intervene in discourses on war and ethnic strife that would otherwise either obscure or exploit violent sexual acts committed against women.

Rape and Representation

Peter Handke was not the only writer to attack the media for its sensationalist, clichéd representations of the war in Yugoslavia in the 1990s. The Berlin-based Austrian author Erica Fischer begins her 1997 book *Am Anfang war die Wut* (In the Beginning There Was Anger) with a critical reading of a November 1992 cover story on mass rapes in Yugoslavia that appeared in the German magazine *Stern*.[13] Washed in red, both the magazine cover and the feature article show multiple photographs of weeping, physically ravaged women, and the article's text contains graphic descriptions of sexual violence committed against the women.[14] Like Handke, Fischer presents the shock tactics used by the magazine as reckless and irresponsible, for some of the women interviewed for the story by the German journalist Alexandra Stiglmayer, Fischer claims, were not Bosnian rape victims but Croatian nationalists fanning the flames of hatred against the Serbs. As much as Fischer herself advocates for greater public awareness of the perilous situation for women in the Balkans, she is also vehemently opposed to the nearly pornographic descriptions of wartime violence that serve to objectify female victimhood and cloud the complex political situation (*AW*, 13–14). Juli Zeh's classification of *Stern* as a porno mag would have rung true for Fischer, who was not the only one to be shocked by the magazine's cover story. The protagonist of Fischer's book, the gynecologist Monika Hauser, also read the article and was so enraged by its content that she decided to open a women's health clinic in Zenica, in the heart of war-torn Bosnia. Hauser's rage, however, was not simply provoked by the stories of the rapes themselves, but also by the sensationalist way they were told and visually represented. As Fischer writes of Hauser's reaction to the *Stern* article, "Ihr Entsetzen über das, was die Zeilen ihr vermitteln, mischt sich mit Wut über die Schamlosigkeit des Mißbrauchs der Frauen durch den Blick der Fotografen. Die drastische Sprache schockiert sie" (*AW*, 14–15; The disgust over what the lines of text communicated to her mixes with anger over the shamelessness of the women's abuse by the photographer's gaze. The extreme language shocks her). The way, form, or narrative mode in which information about rape is conveyed to readers is just as important as the information itself.

Fischer's biography of Hauser demonstrates photojournalism's potential to incite readers to meaningful action, but Fischer also emphasizes the danger that media images will provoke overly emotional—she even uses the term "hysterical"—rather than rational reactions, thereby compromising a nuanced understanding of the rapes and their particular context.[15] Fischer presents the "Betroffenheit" that pervaded the German feminist discourse on Yugoslavia in 1992 and 1993 as the enemy of "kritisches Nachdenken" (critical thinking), and she even goes so far as to argue that the affect of "Betroffenheit" led Western feminists to exploit the stories of Bosnian rape victims to further their own fight against "patriarchal[e] Gewalt" (patriarchal violence) at home (*AW*, 17). In Fischer's narrative, true feminist activism involves gaining knowledge of the specific political and ethnic context of the rapes in Yugoslavia, and, in the case of Hauser, taking action within the conflict zone to help and empower local women.

Considering Fischer's standpoint that the rapes in Bosnia should be viewed through the dual lens of gender and political/ethnic divisions, it is no coincidence that her book also begins with a critical reference to the filmmaker Helke Sander. Also featured in the November 1992 cover story in *Stern*, Sander was surprised by the fact that the Bosnian Muslim rape survivors she interviewed expressed rage rather than shame, defiance rather than guilt. In an editorial comment, she wonders whether the Muslim community will allow the women to take such a strong stance. In Fischer's eyes, this comment stems from Sander's own ignorance of Muslim culture and her inability to see rape survivors as anything other than victims.[16] Indeed, Sander found herself at the center of a controversial debate on wartime rape and its representation after she premiered her groundbreaking film *BeFreier und Befreite* (Liberators and the Liberated; released in English as *Liberators Take Liberties*, 1992) at the Berlin Film Festival earlier that year.[17] Sander's film was the first documentary to openly discuss the mass rapes of German women by Soviet and Allied troops at the end of the Second World War, and it sparked a lively discussion both in Germany and among US scholars of German Studies. The debate centered on the tension in the film between the filmmaker's stated desire to bring a specific historical case of mass rape back into German public consciousness after years of silence versus her gestures to universalize rape as a common war crime perpetrated against women. This tension is evident in the opening lines of the film, in which Sander's voice tells viewers that the film is about mass rapes in 1945 Berlin, yet, even as the film continues to roll footage of the ruined German capital, the voiceover draws a comparison to the contemporary moment, stating, "Alle wußten davon, doch niemand sprach darüber, wie heute in Kuwait und Jugoslawien" (Everybody knew about it, but still no one talked about it, just like today in Kuwait and Yugoslavia).[18] Both critics and fans tend to agree that Sander's film compromises historical specificity in favor of what Pascale Bos has pithily called "the ahistorical sexism approach," an interpretation of wartime rape as a symptom of pervasive misogyny.[19] By depicting rape primarily as a sexist crime and German women exclusively as victims of war, the film's detractors argued, Sander ignored the racist genocidal politics of the Nazi regime, as well as German women's complicity with—or even their active support of—that regime.[20] The film's focus on women as victims and the relative lack of attention paid to questions of racial politics, Bos argues, is symptomatic of how feminist artists and thinkers struggled throughout the 1990s to theorize "both women's political agency and sexist oppression in the context of war, particularly in conjunction with issues of race and ethnicity."[21] Sander, for her part, continued to use the "sexism approach" in her public statements on mass rapes in Yugoslavia, and in her prologue to Alexandra Stiglmayer's 1994 book *Mass Rape*, Sander quickly shifts away from a discussion of the specific ethnic and political dynamics in Yugoslavia, and even away from the war itself, to a plea for broader recognition of "how deep misogyny goes, even in countries that are not at war."[22] The rapes in Bosnia, then, are removed from their specific context and explained as a symptom of men's deep-seated hatred of women.

Although an in-depth analysis of Sander's film falls outside the scope of this essay, the film itself, its reception, and Sander's response to the rapes in Yugoslavia reveal how feminists in 1990s German-speaking Europe struggled, and often failed, to reconcile the gender politics with the specific ethnic or national dynamics of wartime rape. Sander's film and her essay on the rapes in Bosnia also serve here as fitting counterexamples to Fischer's more nuanced engagement with questions of gender and sexuality as well as questions of European politics and ethnic tensions in Yugoslavia. Fischer's book effectively challenges clichéd media representations of the rapes in Bosnia, casts a critical eye on Western European feminist myopia that reads the war in Bosnia simply as another example of patriarchal oppression, and takes an intersectional approach to gender and ethnicity. In other words, it shows that women were raped not only because they were women but also because they were seen as ethnic or political enemies (e.g., ethnic slurs for Bosnian Muslims, "Balija" and "Bula," were repeatedly uttered during rapes by both Serbian and Croatian men, and the term "Ustasha whore"[23] was often used by Serbian rapists, who were conditioned to view Croatian women as fascists).[24] Fischer's is a mixed-genre text, perhaps best classified as documentary literature, that combines the biography of Hauser and the story of her clinic in Bosnia with testimonials of Yugoslav rape survivors (Bosnian, Croatian, and Serbian women alike) and detailed contextual information about the conflict in Bosnia, the ever-changing situation on the ground, and the various responses of European governments and organizations to the conflict. The writing style is similar to that of journalism, yet it avoids sensationalism. Because Fischer's text devotes as much space to the voices of local women who worked in Hauser's clinic as it does to the voices of those who survived multiple rapes, it presents more than a one-dimensional view of Bosnian women as victims. It allows them to be agents alongside the main protagonist, Hauser.

For all its strengths, however, Fischer's text is not without moments of pathos and condescension. Indeed, it ends in a way that reinstates rather than undermines hierarchies between German feminist activists like Hauser and her Bosnian medical team and support staff. Western feminism, presented in such a critical light at the beginning of the book, becomes an ideal that was successfully exported to former Yugoslavia. Fischer proclaims: "Ja, es stimmt, der Krieg hat den Feminismus nach Zenica gebracht" (*AW*, 223; Yes, it's true, the war brought feminism to Zenica). While there is certainly nothing wrong with raising feminist consciousness and empowering local women to speak and act on their own behalf, the fact that Fischer's book goes on to describe the eventual separation of the German headquarters in Cologne of Medica mondiale, Hauser's women's health organization, from the original clinic in Zenica as an "Abnabelung" (cutting of the umbilical cord) clearly depicts the German feminists as mothers and the Bosnian women as infantile daughters whose potential for autonomous action is called into question (*AW*, 229). In terms of narrative tone and structure, Fischer makes it clear by inserting herself into the action from time to time that hers is the authoritative voice shaping the fact-driven narrative. Posed as an alternative to the media stories it so reviles, Fischer's book stands as an example of activist feminist non-fiction that promises to give readers the "true story" of the war in Bosnia. And yet the text does not shy away from melodrama in its recounting of Monika Hauser's emotional and physical breakdown after the war, and in its portrait of Hauser as savior in passages such as this: "Die [bosnischen] Frauen stürzen auf Monika zu, streicheln sie, nehmen sie in den Arm, wischen sich die Tränen von den Wangen. 'Du bist da!'" (*AW*, 132; The [Bosnian] women rush to Monika, caress her, take her in their arms, wipe tears from their cheeks. "You're here!").[25] By making Hauser into an undisputed Balkan hero, Fischer's book leaves no doubt that Western feminist intervention is the right remedy for the mass rapes in Bosnia, a perspective that has been heavily criticized in recent feminist legal scholarship on sexual violence and war.[26]

As my analysis of Fischer's text has suggested, the question of how to represent rape is both a political and an aesthetic one. It is a question that ties content to form, that provokes both a discussion of how rape is explained or understood and a debate regarding the proper mode of representation. The blatant sexual violence of rape presents contemporary writers and filmmakers with a conundrum, for how does one represent wartime atrocities against women in a way that expresses the magnitude of suffering without giving way to sensationalistic, melodramatic, or even pornographic modes of narration? Despite all the criticisms leveled at the content of Helke Sander's film, Richard W. McCormick argues that a close, careful analysis of the film's aesthetic, which uses montage style in an ironic, self-reflexive manner, makes it a successful example of how art can represent rape. Sander's frequent and inquisitive presence in the film does not serve to make her into the authoritative voice of truth; rather, it has the opposite effect, McCormick asserts: "This continual emphasis on the process of meaning construction in the search for historical truth and on her [Sander's] own role therein could easily be accused of creating a too complex film, one that deconstructs or undermines any too definitive conclusion about the events being investigated." However, McCormick goes on to argue that "the film's strength lies in its complexity, its refusal of false clarity."[27] I certainly side with McCormick on this point. As a film that breaks the silence surrounding wartime rape without offering viewers graphic descriptions of the acts of sexual violence themselves, and as a documentary work that raises provocative questions regarding the possible motivations for rape without providing definitive answers, Sander's *BeFreier und Befreite* makes a fascinating case study for the aesthetic representation of rape. In its "refusal of false clarity," its questioning of narrative authority, and its engagement with the idea of silence, Sander's film could also be read as an aesthetic model for Juli Zeh's own approach to the topic of rape in *Die Stille ist ein Geräusch*. In what follows, I examine how Zeh's travelogue represents past sexual violence and continued contentious gender relations in Bosnia without lapsing into the affective modes listed above. Zeh's travel narrative can be seen as an example of what I call an "aesthetics of restraint" in regard to the Balkan wars and in particular to the systematic rape of women, an aesthetic that avoids the affective modes of melodrama and what Zeh classifies as "kitsch" in order to engage more effectively with questions of justice, remembrance, artistic production, the European project, and the central role that gender plays in these questions.

Sounds of Silence

In his 1949 "Lecture on Nothing," the experimental composer John Cage performed a rhythmically composed talk in which he gave silence just as much space as uttered words. "But / now / there are silences / and the words / make / help make / the silences," he said in the opening lines of his lecture.[28] Later in the talk, when musing on musical intervals and tonality, he introduced the concept of deceptive cadences, in which listeners are tricked into anticipating or sensing the presence of a tone that is not played: "there are some / pro-gressions called / de-ceptive cadences. / The idea is this: / progress in such a way / as to imply / the presence / of a tone not actually / present; / then fool everyone by not / landing on it— / land somewhere else. / What is being / fooled / ? / Not the ear / but the mind / ."[29] Much like Cage, Juli Zeh explores what silence can do. As the title of her Bosnian travelogue clearly states, even silence is a sound; what is left unsaid or unarticulated is often just as important as what is said, if not more so.

The measure of restraint exercised by Zeh in her Bosnian travel narrative may seem surprising, particularly to those readers who are more familiar with her novels. In her debut novel and first literary engagement with the war in Yugoslavia, *Adler und Engel* (Eagles and Angels, 2001), Zeh confronted readers with shocking scenes of violence (rape and murder) and self-abnegation, scenes that some critics and scholars even describe as "Tarantino-esque."[30] In their representation of rape, the novel and the travelogue are polar opposites. In the novel, Bosnian rape victims, called "Großmütter" (grandmothers) by the childlike, waifish character Jessie, are reduced to a prematurely aged, traumatized mass of women who huddle together in a Serbian torture facility outside Sanski Most. Jessie's father, Herbert, is an Austrian drug smuggler and dealer who offers the women their only chance of release from the facility: they can work for him as drug mules once they are trained by Jessie. Jessie's own naive promise to free one of the women ends in a scene of graphic violence, in which the Serbian war criminal Arkan cuts off the Bosnian woman's ears before shooting her in the face. Zeh gives her readers desecrated bodies and a nightmarish scene—the novel's protagonist Max aptly calls the episode "ein Horrorfilm" (a horror film).[31] And yet Max enacts his own scene of horror on the psychology student Clara, who accompanies him from Leipzig to Vienna in hopes of uncovering the truth about Jessie's suicide. Mechanically mimicking the actions of Serbian perpetrators, Max shaves the heavily drugged Clara's head and then proceeds to rape her in a numb and fumbling manner with his barely erect penis.[32] The novel's shocking "foregrounding of physicality," Claudia Breger argues, helps to create "a poetics of disturbance, in which a critical response . . . is produced in the mode of sensation rather than thought."[33] Zeh herself claims in a 2005 essay that she gave very little thought to how readers would respond to *Adler und Engel*, whereas she viewed *Die Stille ist ein Geräusch* as an intentional work that required a completely different, more controlled and cerebral method of writing than the novel.[34]

Before she became a renowned writer and public intellectual, Zeh practiced writing as a private pastime, developing her fictional texts piecemeal, like snatches of daydreams, in secrecy. While a student at the Deutsches Literaturinstitut (German Institute for Literature) in Leipzig, Zeh began writing for an audience, and she has since written several essays about the writing process, particularly about the different aesthetic strategies she employs depending on the genre in which she is writing. In the essay "Von der Heimlichkeit des Schreibens" (On the Secrecy of Writing), she writes specifically about the difference between her first novel and her travel narrative on Bosnia. The novel, she admits, is the product of writing done in secret; its fragmentary nature and mosaic-like narrative, even its nightmarish quality, are the results of separate literary pieces being patched together years after their initial conception (208). The writing process of *Die Stille ist ein Geräusch* was much more deliberate and measured, for Zeh intended to publish it for a reading public right from the start:

> Mein Bemühen richtete sich darauf, realen Erlebnissen eine Stimme zu verleihen und mit Hilfe der Sprache möglichst nah an tatsächliche Wahrnehmungen und Empfindungen heranzukommen. Das bedeutete eine völlig neue Form des Arbeitens, bei der schöpferischer Akt und handwerkliche Anstrengung im selben Moment zusammenfielen. (209)

> [My efforts were focused on giving a voice to real experiences and, with the help of language, coming as close as possible to actual perceptions and feelings. That meant a completely new way of working, in which the creative act and deliberate craftsmanship came together in the same moment].[35]

The result is a more overtly political work, a literary, essayistic work that defies easy categorization and that is itself a meditation on the possibilities and limitations of literature.

Zeh explicitly discusses the limits of traditional forms of literary expression in her travelogue when she describes her contact with a community of Bosnian writers living in Sarajevo. Goran, the owner of a bookstore and café in the capital city, laments that much of the literature he sells—most of it war prose—is "Kitsch." Goran tells Zeh, "Der Krieg hat nicht nur Menschen getötet, sondern auch ihre Geschichten" (*SG*, 84; The war didn't just kill people, it killed their stories as well). Haunted by Goran's warning, Zeh imagines the possibilities that other cultural media, such as film, might offer. When she finds herself on a desolate and seemingly endless tree-lined street on the outskirts of Sarajevo, she imagines the following scenario:

> Ich denke mir einen Film aus . . .: Ein Paar geht die Allee entlang. Der Mann hat nach zehn Jahren seine Jugendliebe aufgesucht, in der Hoffnung, die Begegnung würde Gefühle wecken, die ihn Gedichte schreiben lassen, wie sie ihm seit dem Krieg nicht gelungen

sind. Aus dem Flirt am Frühlingsabend wird Vertrautheit und daraus Geständnisse, die Jugendliebe erzählt, wie oft sie während des Kriegs vergewaltigt wurde und wie sie sich selber anbot, um ihr Leben zu retten. Andernfalls hätten sie sich zu diesem Spaziergang nicht wiedertreffen können. Der Dichter erkennt die Wahrheit: Kein einziges Gedicht wird er mehr schreiben bis zum Tod. Er will die Jugendliebe loswerden, aber die Allee nimmt kein Ende. Das ganze wäre in einer Einstellung zu drehen, drei Kameras würden aus Dollys vor, neben und hinter den Spaziergängern fahren. (*SG*, 88)

[I think up a film . . .: A couple walks along a tree-lined street. After ten years' time, the man went searching for his former sweetheart in the hope that meeting up with her would awaken feelings that would allow him to write the poems that he has been unable to write since the war. Their flirtatious behavior on this evening in spring results in greater closeness, out of which come confessions. His former sweetheart tells him how often she was raped during the war and how she offered herself freely in order to save her own life. Had she not done it, they could never have met up and taken this walk. The poet realizes the truth: He will never write another poem as long as he lives. He wants to be rid of his former sweetheart, but the street is endless. The whole thing would be filmed in one continuous shot, and three cameras on dollies would film in front, next to, and behind the strolling couple.]

Initially desired by the poet as a potential muse, the woman in Zeh's film scenario loses her desirability and her ability to inspire when she reveals herself as a rape survivor. She becomes a burden for the poet, just as rape becomes a burden for artistic production itself. While Zeh's vision of a minimalist mise-en-scène comprising the tree-lined street and the lone couple departs from the object-laden, claustrophobic interiors of classic melodrama, the woman's confession of her sexual debasement and the poet's tragic "cycle of non-fulfillment," both artistic and emotional, push Zeh's screenplay to the verge of melodrama.[36] The narrative voice immediately pulls back from the melodramatic mode, quickly abandoning that particular experiment to offer some sardonic, self-deprecating remarks, switching back to her travel experiences and cultural observations. It is in these gestures of pulling back from melodramatic expression or graphic descriptions of violence and in the self-conscious avoidance of "kitsch" that what I am calling Zeh's aesthetics of restraint resides. In reading some of the war stories she has bought at Goran's bookstore, Zeh has nightmarish visions that rob her of sleep and cause her to seek solace in the life-affirming antics of her dog, Othello. But this flight from visions of horror into a cheery, life-affirming narrative, Zeh admits, places her squarely in the realm of kitsch: "Und schon sitze ich mitten im Kitsch, von dem Goran gesprochen hat. Aber es beruhigt" (*SG*, 95; And now here I am, sitting right in the middle of the kitsch that Goran talked about. But it's comforting).[37] Kitsch may be comforting, as Zeh mentions, but it does not make for good literature, nor does an overexposure to the violent memories of war, for the nightmares they bring can cause an intense desire to forget, an emotional numbness, a flight into oblivion. As Andreas Huyssen argues in his book *Present Pasts*, if we let the media (be it journalism, digital media, literature, or film) carry the full burden of representing historical trauma for us, we become increasingly distant from or numb to actual events. Active, discerning readers, however, will engage critically with different types of media and with the traumatic past, without losing their sense of the present or the future.[38]

As a meditation on the aesthetic representation of gendered violence and war, Zeh's travelogue is pitched to a curious and discerning reader. As a medium that requires both the reader and the writer to remain open to spontaneous discovery, the travelogue is the account of a journey that is simultaneously physical and intellectual. For readers who wish to learn more about the region or make the trip to Bosnia themselves, *Die Stille ist ein Geräusch* is also the only text by Zeh that has its own accompanying website where readers can access geopolitical information about the Yugoslav wars, excerpts from the travelogue itself, and Zeh's personal photos, trip itinerary, and pragmatic travel advice.[39] The book transcends its physical limits—and the limits of genre—and becomes a mixed-media or "intermedial" text that embraces different modes of reading and perspectives on the Bosnian conflict and on postwar Bosnia.[40]

The narrative perspective is clearly a gendered one that asks the reader to contemplate the place of women in twenty-first-century Bosnia. Mobilizing the politics of the gaze, Zeh cannily portrays her pervasive unease as a woman traveling alone in desolate communities that seem to be populated only by men—men who sit on plastic chairs in front of their houses and cafés and stare rather suggestively at Zeh. Refusing to be objectified or intimidated, she stares back at them until they lower their gaze or even hide their faces behind other men (*SG*, 158–59). Despite the author's courage, the absence of Bosnian women helps convey the eerie, threatening mood of this scene and of the text in general. "Wo sind eigentlich die anderen Frauen?" (Where are the other women?), Zeh asks, causing readers to ponder the long-term effects that the wartime rapes might have had on Bosnian gender demographics (*SG*, 159).

The text's openness to critical contemplation on the part of the reader is a result of both narrative complexity and the narrative voice's restraint in regard to its own authority. True, Zeh the traveler exhibits moments of great strength and courage, as evidenced in the above example, but just as often she is vulnerable, frustrated, and disoriented. As Jürgen Brokoff has suggested, the narrative voice that structures the text is often distanced, or dissociated, from what Brokoff calls the text's "protagonist," the active traveler. This dissociation of the protagonist from the narrator, this split first-person perspective, Brokoff argues, opens up space between the traveler's actions and the narrative voice's critical reflections on politics and aesthetics, thereby activating the reader.[41] Through this split perspective, Zeh creates a first-person narrative in which the "I" often pulls back in order to make room for other voices, other stories, and other images: these are, of course, structured by the narrator, yet are not dominated by her.[42] With the exception of the brief screenplay about the poet and his childhood sweetheart that I quote above, in which Zeh as narrator envisions a Bosnian rape survivor, Zeh never tries to narrate the rape of a Bosnian woman, and she reminds readers that her authorial perspective can not and will not offer such a narrative. In this respect, Zeh sets her work clearly apart from 1990s feminist narratives such as Erica Fischer's, in which Fischer adopts a very clear position of Western narrative authority. Zeh may imagine herself as a potential victim of rape, as she does several times in the travelogue, and she may even allow herself to stand in as a woman victim of war at the request of a bereaved relative, as I will explain below. Yet, she admits,

> Gewissen Ereignissen gegenüber werde ich immer dreitausend Kilometer weg sitzen, genau da, wo ich saß, als sie stattfanden. Am Ort des Verbrechens zu stehen ändert nichts. (*SG*, 158)

> [In the case of certain events, I will always sit 3,000 kilometers away, just as far away as I was when they happened. Standing at the scene of the crime doesn't change anything.]

By admitting to her own distance from the experience of wartime rape and by refusing to use her Western European perspective as grounds for authority, Zeh becomes a more credible, trustworthy guide, one who challenges readers to question the notion that travel to previously war-torn regions will result in the unearthing of truths or to a greater understanding of the crimes humans commit against one another.[43]

In her analysis of Zeh's travelogue, Gordana Grozdanic unfairly criticizes Zeh for relying too much on her own narrative authority, for privileging her own eye-witness account over "ortsgebunden[en] ... Referenzen" (local sources).[44] By silencing the voices of Bosnians, Grozdanic argues, Zeh fails to honor the specific context of her work. Brokoff, on the other hand, praises Zeh for doing exactly the opposite: "Die eigene Rede setzt aus, pausiert, um den Anderen, der mehr zu erzählen weiß, zu Wort kommen zu lassen" ([Zeh's] own voice suspends itself, pauses, in order to let the other, who has more to tell, speak).[45] I propose a different reading, one that shows that some of the most harrowing moments in the text are ones of silence, ones that offer visual snapshots of grief and loss against the implicit backdrop of wartime violence against women.

On her first night in Bosnia, Zeh meets Dario, a Croatian man whose sister was killed and possibly also raped in the war. After the long silence that follows Dario's brief description of his home being under siege, he expresses his wish for Zeh, who is the same age and physical build as his sister, to dress in his sister's clothes and stand silently at the window, smoking a cigarette and dropping ashes on the floor. This wish, incidentally, is never voiced in the text. We only know that Dario has a request, and then Zeh describes the scene, relying on the reader to fill in the gaps. What she does articulate is the silence: "Es ist vollkommen still" (It is completely quiet). The only sounds that punctuate the silence are the beating of Zeh's heart, the breathing of her dog, and Dario's occasional sniffling (*SG*, 33–34). The scene stands out as the sole example of Zeh embodying the absent woman, of bringing a suffering woman briefly back to life. In two later examples, she is first an astute observer describing what she sees and then a dreamer struggling in vain to make sense of her experiences. The result is two somber, haunting snapshots of young women: one is a girl in a wheelchair whose body is present but whose mind has taken her elsewhere. "Obwohl ich sie mit ausgestrecktem Arm berühren könnte," writes Zeh, "kann man nicht weiter weg sein als sie" (*SG*, 237; Even though I could touch her with my outstretched arm, no one could be farther away than she). The second young woman, who appears only in a dream, looks at Zeh in a way that shocks the writer into silence. "Nur einmal schaut eine junge Frau mit verwegener, sonnengebleichter Frisur mich an, so auffordernd, dass ich vor Schreck keine Wörter finde" (*SG*, 150; Just once a young woman with rakish, sun-bleached hair looks at me in such a way, so imploringly, that, startled, I'm at a loss for words). That particular chapter ends there, with the loss for words, with silence.

If silence is a sound, then the absence of women—whether real or virtual—conveys the ever-present memory of wartime trauma. Silence, for Zeh, is not the same as silencing, but it is a key element in the aesthetics of restraint that she develops in her Bosnian travelogue. The text expresses the failing of words and the limits of literature with great poignancy and humanity. While Grozdanic would have Zeh channel Bosnian voices to give her readers a more coherent picture of the Yugoslav conflicts and their context, Zeh harbors no illusions about her own limited perspective, and she eschews any claims to expertise. "Keine meiner Fragen habe ich beantwortet" (I haven't answered any of my questions), she states at the end of the journey, but she admits a few chapters earlier that, unlike a journalist, she was never looking for answers (*SG*, 263, 234). Still, the questions raised by Zeh's text challenge readers to think about how literature can convey the horrors of rape and still preserve the dignity of those who survive it. The answer Zeh's text seems to convey is to use restraint.

In their recent study *Rape in Wartime*, the historians Raphaëlle Branche and Fabrice Virgili stress the importance of restraint as an aesthetic approach to rape. While they lament the omission or silencing of rape in many historical accounts of war, they also assert that writing about rape requires caution. They identify two basic "requirements" for writers to consider: first, "rape needs to be addressed in plain language," and second, those who write about rape should "not . . . indulge in rhetoric that can all too easily" evoke "emotional or ideological" responses in readers.[46] Juli Zeh's travelogue *Die Stille ist ein Geräusch* neither omits nor exploits the crime of wartime rape. Instead, it engages with the idea of silence in two key ways: on the one hand, her book breaks the silence that descended upon the rapes of Bosnian women once the Yugoslav conflicts drew to a close. In contrast to well-known writers such as Peter Handke, whose extensive work on the Yugoslav wars ignores rape, Zeh repeatedly and soberly names the crime and marks it as gendered, addressing feminist concerns regarding women's violent oppression by men. Her twenty-first-century travelogue thereby engages in dialogue with Erica Fischer's and Helke Sander's work from the 1990s. On the other hand, Zeh reinstates the concept of silence as part of an aesthetics of restraint that refuses to indulge in melodramatic or sensational modes of narration. It is the author's open struggle to find a fitting mode of representation for rape, played out in the pages of her travelogue, as well as her refusal to adopt a position of Western authority, that separates her own feminist work from those who came before her.

Epilogue in the Disco: Living Loudly

In an essay published in the German women's magazine *Brigitte* the same year that her travelogue appeared, Zeh describes a night in a Bosnian disco that was anything but silent. DJ Jasmina, the only woman DJ in Bosnia, appears only briefly in *Die Stille ist ein Geräusch*, but she is given much clearer contours in Zeh's essay. Having returned to Bosnia after living in Germany for most of the war, Jasmina is determined to remain there and to use culture as a uniting force between Bosnian Muslims, Serbs, Croats, and Kosovars. Undeterred by those who complain that chaos reigns in former Yugoslavia and that opportunities for young people are limited, Jasmina counters: "Man kann es aber auch anders sehen: Nirgendwo sonst kannst du so leicht etwas Neues, Eigenes schaffen. Ich will hier nicht weg" (One can look at it another way: nowhere else is it so easy to create something new, something that's your own. I don't want to leave).[47] With her vibrant presence, the Jasmina of Zeh's essay replaces the silence of Zeh's more sober travel text with loud disco music, to which a community of young Bosnians and Western Europeans dance together. As the legal scholar Wolfgang Vitzthum asks in reference to Zeh's Bosnian texts: "Wird hier auf dem so schicksalsdunklen wie überlebungskräftigen Balkan der europäische Mensch geboren?" (Is it here in the ill-fated yet tenacious Balkans that the European human being will be born?).[48] Again, Zeh's text only hints at an answer, but even more important than providing an answer, it makes readers envision a Europe in which Eastern Europeans shape their own destinies, where East and West inspire each other in equal measure, and where a woman, quite literally, sets the tone.

Notes

[1] Juli Zeh, *Die Stille ist ein Geräusch: Eine Fahrt durch Bosnien* (Repr., Munich: btb, 2003), 230–31. Further references to this work are given in the text, using the abbreviation *SG*. Unless indicated otherwise, all translations in this chapter are my own. On the Srebrenica and Višegrad massacres, respectively, see Misha Glenny, *The Fall of Yugoslavia: The Third Balkan War*, 3rd rev. ed. (New York: Penguin, 1996), 273, 168–69.

[2] For an analysis of Zeh's intertextual references to Enzensberger and Conrad, see Jürgen Brokoff, "'Zusehen, wie alles grundlos zwischen Gut und Böse pendelt': Ethik und Ästhetik der Darstellung in Juli Zehs Bosnientext *Die Stille ist ein Geräusch*," in *Spielräume: Ein Buch für Jürgen Fohrmann*, ed. Jürgen Brokoff, Elke Dubbels, and Andrea Schütte (Bielefeld: Aisthesis, 2013), 263–77, here 263–64. Recounting her visit to the Sarajevo Film Festival in *Die Stille*, Zeh mentions Danis Tanovic's critically acclaimed film on the Yugoslav wars, *No Man's Land* (2001) (117).

[3] Peter Handke, *Eine winterliche Reise zu den Flüssen Donau, Save, Morawa und Drina oder Gerechtigkeit für Serbien* (Frankfurt am Main: Suhrkamp, 1996), translated as *A Journey to the Rivers: Justice for Serbia*, trans. Scott Abbott (New York: Viking, 1997). The particular episode to which Zeh refers appears on page 121 in the German version. Handke's text appeared in two weekend editions of the *Süddeutsche Zeitung* in early January 1996. The literature on the controversy that followed the work's publication is vast. The following texts offer clear, concise analyses of the debate and of Handke's larger body of work on Yugoslavia: Scott Abbott, "Handke's Yugoslavia Work," in *The Works of Peter Handke: International Perspectives*, ed. David N. Coury and Frank Pilipp (Riverside, CA: Ariadne, 2005), 359–86; Gordana-Dana Grozdanic, "Peter Handke: 'Entwurf Jugoslawien,'" chapter 4 in *Der Balkankrieg als literarisches Phaenomen: Auseinandersetzungen deutschsprachiger Autoren* (PhD diss., University of Pennsylvania, 2008), 123–77.

[4] Handke did eventually visit the Serbian zone in Bosnia, known as the Republika Srpska, and write about it in his *Sommerlicher Nachtrag zu einer winterlichen Reise* (Frankfurt am Main: Suhrkamp, 1996).

[5] See, for example, Peter Schneider's scathing critique of Handke, "Der Ritt über den Balkan," in *Die Angst des Dichters vor der Wirklichkeit: 16 Antworten auf*

Peter Handkes Winterreise nach Serbien, ed. Tilman Zülch (Göttingen: Steidl, 1996), 25–34.

[6] Handke, *Eine winterliche Reise*, 50; *A Journey to the Rivers*, 26. In terms of political culpability for the war in Yugoslavia, the German example is particularly telling. Under the leadership of Helmut Kohl and Hans-Dietrich Genscher, the German federal government exacerbated the Yugoslav crisis through its hasty recognition of its former ally Croatia as an independent nation, a diplomatic move that undermined the legitimacy of the Yugoslavian multiethnic state, set in motion the expulsion of Serbs from Croatia, and made Germany's role in the conflict particularly fraught. See Glenny, *The Fall of Yugoslavia*, 163.

[7] Handke, *Eine winterliche Reise*, 124; *A Journey to the Rivers*, 76.

[8] Zeh, "Wie eine Gehirnwäsche," interview mit Juli Zeh, *Die Tageszeitung* (*taz*), 27 July 2002. Emphasis added.

[9] Although statistics on the number of rapes are still fairly unreliable, it is estimated that between 20,000 and 60,000 women were the victims of sexual brutality, often repeatedly and for prolonged periods of time. For statistics from Amnesty International and United Nations reports, see the Women's Media Center's Women under Siege Project, accessed August 1, 2014, http://www.womenundersiegeproject.org/conflicts/profile/bosnia.

[10] Clear references to rape appear on pages 40, 88, 90, 94, 142, 192, and 233 in Zeh, *Die Stille ist ein Geräusch*. The passages to which I refer above appear on pages 248–50, 66, 158–59, and 88.

[11] For secondary literature on Zeh's *Die Stille ist ein Geräusch*, see Brokoff, "'Zusehen, wie alles grundlos zwischen Gut und Böse pendelt'"; Grozdanic, *Der Balkankrieg als literarisches Phaenomen*, 203–14; Karoline von Oppen, "Nostalgia for Orient[ation]: Travelling through Former Yugoslavia with Juli Zeh, Peter Schneider, and Peter Handke," *Seminar* 41 (September 2005): 246–60; Wolfgang Graf Vitzthum, "Gerechtigkeit für Bosnien? Zu Juli Zehs Bildern vom Balkan," in *Fiktionen der Gerechtigkeit: Literatur—Film—Philosophie—Recht*, ed. Susanne Kaul and Rüdiger Bittner (Baden-Baden: Nomos, 2005), 117–33; and Thomas Weitin, "Ermittlung der Gegenwart: Theorie und Praxis unsouveränen Erzählens bei Juli Zeh," in *Postsouveränes Erzählen* (Stuttgart: Metzler, 2012), 67–85, especially 80–85. Of these scholars, only Oppen even mentions gender as a thematic element in Zeh's text, and she does so only in reference to Zeh's harassment by a Turkish man ("Nostalgia for Orient[ation]," 250–51).

[12] Patricia Herminghouse, "The Young Author as Public Intellectual: The Case of Juli Zeh," in *German Literature in a New Century: Trends, Traditions, Transitions, Transformations*, ed. Katharina Gerstenberger and Patricia Herminghouse (New York: Berghahn Books, 2008), 280–81. The text that Herminghouse cites as evidence of Zeh's "postfeminism" is her satirical mock interview "Sind wir Kanzlerin?" reprinted in the essay collection *Alles auf dem Rasen: Kein Roman* (Doing it on the Grass: Not a Novel, 2006; repr., Munich: btb, 2008), 29–36, in which Zeh expresses gratitude toward second-wave German feminists such as Alice Schwarzer yet immediately distances herself from them (32). Even so, by interviewing a young writer named JuLi for a fictitious women's magazine and thereby acting as both interviewer and interviewee, Zeh does foreground her

own gender in this political commentary on the chancellorship of Angela Merkel. Zeh's novels also include gender-bending characters, including quite a few men who depart from traditional masculine roles and traits. For a reading of characters who defy easy gender categorization, see Sonja Klocke's analysis of Zeh's acclaimed novel *Spieltrieb* (2004), "Transnational Terrorism, War, and Violence: Globalization and Transborder Exchanges in Juli Zeh's *Spieltrieb*," *Seminar* 47 (September 2011): 525–26.

[13] Erica Fischer, *Am Anfang war die Wut: Monika Hauser und Medica mondiale; Ein Frauenprojekt im Krieg* (Cologne: Kiepenheuer & Witsch, 1997). Further references to this work are given in the text using the abbreviation *AW*. Fischer was one of the founding members of the "new women's movement" in Vienna in the 1970s and has been active in the German feminist movement since she moved to Berlin in the 1990s. She is best known as the author of *Aimée und Jaguar: Eine Liebesgeschichte, Berlin 1943* (Cologne: Kiepenheuer & Witsch, 1994), a work of creative non-fiction that tells the story of an unlikely and ill-fated romance between a German and a German-Jewish woman in wartime Berlin.

[14] "Jugoslawien: Vergewaltigung als Waffe; Der Krieg gegen die Frauen; Opfer berichten," Cover story, *Stern*, 26 November 1992, 49–63.

[15] Journalists, of course, did play an important role in promoting widespread awareness of the rapes in Bosnia and of the Yugoslav wars in general, with German journalists at the forefront. Implicitly referencing the *Stern* article, Alexandra Stiglmayer proudly states: "The news about mass rapes in Bosnia-Herzegovina spread like wildfire in the German media in November 1992, and soon the wave of outrage spilled over to other European countries and the United States." Stiglmayer, "The Rapes in Bosnia-Herzegovina," in *Mass Rape: The War against Women in Bosnia-Herzegovina*, ed. Alexandra Stiglmayer, trans. Marion Faber (Lincoln: University of Nebraska Press, 1994), 161. See also the foreword by the Pulitzer-Prize-winning journalist Roy Gutman in the same volume, ix–xiii. The German version of the book, *Massenvergewaltigung: Krieg gegen die Frauen*, was published in 1993 and is no longer in print.

[16] After quoting Sander, Fischer practically growls: "Die meisten Menschen in Deutschland hatten zwar bis Kriegsausbruch keine Ahnung, daß in Bosnien Moslems leben, jetzt aber wissen es auf einmal alle ganz genau: Die bosnischen Musliminnen haben keine Chance" (*AW*, 14; Before the war broke out, most people in Germany had no idea that Muslims even live in Bosnia, but as of now they all know quite well: the Bosnian Muslim women don't have a chance).

[17] For the film's screenplay and additional documents and essays, see Helke Sander and Barbara Johr, eds., *BeFreier und Befreite: Krieg, Vergewaltigung, Kinder* (Munich: Kunstmann, 1992).

[18] Sander and Johr, *BeFreier und Befreite*, 109.

[19] Pascale R. Bos, "Feminists Interpreting the Politics of Wartime Rape: Berlin, 1945; Yugoslavia, 1992–1993," *Signs* 31 (Summer 2006): 1010. For the scholarly debate on Sander's film and Sander's response to it, see the special issue of the journal *October* dedicated to the film, which includes essays by Andreas Huyssen, Gertrud Koch, David Levin, and Eric Santner, among others. Stuart Liebman and Annette Michelson, eds., *October: Berlin 1945; War and Rape; "Liberators Take*

Liberties," *October* 72 (1995). Richard W. McCormick offers a clear and thorough summary of the debate in his article "Rape and War, Gender and Nation, Victims and Victimizers: Helke Sander's *BeFreier und Befreite*," *Camera Obscura* 46 (2001): 98–141.

[20] See especially Gertrud Koch, "Blood, Sperm, and Tears," trans. Stuart Liebman, *October* 72 (1995): 27–41.

[21] Bos, "Feminists Interpreting the Politics of Wartime Rape," 997.

[22] Helke Sander, prologue, in Stiglmayer, *Mass Rape*, xvii–xxiii; here, xx.

[23] Ustasha (literally "insurgence") was a Croatian fascist movement in existence from 1929 to 1945.

[24] On the use of ethnic and political slurs in visual propaganda during the war in Bosnia, see Catherine A. McKinnon, "Turning Rape into Pornography: Postmodern Genocide," in Stiglmayer, *Mass Rape*, 75.

[25] The section on Hauser's breakdown is on page 218.

[26] See Tonia St. Germain and Susan Dewey's introduction to their edited volume *Conflict-Related Sexual Violence: International Law, Local Responses* (Sterling, VA: Kumarian, 2012), 1–12, for a clear critique of the dominance of Western European and US feminist perspectives in the legal discourse on wartime rape and post-conflict justice.

[27] McCormick, "Rape and War, Gender and Nation, Victims and Victimizers," 116.

[28] John Cage, "Lecture on Nothing," reprinted in *Silence: Lectures and Writings by John Cage* (Middletown, CT: Wesleyan University Press, 1973), 109. I have inserted backslashes to indicate the visual gaps that represent the silences in Cage's talk. While this may seem like an odd reference, Cage's "Lecture on Nothing" and the accompanying essays in his volume had a significant impact on avant-garde literature and art.

[29] Cage, "Lecture on Nothing," 116, orthography as in the original.

[30] Juli Zeh, *Adler und Engel* (2001; repr., Munich: btb, 2003). The term "Tarantino-esque" refers of course to the US screenwriter and film director Quentin Tarantino, well known for his use of excessive violence. See Claudia Breger's reading of *Alder und Engel* in *An Aesthetics of Narrative Performance: Transnational Theater, Literature, and Film in Contemporary Germany* (Columbus: Ohio State University Press, 2012), 124.

[31] Zeh, *Adler und Engel*, 299, 305–6, 310.

[32] Ibid., 393–97, 411–13. Max surprises himself by his ability to penetrate Clara, since he has been impotent since Jessie's death. Impotence is a recurring motif in Zeh's early novels; on the impotence of the character Alev in *Spieltrieb*, see Klocke, "Transnational Terrorism, War, and Violence," 526.

[33] Breger, *An Aesthetics of Narrative Performance*, 125, 130. Zeh also foregrounds physicality in the travelogue when she describes how her body responds to the extreme summer heat, the fatigue brought on by multiple sleepless nights, and the stress of her travels. In her chapter entitled "Panik," she wakes up to find "dass in der Nacht mein linkes Auge geplatzt ist" (*SG*, 213; that my left eye

exploded overnight). Zeh's fascination with the body pushed to its physical limits is another recurring motif in her work, and it is one of the only things that *Adler und Engel* and *Die Stille ist ein Geräusch* have in common.

[34] Zeh, "Von der Heimlichkeit des Schreibens," 2005; reprinted in *Alles auf dem Rasen*, 201–13.

[35] In translating this passage, I took some creative liberties with "handwerkliche Anstrengung," since "deliberate craftsmanship" seemed to capture the meaning better than "the efforts of the craft."

[36] I take my definition of classic melodrama from Thomas Elsaesser, "Tales of Sound and Fury: Observations on the Family Melodrama," reprinted in *Imitations of Life: A Reader on Film and Television Melodrama*, ed. Marcia Landy (Detroit: Wayne State University Press, 1991), 84–85. I am grateful to Barbara Mennel for directing me to this text.

[37] In another essay on her studies at the Literaturinstitut in Leipzig, Zeh describes how she developed a strict inner editor that helped her avoid "Kitschgefahr" (the danger of kitsch) in her writing. See Zeh, "Marmeladenseiten," 2003, reprinted in *Alles auf dem Rasen*, 189.

[38] Andreas Huyssen, *Present Pasts: Urban Palimpsests and the Politics of Memory* (Stanford, CA: Stanford University Press, 2003), 17–19. See, for instance, Huyssen's point that "many of the mass-marketed memories we consume are 'imagined memories' to begin with, and thus more easily forgettable than lived memories" (17). He urges readers not to view media representations through the "high art/low art" paradigm, yet he does argue that the "question of quality remains," and that readers should analyze "the specific strategies of representation and commodification pursued" as well as "the context in which they are staged" (19).

[39] The website, although a bit dated in format, is still active. See *Die Stille ist ein Geräusch*, accessed July 30, 2014, http://www.stille-ist-geraeusch.de/.

[40] I take the term "intermedial" from Claudia Breger's assertion that contemporary German literature such as Zeh's employs "programmatically intermedial affiliations." See Breger, *An Aesthetics of Narrative Performance*, 45.

[41] Brokoff, "'Zusehen, wie alles grundlos zwischen Gut und Böse pendelt,'" 273, 275.

[42] Ibid., 276.

[43] Zeh discusses the critical, creative potential of first-person narratives, as opposed to the more authoritative (even authoritarian) third-person narratives, in her essay "Sag nicht ER zu mir," 2002, reprinted in *Alles auf dem Rasen*, 220–34. For other articulations on what I would call Zeh's "anti-authoritative" narration, which I see as a key aspect of her aesthetics of restraint, see Breger, who calls Zeh's writing in *Adler und Engel* "an aesthetics of precarious narration" (*An Aesthetics of Narrative Performance*, 131), and Weitin, who claims that Zeh employs a strategy of "offensiv unzuverlässige Ich-Erzählungen" (deliberately unreliable first-person narratives; "Ermittlung der Gegenwart," 84). Existing scholarship on Zeh has also pointed out her self-conscious criticism of the West and the ability of her narratives to undermine ideas of Western superiority, be it moral, economic, or political. See Brokoff, "'Zusehen, wie alles grundlos zwischen Gut und Böse

pendelt,'" 272; Klocke, "Transnational Terrorism, War, and Violence, 523; and Oppen, "Nostalgia for Orient[ation]," 248.

⁴⁴ Grozdanic, *Der Balkankrieg als literarisches Phaenomen*, 214.

⁴⁵ Brokoff, "'Zusehen, wie alles grundlos zwischen Gut und Böse pendelt,'" 276. It is also important to note, as Brokoff does, that two years after the publication of *Die Stille ist ein Geräusch* Zeh coedited a volume of stories written by Bosnian writers, translated for a German audience. See Zeh, David Finck, and Oskar Terš, ed., *Ein Hund läuft durch die Republik: Geschichten aus Bosnien* (A Dog Runs through the Republic: Stories from Bosnia) (Frankfurt am Main: Schöffling, 2004).

⁴⁶ Raphaëlle Branche, Isabelle Delpla, John Horne, Pieter Lagrou, Daniel Palmieri, and Fabrice Virgili, "Writing the History of Rape in Wartime," in *Rape in Wartime*, ed. Raphaëlle Branche and Fabrice Virgili (Basingstoke, UK: Palgrave Macmillan, 2012), 15.

⁴⁷ Zeh, "Jasmina and Friends," *Brigitte*, October 2002, reprinted in *Alles auf dem Rasen*, 270.

⁴⁸ Vitzthum, "Gerechtigkeit für Bosnien?" 126.

Bibliography

Primary Literature

Akyün, Hatice. *Ali zum Dessert: Leben in einer neuen Welt*. Munich: Wilhelm Goldman Verlag, 2008.

———. *Einmal Hans mit scharfer Soße: Leben in zwei Welten*. 2nd ed. Munich: Wilhelm Goldman Verlag, 2007.

———. *Ich küss dich, Kismet: Eine Deutsche am Bosporus*. Cologne: Kiepenheuer & Witsch, 2013.

Alanyali, Iris. *Die blaue Reise*. Reinbek bei Hamburg: Rowohlt, 2006.

Ayşe (pseud.), and Renate Eder. *Mich hat keiner gefragt: Zur Ehe gezwungen—eine Türkin in Deutschland erzählt*. Munich: Blanvalet Verlag, 2005.

Balàka, Bettina. *Kassiopeia*. Innsbruck: Haymon, 2012.

Berg, Sibylle. *Vielen Dank für das Leben*. Munich: Carl Hanser Verlag, 2012.

Çileli, Serap. *Wir sind eure Töchter nicht eure Ehre*. Munich: Blanvalet, Random House, 2006.

Erpenbeck, Jenny. *Aller Tage Abend*. Munich: Knaus, 2012.

———. *Heimsuchung*. Frankfurt am Main: Eichborn, 2008.

Güngör, Dilek. *Ganz schön deutsch*. Munich: Piper, 2007.

———. *Unter uns*. Berlin: Ebersbach, 2004.

Hacker, Katharina. *Die Habenichtse*. Frankfurt am Main: Suhrkamp, 2006.

Hagena, Katharina. *Der Geschmack von Apfelkernen*. Cologne: Kiepenheuer & Witsch, 2008.

Handke, Peter. *Eine winterliche Reise zu den Flüssen Donau, Save, Morawa und Drina oder Gerechtigkeit für Serbien*. Frankfurt am Main: Suhrkamp, 1996.

Hegemann, Helene. *Axolotl Roadkill*. Berlin: Ullstein, 2010.

Heidenreich, Gisela. *Das endlose Jahr: Die langsame Entdeckung der eigenen Biographie—ein Lebensborn-Schicksal*. Frankfurt am Main: Fischer, 2004.

Hermann, Judith. *Sommerhaus, später*. Frankfurt am Main: Fischer, 1998.

James, Sabatina (pseud.). *Sterben sollst du für dein Glück: Gefangen zwischen zwei Welten*. Munich: Knaur Taschenbuch Verlag, 2004.

Jonuleit, Anja. *Herbstvergessene*. Munich: DTV, 2010.

Kalkan, Hülya. *Ich wollte nur frei sein: Meine Flucht vor der Zwangsehe*. Berlin: Ullstein Taschenbuch, 2006.

Kelek, Necla. *Die fremde Braut: Ein Bericht aus dem Inneren des türkischen Lebens in Deutschland*. Cologne: Kiepenheuer & Witsch, 2005.

Krechel, Ursula. *Landgericht*. Salzburg: Jung und Jung, 2012.
Pehnt, Annette. *Chronik der Nähe*. Munich: Piper, 2012.
Ray, Lady Bitch. *Bitchsm*. Stuttgart: Vagina Style Verlag/Panini Books, 2012.
Richter, Nikola. *Die Lebenspraktikanten*. Frankfurt am Main: Fischer, 2006.
Roche, Charlotte. *Feuchtgebiete*. Cologne: DuMont, 2008.
———. *Schoßgebete*. Munich: Piper, 2011.
Schalansky, Judith. *Blau steht dir nicht: Matrosenroman*. Reprint. Frankfurt am Main: Suhrkamp, 2011.
———. *Der Hals der Giraffe: Bildungsroman*. Berlin: Suhrkamp, 2011.
———. *Taschenatlas der abgelegenen Inseln: Fünfzig Inseln, auf denen ich niemals war und niemals sein werde*. Reprint. Frankfurt am Main: Fischer, 2011.
Schoch, Julia. *Mit der Geschwindigkeit des Sommers*. Munich: Piper, 2009.
———. *Selbstporträt mit Bonaparte*. Munich: Piper, 2012.
———. *Verabredungen mit Mattok*. Munich: Piper, 2004.
Senfft, Alexandra. *Schweigen tut weh: Eine deutsche Familiengeschichte*. Berlin: List, 2008.
Sezgin, Hilal. *Typisch Türkin?* Freiburg: Herder, 2006.
Strubel, Antje Rávic. *Kältere Schichten der Luft*. Frankfurt am Main: Fischer, 2007.
———. *Unter Schnee: Episodenroman*. Munich: dtv, 2001.
Von Braun, Christina. "Fort da: Die Wiedergänger des kulturellen Gedächtnisses." In *[Auslassungen]: Leerstellen als Movens der Kulturwissenschaft*, edited by Natascha Adamowsky and Peter Matussek, 265–70. Würzburg: Königshausen & Neumann, 2004.
———. *Nicht Ich: Logik—Lüge—Libido*. Frankfurt am Main: Neue Kritik, 1985.
———. *Stille Post: Eine andere Familiengeschichte*. 3rd ed. Berlin: List, 2011.
Y., Inci. *Erstickt an euren Lügen: Eine Türkin in Deutschland erzählt*. Munich: Piper Verlag, 2005.
Zaimoglu, Feridun. *Kanak Sprak/Koppstoff: Die gesammelten Mißtöne vom Rande der Gesellschaft*. Cologne: Kiepenheuer & Witsch, 2011.
Zeh, Juli. *Adler und Engel*. 2001. Reprint. Frankfurt am Main: btb, 2003.
———. *Alles auf dem Rasen: Kein Roman*. Munich: btb, 2008.
———. *Die Stille ist ein Geräusch: Eine Fahrt durch Bosnien*. Frankfurt am Main: btb, 2003.

Secondary Literature

Adelson, Leslie. *The Turkish Turn in Contemporary German Literature: Toward a New Critical Grammar of Migration*. New York: Palgrave Macmillan, 2005.
Aune, Kristin, Sonya Sharma, and Giselle Vincent, eds., *Women and Religion in the West: Challenging Secularization*. Aldershot, UK: Ashgate, 2008.

Baer, Hester. "Frauenliteratur 'after Feminism': Rereading Contemporary Women's Writing." In *Über Gegenwartsliteratur/About Contemporary Literature: Festschrift für/for Paul Michael Lützeler*, edited by Mark W. Rectanus, 69–86. Bielefeld: Aisthesis, 2008.

———. "German Feminism in the Age of Neoliberalism: Jana Hensel and Elisabeth Raether's *Neue deutsche Mädchen.*" *German Studies Review* 35, no. 2 (2012): 355–74.

———. "Introduction: Resignifications of Feminism in Contemporary Germany." In "Contemporary Women's Writing and the Return of Feminism in Germany," special issue, *Studies in Twentieth and Twenty-First Century Literature* 35, no. 1 (2011): 8–17.

———. "Sex, Death, and Motherhood in the Eurozone: Contemporary Women's Writing in German." *World Literature Today* (May–June 2012), 59–65.

Bartel, Heike, and Elizabeth Boa, eds. *Pushing at Boundaries: Approaches to Contemporary Women Writers from Karen Duve to Jenny Erpenbeck.* Amsterdam: Rodopi, 2006.

Berlant, Lauren G. *Cruel Optimism.* Durham, NC: Duke Unversity Press, 2011.

Bethman, Brenda. "Generation Chick: Reading *Bridget Jones's Diary, Jessica, 30.*, and *Dies ist kein Liebeslied* as Postfeminist Novels." In "Contemporary Women's Writing and the Return of Feminism in Germany," special issue, *Studies in Twentieth and Twenty-First Century Literature* 35, no. 1 (2011): 136–54.

Biendarra, Anke S. "Gen(d)eration Next: Prose by Julia Franck and Judith Hermann." *Studies in Twentieth and Twenty-First Century Literature* 28, no. 1 (2004): 211–39.

Braithwaite, Ann. "The Personal, the Political, Third-Wave and Postfeminisms." *Feminist Theory* 3, no. 3 (2002): 335–44.

Breger, Claudia. *An Aesthetics of Narrative Performance: Transnational Theater, Literature, and Film in Contemporary Germany.* Columbus: Ohio State University Press, 2012.

Butler, Judith. *Bodies That Matter: On the Discursive Limits of "Sex."* New York: Routledge, 1993.

———. *Excitable Speech: A Politics of the Performative.* New York: Routledge, 1997.

———. *Gender Trouble: Feminism and the Subversion of Identity.* New York: Routledge, 1990.

———. *Undoing Gender.* New York: Routledge, 2004.

Catling, Jo, ed. *A History of Women's Writing in Germany, Austria and Switzerland.* Cambridge: Cambridge University Press, 2000.

Cheesman, Tom. *Novels of Turkish German Settlement: Cosmopolite Fictions.* Rochester, NY: Camden House, 2007.

Cohen-Pfister, Laurel, and Susanne Vees-Gulani, eds. *Generational Shifts in Contemporary German Culture.* Rochester, NY: Camden House, 2010.

Dorn, Thea. *Die neue F-Klasse: Wie die Zukunft von Frauen gemacht wird*. Munich: Piper, 2007.

Duggan, Lisa. *The Twilight of Equality? Neoliberalism, Cultural Politics, and the Attack on Democracy*. Boston: Beacon, 2003.

Eigler, Friederike. *Gedächtnis und Geschichte in Generationenromanen seit der Wende*. Berlin: Erich Schmidt, 2005.

Eismann, Sonja, ed. *Hot Topic: Popfeminismus heute*. Mainz: Ventil Verlag, 2007.

El-Tayeb, Fatima. *European Others: Queering Ethnicity in Postnational Europe*. Minneapolis: University of Minnesota Press, 2011.

Ferree, Myra Marx. "Gender Politics in the Berlin Republic: Four Issues of Identity and Institutional Change." *German Politics & Society* 28, no. 1 (2010): 189–214.

———. *Varieties of Feminism: German Gender Politics in Global Perspective*. Stanford, CA: Stanford University Press, 2012.

Ferriss, Suzanne, and Mallory Young. *Chick Lit: The New Woman's Fiction*. New York: Routledge, 2006.

Frederiksen, Elke, and Martha Wallach, eds. *Facing Fascism and Confronting the Past: German Women Writers from Weimar to the Present*. Albany, NY: SUNY Press, 2000.

Fuchs, Anne. *Phantoms of War in Contemporary German Literature, Films and Discourse*. New Perspectives in German Political Studies. Basingstoke, UK: Palgrave Macmillan, 2010.

Genz, Stéphanie, and Benjamin A. Brabon, eds. *Postfeminism: Cultural Texts and Theories*. Edinburgh: Edinburgh University Press, 2009.

Gerstenberger, Katharina. *Writing the New Berlin*. Rochester, NY: Camden House, 2008.

Gerstenberger, Katharina, and Patricia Herminghouse, eds. *German Literature in a New Century: Trends, Traditions, Transitions, Transformations*. New York: Berghahn Books, 2008.

Gill, Rosalind, and Christina Scharff, eds. *New Femininities: Postfeminism, Neoliberalism, and Subjectivity*. London: Palgrave Macmillan, 2011.

Haaf, Meredith, Susanne Klingner, and Barbara Streidl. *Wir Alphamädchen: Warum Feminismus das Leben schöner macht*. Hamburg: Hoffmann & Campe, 2008.

Hains, Brigid, and Margaret Littler. *Contemporary Women's Writing in German: Changing the Subject*. Oxford: Oxford University Press, 2004.

Halberstam, Judith. *Female Masculinity*. Durham, NC: Duke University Press, 1998.

Hawkesworth, Mary. *Feminist Inquiry: From Political Conviction to Methodological Innovation*. New Brunswick, NJ: Rutgers University Press, 2006.

Heffernan, Valerie, and Gillian Pye, eds. *Transitions: Emerging Women Writers in German-Language Literature*. Amsterdam: Rodopi, 2013.

Hensel, Jana, and Elisabeth Raether. *Neue deutsche Mädchen*. Reinbek bei Hamburg: Rowohlt, 2008.

Hill, Alexandra Merley. "'Female Sobriety': Feminism, Motherhood, and the Works of Julia Franck." *Women in German Yearbook* 24 (2008): 209–28.
———. "Motherhood as Performance: (Re)Negotiations of Motherhood in Contemporary German Literature." In "Contemporary Women's Writing and the Return of Feminism in Germany," special issue, *Studies in Twentieth and Twenty-First Century Literature* 35, no. 1 (2011): 74–94.
———. *Playing House: Motherhood, Intimacy, and Domestic Spaces in Julia Franck's Fiction*. Oxford: Peter Lang, 2012.
Hirsch, Marianne. *The Mother/Daughter Plot: Narrative, Psychoanalysis, Feminism*. Bloomington: Indiana University Press, 1989.
Huth-Hildebrandt, Christine. *Das Bild von der Migrantin: Auf den Spuren eines Konstrukts*. Frankfurt am Main: Brandes & Apsel, 2002.
Jeremiah, Emily. *Nomadic Ethics in Contemporary Women's Writing in German: Strange Subjects*. Rochester, NY: Camden House, 2012.
———. *Troubling Maternity: Mothering, Agency, and Ethics in Women's Writing in German of the 1970s and 1980s*. London: Maney, 2003.
Leydesdorff, Selma, Luisa Passerini, and Paul Richard Thompson, eds. *Gender and Memory*. New Brunswick, NJ: Transaction, 2005.
Lutz, Helma, María Teresa Herrera Vivar, and Linda Supik. *Fokus Intersektionalität: Bewegungen und Verortungen eines vielschichtigen Konzepts*. Wiesbaden: VS Verlag, 2010.
Marven, Lyn. "German Literature in the Berlin Republic—Writing by Women." In *Contemporary German Fiction: Writing the Berlin Republic*, edited by Stuart Taberner, 159–76. Cambridge: Cambridge University Press, 2007.
McCall, Leslie. "The Complexity of Intersectionality." *Signs: Journal of Women in Culture and Society* 30, no. 3 (2005): 1771–1800.
Moi, Toril. "'I Am Not a Woman Writer': About Women, Literature, and Feminist Theory Today." *Feminist Theory* 9, no. 3 (2008): 261.
Palatschek, Sylvia, and Sylvia Schraut, eds. *The Gender of Memory: Cultures of Remembrance in Nineteenth- and Twentieth-Century Europe*. Frankfurt am Main: Campus, 2007.
Roebling, Irmgard, and Wolfram Mauser, eds. *Mutter und Mütterlichkeit: Wandel und Wirksamkeit einer Phantasie in der deutschen Literatur*. Würzburg: Königshausen & Neumann, 1996.
Smith-Prei, Carrie. "'Knaller Sex für alle': Popfeminist Body Politics in Lady Bitch Ray, Charlotte Roche, and Sarah Kuttner." In "Contemporary Women's Writing and the Return of Feminism in Germany," special issue, *Studies in Twentieth and Twenty-First Century Literature* 35, no. 1 (2011): 18–39.
Smith-Prei, Carrie, and Maria Stehle, "*Awkwardness* als Provokation: Gedankenspiele zu Popfeminismus, Körperpolitik und der Vermarktung literarischer Frauen." In *Fiktionen und Realitäten*, edited by Marion Schulz and Brigitte Jirku, 215–30. Frankfurt am Main: Peter Lang, 2013.
Stehle, Maria. *Ghetto Voices in Contemporary German Culture: Textscapes, Filmscapes, Soundscapes*. Rochester, NY: Camden House, 2012.

———. "Pop, Porn, and Rebellious Speech." *Feminist Media Studies* 12, no. 2 (2012): 229–47.
Stephan, Inge, Regula Venske, and Sigrid Weigel. *Frauenliteratur ohne Tradition?* Frankfurt am Main: Fischer, 1987.
Stöcker, Mirja, ed. *Das F-Wort: Feminismus ist sexy*. Königstein: Helmer, 2007.
Tasker, Yvonne, and Diane Negra, eds. *Interrogating Postfeminism: Gender and the Politics of Popular Culture*. Durham, NC: Duke University Press, 2007.
Weber, Beverly. "Freedom from Violence, Freedom to Make the World: Muslim Women's Memoirs, Gendered Violence, and Voices for Change in Germany." *Women in German Yearbook* 25 (2009): 199–222.
———. *Violence and Gender in the "New" Europe: Islam in German Culture*. New York: Palgrave Macmillan, 2013.
———. "Work, Sex, and Socialism: Reading beyond Cultural Hybridity in Emine Sevgi Özdamar's *Die Brücke vom Goldenen Horn*." *German Life and Letters* 63, no. 1 (January 2010): 37–53.
Weedon, Chris, ed. *Post-War Women's Writing in German: Feminist Critical Approaches*. Providence, RI: Berghahn Books, 1997.
Weigel, Sigrid. *Die Stimme der Medusa: Schreibweisen in der Gegenwartsliteratur von Frauen*. Dülmen-Hiddingsel, Germany: Tende, 1987.
Yeşilada, Karin. "Die geschundene Suleika: Das Eigenbild der Türkin in der deutschsprachigen Literatur türkischer Autorinnen." In *Interkulturelle Konfigurationen: Zur deutschsprachigen Erzählliteratur von Autoren nichtdeutscher Herkunft*, edited by Mary Howard, 95–114. Munich: Iudicium Verlag, 1997.
———. "'Getürkt' oder nur 'anders'? Das Türkenbild in der türkisch-deutschen Satire." In *The Image of the Turk in Europe from the Declaration of the Republic in 1923 to the 1990s*, edited by Nedret Kuran Borçoğlu, 205–20. Istanbul: Isis, 2000.
———. "'Nette Türkinnen von nebenan'—Die neue deutsch-türkische Harmlosigkeit als literarischer Trend." In *Von der nationalen zur internationalen Literatur: Transkulturelle deutschsprachige Literatur und Kultur im Zeitalter globaler Migration*, edited by Helmut Schmitz, 117–42. Amsterdamer Beiträge zur neueren Germanistik 69. Amsterdam: Rodopi, 2009.
Yildiz, Yasemin. "Governing European Subjects: Tolerance and Guilt in the Discourse of 'Muslim Women.'" *Cultural Critique* 77 (Winter 2011): 70–101.
———. "Turkish Girls, Allah's Daughters, and the Contemporary German Subject: Itinerary of a Figure." *German Life and Letters* 62, no. 4 (October 2009): 465–81.

Contributors

HESTER BAER is an associate professor of German and film studies at the University of Maryland, College Park. She is the author of *Dismantling the Dream Factory: Gender, German Cinema, and the Postwar Quest for a New Film Language* (2009), and the editor of a special issue of *Studies in Twentieth & Twenty-First Century Literature* titled "Contemporary Women's Writing and the Return of Feminism in Germany" (2011).

NECIA CHRONISTER is an assistant professor of German at Kansas State University. She has published on Angela Krauss in the *Women in German Yearbook* (2012) and on East German property disputes in the volume *Heimat Goes Mobile: Hybrid Forms of Home in Literature and Film* (2013).

HELGA DRUXES is a professor of German at Williams College. She is the author of *Resisting Bodies: The Negotiation of Female Agency in Twentieth-Century Women's Fiction* (1996) and of numerous articles on German literature.

VALERIE HEFFERNAN is Head of German at the National University of Ireland Maynooth. She is the author of *Provocation from the Periphery: Robert Walser Re-Examined* (2007) and the coeditor of the volume *Transitions: Emerging Women Writers in German-Language Literature* (2013).

ALEXANDRA MERLEY HILL is an assistant professor of German at the University of Portland. She is the author of *Playing House: Motherhood, Intimacy, and Domestic Spaces in Julia Franck's Fiction* (2012) and the coeditor of *Germany in the Loud Twentieth Century* (2011).

LINDSAY LAWTON received her PhD from the Department of German, Scandinavian, and Dutch at the University of Minnesota in 2014. Her dissertation focuses on the production and consumption of contemporary memoirs by Muslim women in Germany and Austria.

SHERIDAN MARSHALL works as a freelance translator and editorial consultant for *New Books in German*. She is the author of *Forgetting to Remember: Religious Remembrance and the Literary Response to the Holocaust* (2014).

MIHAELA PETRESCU teaches German at the University of Pittsburgh. She has published on vamps and jazz dancing, male dance instructors during the Weimar Republic, satiric representations of Brigitte Helm and Marlene Dietrich, and recent Romanian cinema in book chapters and journals including *New German Critique*, *Monatshefte*, and *Seminar*.

JILL SUZANNE SMITH is associate professor of German at Bowdoin College. She is the author of *Berlin Coquette: Prostitution and the New German Woman* (2013). She has published articles in the *Journal of Modern Jewish Studies* and *The German Quarterly*. She is currently working on a book project that examines German and Austrian cultural representations of the Bosnian crises of the early 1990s.

CARRIE SMITH-PREI is an associate professor of German at the University of Alberta. She is the author of *Revolting Families: Toxic Intimacy, Private Politics, and Literary Realisms in the German Sixties* (2013) and the coeditor of *Bloom and Bust: Urban Landscapes in the East since German Reunification* (2014) and a special issue of *Germanistik in Ireland*, "Sexual-Textual Border-Crossings: Lesbian Identity in German-Language Literature, Film, and Culture" (2010).

MARIA STEHLE is an associate professor of German at the University of Tennessee Knoxville. She is the author of *Ghetto Voices in Contemporary German Culture* (2012) and articles on race, gender, and feminism in the *European Journal of Cultural Studies*, *Feminist Media Studies*, and *The German Quarterly*, among others.

KATHERINE STONE completed her PhD at the University of Cambridge. Her dissertation is titled "Gender and German Memory Cultures: Representations of National Socialism in post-1945 German Women's Writing." She is currently a postdoctoral research assistant at the National University of Ireland Maynooth.

Index

adolescence, 41, 136–39, 145, 149
aesthetics, 2, 5, 7–8, 135–40, 149, 182, 185
aesthetics of restraint, 13, 183–90, 195n43
Akyün, Hatice, 3, 12, 113
Akyün, Hatice, works by: *Ali zum Dessert*, 113, 123–26; *Einmal Hans mit scharfer Soße*, 113, 115–23; *Ich küss dich, Kismet*, 128n3
Alanyali, Iris, 113–14, 130n33
Ateş, Seyran, 103, 114, 123
#Aufschrei, 5
awkwardness, 6, 13, 132–35, 146–48
Ayşe (pseud.), 95, 97, 100–103, 105

Bachmann, Ingeborg, 6, 32, 71n5
Balàka, Bettina, 12, 75
Balàka, Bettina, works by: *Kassiopeia*, 85–88, 92
Balkan wars, 13, 178, 183
Berg, Sibylle, 12, 75, 88–92
Berg, Sibylle, works by: articles in *Spiegel Online*, 90; *Vielen Dank für das Leben*, 88–92
Berlant, Lauren, 134, 135
birthrate, declining. *See* demography debate
bodies, 2, 3, 11, 14, 18, 20, 32, 60, 118, 141, 144–46, 150, 154, 159
Braun, Christina von, 11, 54–56
Braun, Christina von, works by: *Stille Post*, 54, 58–62, 65–66, 69–70
Butler, Judith, 2, 9, 17n33, 19–20, 22–25, 27, 30, 32, 56, 66, 68–69

chick lit, 6–8, 115, 123–24, 126, 129n12
chick lit alla turca, 16, 115, 126, 129n13

Chinese whispers. *See* telephone
Christianity, 12, 74–79, 89, 91–92, 97
Çileli, Serap, 100, 103, 105
class, 2, 8, 10, 14, 17n33, 99, 104–5, 107–9, 120, 156–57, 159, 161–62, 171
communism, 58, 75, 84–85, 123, 130n35, 154–73
confounding gender, 10, 11, 13, 14
cruel optimism, 134–35, 139–40, 143–45, 149

daughters, 11, 38–52, 54, 58, 60, 63–65, 79–88, 101, 105, 124, 126, 143, 166
demography debate, 3–4, 38, 45, 125–26
Deutsche Islam-Konferenz. *See* German Islam Conference
discrimination, 12, 96, 99, 121, 130n27, 148
drag, 29, 30, 32

education, 47, 100, 107, 165, 172
Eismann, Sonja, 4–5, 113, 134
Erpenbeck, Jenny, 3, 12, 75, 76
Erpenbeck, Jenny, works by: *Aller Tage Abend*, 80–85, 87–88, 89, 91–92; *Heimsuchung*, 80
exile, 76, 78, 166

family narratives, 11, 37–52, 54–70
fathers, 15n11, 45, 58, 67, 69, 82, 96
Femen, 5
feminism(s), 1–14, 19, 37, 49, 54, 59, 61, 64, 70, 113, 115, 117–18, 123, 126, 132–50, 172, 178–82. *See also* popfeminism; postfeminism
Ferree, Myra Marx, 7, 15n10, 17n33, 150n4

Franck, Julia, 3, 6, 7, 32
Frauenliteratur, 6
Fräuleinwunder, 6–8, 28

gender binary, 1, 19, 21, 23, 32, 61–62, 66
gender norms, 2, 4, 9–10, 11, 13, 56, 65–70, 96, 133, 149, 167, 171
gender roles, 4, 28, 31, 55, 65, 69, 79, 101
gender transition, 11, 18, 27, 32–33
generations, 4, 5, 11, 37–52, 54–70, 75, 80–84, 89, 91, 101, 114, 122–25, 136, 162, 163, 169, 170, 172
German Democratic Republic (GDR), 7, 21, 85, 88, 155, 157, 163–72
German Islam Conference, 103, 111n35, 123
grandmothers, 39–50, 57, 60, 64–65, 81–88, 142, 168, 184
Grossmütterliteratur, 82
guest workers, 99, 114, 122–25, 128n7, 131n41. *See also* labor
Güngör, Dilek, 113, 114

Hacker, Katharina, 3, 6, 13, 154, 156, 162, 171, 173
Hacker, Katharina, works by: *Die Habenichtse*, 156–59, 162, 171
Hagena, Katharina, 3, 11
Hagena, Katharina, works by: *Der Geschmack von Apfelkernen*, 39, 41–42, 45–46, 48, 49, 51–52
Halberstam, Judith/Jack, 32, 140
Handke, Peter, 175–79, 190
hate speech, 20, 23–24
Hawkesworth, Mary, 10
headscarf, 99, 115–17, 146, 153n40
Hegemann, Helene, 3, 5, 12, 132, 135–36, 149–50
Hegemann, Helene, works by: *Axolotl Roadkill*, 133, 135–40, 145
Heidenreich, Gisela, 11, 54–57, 61, 66
Heidenreich, Gisela, works by: *Das endlose Jahr*, 54–57, 62–64, 67–68, 70
Herman, Eva, 3

Hermann, Judith, 3, 11, 18–19, 27–33
heteronormativity, 19, 32, 101, 102, 138, 169
Hirsch, Marianne, 11, 48–52, 62, 70
historia matria, 39–44, 48, 51–52
Holocaust, 60, 75–76, 79–80, 92, 122
honor killing, 95, 111n27, 122, 146
Hot Topic: Popfeminismus heute. *See* Eismann, Sonja

intersectionality, 1, 8–10, 12, 99, 114, 124, 127n2, 148, 181
Islam, 12, 74, 93n4, 95–109, 110n3, 114, 116
Islamophobia, 3, 99

James, Sabatina, 97, 102–7, 111n27
Jews, 43, 59, 60, 69, 74–92, 156, 158, 193n13
Jonuleit, Anja, 3, 11, 45
Jonuleit, Anja, works by: *Herbstvergessene*, 39–40, 42–44, 46–48, 49, 50–52
Judaism, 12, 76, 85, 88, 91–92

Kelek, Necla, 98, 103, 104, 105, 110n14, 114, 122, 123
Kindertransport, 79
Krechel, Ursula, 3, 6, 12
Krechel, Ursula, works by: *Das Landgericht*, 75, 76–81, 88, 92

labor, 2, 3, 10, 12, 96, 99, 108, 114, 124, 161, 162
Lady Bitch Ray, 12, 129n18, 132, 146–47, 148–49
Lady Bitch Ray, works by: *Bitchsm*, 133, 146–48
Lebensborn program, 39, 42–43, 56–57, 63–64, 67, 72n12

marketing, 7, 12, 16n24, 95–97, 108–9, 154
McCall, Leslie, 9–10
memoir, 11, 12, 42, 49, 50, 54, 56, 59, 69–70, 95–109, 110n3

memory, 11, 30, 51, 54–70, 75, 86–87, 92, 158, 178, 189
Moi, Toril, 2, 13
Morgner, Irmtraud, 6, 32
motherhood, 11, 12, 37–52, 54–71, 76–91, 96, 101, 114–17, 121, 123–27, 131n39, 141–45, 165–66, 170, 182

National Socialism, 11, 12, 21, 54, 58, 64, 67, 77, 79, 86
neoliberalism, 1, 7–8, 13, 14, 113, 120, 125, 128n11, 134–35, 142, 154–73
Neue deutsche Mädchen, 4, 127n1, 150n5

Özdamar, Emine Sevgi, 6, 32

performativity, gender, 1, 9, 11, 19, 56, 66, 68, 70
popfeminism, 4–5, 12, 113–27, 127n2, 129n15, 130n26, 132–50
pornography, 111n27, 141, 145–46, 148, 152n29, 176, 179, 183
postfeminism, 1, 4, 6, 15n12, 132, 140, 178, 192
precarity, 3, 14, 160–62, 170
public vs. private, 37, 59, 70, 75
Pussy Riot, 5

queer child, 138
queer theory, 1, 8, 9, 11, 22, 32, 140
queering, 19, 23, 27, 28, 30
queerness, 20, 21, 24, 31

Rabenmütter, 44, 166
race, 2, 8, 10, 12, 13, 14, 56, 69, 99, 113, 121, 127n2, 133, 146, 181
rape, 13, 87, 101, 178–90, 192n9, 193n15, 194n26
reader, role of, 11, 12, 18–33, 35n22, 35n24, 62, 98, 121, 133, 137–44, 149, 154, 163, 173, 180, 187–89
religious turn, 74
Richter, Nikola, 3, 13, 154, 156

Richter, Nikola, works by: *Die Lebenspraktikanten*, 159–63, 172–73
Roche, Charlotte, 3, 4, 5, 12, 129n18, 132–33, 149, 150, 152n29
Roche, Charlotte, works by: *Feuchtgebiete*, 133, 140–44, 145, 152n28; *Schoßgebete*, 133, 140–41, 143–44, 145, 152n28

Sander, Helke, 180–83, 190, 193n16–17
Sarrazin, Thilo, 4, 99
Schalansky, Judith, 3, 154–55, 172–73
Schalansky, Judith, works by: *Atlas der abgelegenen Inseln*, 163–64, 167, 169; *Blau steht dir nicht*, 163, 167–69; *Der Hals der Giraffe*, 163–67
Schoch, Julia, 3, 13, 154–55, 169–70, 172–73
Schoch, Julia, works by: *Mit der Geschwindigkeit des Sommers*, 170; *Selbstporträt mit Bonaparte*, 170–71; *Verabredungen mit Mattok*, 170
Schwarzer, Alice, 4, 5, 15, 134, 148, 150, 152n33, 192
Senfft, Alexandra, 11, 54–56
Senfft, Alexandra, works by: *Schweigen tut weh*, 54, 57–58, 61, 62, 63, 64–65, 66, 68–70
September 11, 2001 106, 158
sexual violence. *See* rape
sexuality, 1, 2, 3, 4, 8, 9, 10, 11, 12, 13, 21, 32, 34, 96, 99, 101, 102, 105, 109, 111, 113, 115, 118, 127, 133, 135, 137–38, 140, 142, 147–49, 152, 181
Sezgin, Hilal, 113–14, 128n5
silence, 42, 62, 64, 80, 99, 104, 180, 183–84, 189–90, 194n28
Strubel, Antje Rávic, 3, 11
Strubel, Antje Rávic, works by: *Kältere Schichten der Luft*, 18–19, 21–27, 30, 32; *Unter Schnee*, 21
suicide, 39, 42, 84, 155, 170, 184
Suleika, 103, 111n30, 114, 128

telephone (game), 54, 60, 66

touching tales, 114, 123, 125, 128n8
trauma, 39, 42–44, 48, 55, 57–58, 61, 63–65, 69–70, 143, 184, 187, 189
trivial literature, 6, 109
Turkish-Germans, 12, 95–109, 112–27, 146–49

United States, 21, 60, 112, 120, 127, 129, 166, 193

victimhood, 11, 12, 78–82, 97–109, 113–15, 121, 126, 136, 148, 163, 177, 179–84, 188, 192n9
violence, 2, 5, 13, 20, 44, 82–84, 90, 95–96, 106–7, 109, 114, 122, 158–59, 162, 175–91, 192n9, 193n15, 194n26, 194n30. *See also* rape

Wir Alphamädchen, 4, 125, 145
Wolf, Christa, 6, 32, 71n5
women's writing, 1–3, 6–8, 14, 51, 54
Woolf, Virginia, 30, 32
World War II, 11, 37–45, 51–52, 54, 56–65, 67, 69, 75–80, 85–89, 156–57, 180–81

Y, Inci, 95, 101, 105, 109

Zeh, Juli, 3, 13, 14n6, 175
Zeh, Juli, works by: *Adler und Engel*, 184; *Die Stille ist ein Geräusch*, 175–79, 184–91

www.ingramcontent.com/pod-product-compliance
Lightning Source LLC
Chambersburg PA
CBHW030652230426
43665CB00011B/1053